ROUTLEDGE LIBRARY EDITIONS:
LITERARY THEORY

Volume 7

BRITISH POST-STRUCTURALISM

T0347414

BRITISH POST-STRUCTURALISM
Since 1968

ANTONY EASTHOPE

Routledge
Taylor & Francis Group

LONDON AND NEW YORK

First published in 1988 by Routledge

This edition first published in 2017
by Routledge
2 Park Square, Milton Park, Abingdon, Oxon OX14 4RN

and by Routledge
711 Third Avenue, New York, NY 10017

Routledge is an imprint of the Taylor & Francis Group, an informa business

British Library Cataloguing in Publication Data
A catalogue record for this book is available from the British Library

ISBN: 978-1-138-69377-7 (Set)
ISBN: 978-1-315-52921-9 (Set) (ebk)
ISBN: 978-1-138-68535-2 (Volume 7) (hbk)
ISBN: 978-1-138-68539-0 (Volume 7) (pbk)

Publisher's Note
The publisher has gone to great lengths to ensure the quality of this reprint but points out that some imperfections in the original copies may be apparent.

Disclaimer
The publisher has made every effort to trace copyright holders and would welcome correspondence from those they have been unable to trace.

BRITISH
POST-STRUCTURALISM
SINCE 1968

ANTONY EASTHOPE

London and New York

First published in 1988

Paperback edition first published in 1991 by
Routledge
11 New Fetter Lane, London EC4P 4EE

Simultaneously published in the USA and Canada by
Routledge
a division of Routledge, Chapman and Hall, Inc.
29 West 35th Street, New York NY 10001

Typeset by LaserScript Ltd, Mitcham, Surrey
Printed and bound in Great Britain by
Biddles Ltd, Guildford and King's Lynn

British Library Cataloguing in Publication Data

Easthope, Antony
    British post-structuralism since 1968.
    1. British culture. Deconstruction
    I. Title
    306

Library of Congress Cataloging in Publication Data

Easthope, Antony.
    British post-structuralism since 1968 / Antony Easthope.
        p.   cm.
    Includes bibliographical references and index.
    1. Structuralism.   2. Philosophy, British—20th century.
    3. Deconstruction.   4. Great Britain—Intellectual life—20th
    century.   I. Title.
    B1616.S87E27   1991
    149'.96'0941—dc20   90-27230

ISBN 0 415 06204 7

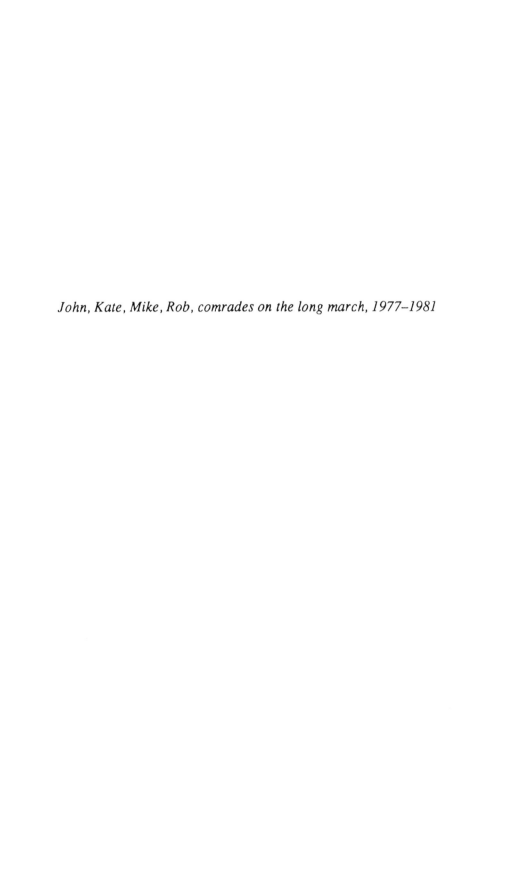

John, Kate, Mike, Rob, comrades on the long march, 1977–1981

Anything that happens to mind in England has usually happened somewhere else first.

Ezra Pound: *How to read* (1931)

Contents

Acknowledgements

I would like to thank the Department of English of the University of Adelaide for electing me to a Distinguished Visiting Scholarship during the tenure of which I was able to start writing this book in the beautiful autumnal weather of March and April 1986. I am grateful also to my colleagues in the Department of English and History at Manchester Polytechnic who supported my leave of absence.

Preface

*'Got one,' Algie Wyatt underlined a phrase on the page
before him.*

*'What?' asked Lidia Korabetski, looking up from the
passage she was translating.*

*'Contradiction in terms.' Algie was collecting
contradictions in terms: to a nucleus of 'military
intelligence' and 'competent authorities' he had added such
discoveries as the soul of efficiency, easy virtue, enlightened
self-interest, Bankers Trust, and Christian Scientist.*

'What?' Lidia asked again.

'Cultural mission,' *replied Algie.*

To this collection of seeming contradictions recorded by Shirley
Hazzard in *People in glass houses* we might now add 'British
Post-structuralism'. My aim is to render the concept less
paradoxical, less of an oxymoron.

This book will review and criticise recent British theoretical
writing in a number of fields. As such, it seeks to do three things.
One is to give a clear, explicit and, as far as possible,
straightforward introduction to a range of work. Those who like
their post-structuralism opaque must seek their pleasures
elsewhere. My own view is that since complete transparency of
writing is in any case impossible a theoretical intervention may
help its reader best by making its arguments and assumptions as
explicit as it can. Every account of a text is of course just that: an
account of a text, a reading, an interpretation. Nevertheless, the
readings given here will tend away from being critical readings,
seeking as far as they can to represent an argument and a text as it
would represent itself.

A second aim is to draw attention to a number of books and
essays that have not been fully recognised before or have not been
read alongside each other before. There is a great difference here
between academic habits in North America and in Britain.
Relatively, the United States lives in a state of active critical
self-consciousness in which it is not unusual for books to be
published about contemporary theoretical writing. This doesn't
happen much in England but I think it should. The present text

hopes to stimulate writers by pointing out the positions they hold and suggesting links between those positions and other work.

But trying to draw even a provisional map of a field cannot be a neutral and objective activity. To write a history — especially a history that only goes back to 1974 — means constructing that history. *British post-structuralism* will welcome the necessity to be polemic, to mark out a preference and name a tradition. It will argue that, working with a surprising though rarely acknowledged level of collective endeavour, recent British writing (1) has made distinct and important innovations in the trajectory of post-structuralism, and (2) that these innovations especially concern the critique of the subject and, in the area of textual studies, the analysis of texts as offering a position to the subject. The work has also posed important problems in epistemology, and these too will be reviewed.

Such work has not always been recognised outside England. Part of my project is to call attention to theoretical writing in a particular tradition. It thus to some degree arises from dissatisfaction with a paragraph such as the following:

> For a detailed Marxist analysis of the 'disintegrated subject', see Rosalind Coward and John Ellis, *Language and Materialism: Developments in Semiology and the Theory of the Subject* (London: Routledge and Kegan Paul, 1977). This book is the work of avant-garde British critics, who attend carefully to semiological and deconstructive theories. (Apparently, deconstruction came to the attention of British intellectuals in the early 1970s. We may expect a flowering of this interest and further publications during the 1980s). (Leitch 1983, p. 277, fn. 13)

Deconstruction, the movement developed out of the American reading of the work of Jacques Derrida, did not come to the attention of British intellectuals in the early 1970s, either really or apparently; nor, for reasons which will be discussed, has American deconstruction had any serious impact in English culture even now. But post-structuralist ideas most certainly exerted a deep influence in certain areas from the late 1960s onward, though in a particular way and in a particular context. A third purpose in writing ensues from this.

It is to argue through and illustrate a theoretical assertion. This can be stated simply and openly: 'ideas' take on meaning according to the discursive context or historical tradition within which they are taken up. The same ideas developed in different national cultures (and we are stuck with those for some time to come) are not, in fact, the same ideas. That body of French critical writing produced especially in the decade between 1962 and 1972 and now referred to as "post-structuralist" (a term they hardly use in France) acquired a specific force, quality and implication when it was translated and imported into the United States. And again, differently, into Britain. Whereas the 'new ideas' and the 'new criticism' were assimilated in America to a liberal and libertarian tradition, in Britain they acquired a radical and political force because they were adopted· into the British Marxist and left-culturalist inheritance.

Marxism denies that individuals create society, think things up, and proposes that it is not people's consciousness that determines their social being but rather it is their social being that determines their consciousness. In so far as it deconstructs the idea of the sovereignty of the individual, post-structuralism was seen to correspond to the Marxist tradition, expanding and supporting it. In Britain post-structuralism has been largely deployed in what is a frankly political form of discourse, as a mode for critique of the transcendental subject, the bourgeois subject.

This helps to explain the particular trajectory followed by British post-structuralism, and again its difference from North American versions. Put at its simplest, intellectuals who were already Marxists read texts by Louis Althusser in the 1960s and 1970s, and were led from there and the analysis of ideology to the psychoanalytic writings of Jacques Lacan. In North America, because of the 1966 Baltimore conference and the subsequent publication in 1970 of Macksey and Donato's *The structuralist controversy* (containing, quite out of sequence, Derrida's work in progress, the essay "Structure, sign, and play in the discourse of the human sciences"), post-structuralism there went to Derrida first and then to the psychoanalytic theories of Jacques Lacan, so managing to by-pass almost altogether the work of the French Marxist theorist, Louis Althusser (though there are now some indications that this omission is being remedied).

The conjunction in Britain between post-structuralism and Marxism also accounts for a major difference in the dissemination of the new theories here. During the late 1960s and early 1970s a whole series of the human sciences had experienced some intervention from Althusserian Marxism. As taken up by the left, post-structuralism came to occupy much the same space as that of its host culture, Marxism. Accordingly in Britain it has gained a broad range of purchase in a number of different disciplines across the academic spectrum: in film theory and cultural studies, the social sciences and history writing, in art history, musicology and of course the study of literature. This remarkable effect will be explored more fully in the chapters which follow.

The fact of this symbiosis with Marxism poses a difficulty for the writing of any book on British developments. Post-structuralism will have to be described in some degree of separation from the Marxism on which it depends, a separation I have tried to maintain while recognising that what is needed is a preliminary history of British Marxism since 1965. That is for someone else to write, the sooner the better.

British post-structuralism has had considerable influence on feminist writing. There are three possible strategies a male writer can take up in writing about feminism. One is to say nothing about it — ignoring it; another is to say a little about it — marginalising it; a third is to say a lot about it — appropriating it. I think it is no harm for a male writer to find himself once again in an impossible position. *British post-structuralism* contains no separate section on 'feminist criticism' and work is discussed as it occurs in each different area. In any case, for an excellent account of the relations between feminism and post-structuralism the reader may turn confidently to Chris Weedon's recently published *Feminist practice and poststructuralist theory*.

The name "British" is an embarrassment, since it is the cover under which English imperialism imposed itself on Ireland, Wales and Scotland. This book should be called "English post-structuralism" and this is what is meant, even though the conventional usage "British" has been retained.

1

Beginnings: On the Left

English separateness and provincialism; English backwardness and traditionalism; English religiosity and moralistic vapouring, paltry English "empiricism" or instinctive distrust of reason ...

Tom Nairn

In 1870 the British economy faced a choice: either to develop new industries — chemicals, even the new electrical industry — and compete there with the rising economies of Germany and the United States; or to sell its existing commodities to the protected market of the Empire. The gods give in to those they wish to destroy; the soft option was chosen, and this, in part, accounts for the chronic crisis afflicting the British economy ever since.

In 1974 British Marxism reached its peak, both in theory and practice. Whereas other national cultures went through a form of political and ideological crisis during the 1960s, as did France in 1968, Britain's corresponding experience did not arrive until six years later. The long-term economic decline was focused that year in the attempt by the Conservative government to hold down wages in the hope of diverting capital into serious investment and renewal. This brought the government into collision with industrial workers and in particular the coal miners, whose demand for a pay rise was refused in October 1973. They banned overtime working, which immediately cut the supply of coal during the winter so that by Christmas the lights started to go off. From 2 January 1974 the government reduced the working week to three days in order to save gas and electricity (general production, however, only fell by 10 per cent). Strongly supported by workers in other industries, the

1

miners held a ballot about a possible strike and on 4 February, when the result was declared, 81 per cent had voted for all-out action. In a final attempt to defeat the miners, on 7 February the government called a General Election over the question, "Who governs Britain?", thus at a stroke turning an industrial action into a political issue, something the Left had been trying to do since Chartism.

The Tories narrowly lost the election. The incoming right-wing Labour government first paid off the miners and then spent the next twelve months defusing and deflecting the radical energies released by this combined economic and political crisis, a mobilisation extending from the many other industrial workers who had acted in support of the miners across to the many socialists who had been active in pressing the Labour Party to implement its "Alternative Economic Strategy" (see Hodgson 1981 and 1984). (How different the situation in 1974 from that of the coal dispute of 1984–5 when another strike was undertaken, though this time without a ballot, without significant help from other manual workers, and, according to polls, without at any time the support of more than 28 per cent of the electorate.)

The year 1974, then, can be seen in retrospect as the 'moment' of British intellectual Marxism. Since that is the parent culture onto which post-structuralism became grafted, this chapter will attempt to give a schematic and provisional outline of its main features (an adequate history of British Marxism from 1960 to 1985 has yet to be written). Two separate currents of British Marxism flow into the conjuncture of 1974. One, typified by the work of Raymond Williams, was left-liberal, culturalist and empiricist; another, deriving from the promotion of Althusserian Marxism by the New Left from the mid-1960s on, seeks to be, in contrast, theoretical, scientific and rationalist.

Two areas of controversy between them come to impinge particularly on post-structuralism. One is the question of how to conceptualise the way human action is determined by economic structures, how far social and ideological superstructures maintain a 'relative autonomy' in relation to the economic base. And connected to that is the question of the subject, specifically whether the subject is understood according to a humanist conception as freely choosing and constitutive or as structurally determined and constituted, 'a support for a position'. This question in turn frames accounts of the literary text and the degree to which it is actively interpreted by the reader as against imposing itself on the reader. These topics provide an arena for contention between the culturalist

2

and theoretist wings of British Marxism during the years before and after 1974. But around 1974 the two tendencies temporarily coalesce.

Raymond Williams and the traditional Left

Published in 1958, Raymond Williams's *Culture and society, 1780–1950* takes off from dissatisfaction with the notion of culture put forward ten years earlier in T. S. Eliot's *Notes towards the definition of culture*. Eliot defines "culture" not in terms of an individual or a class but as the development "of a *whole society*" (1948, reprinted 1962, p. 21). In what has become a famous passage, Eliot's *Notes* summarise his idea of culture in a collage of images and impressions:

> Culture...includes all the characteristic activities and interests of a people: Derby Day, Henley Regatta, Cowes, the twelfth of August, a cup final, the pin table, the dart board, Wensleydale cheese, boiled cabbage cut into sections, beetroot in vinegar, nineteenth-century Gothic churches, and the music of Elgar. (p. 31)

Informal, consumerist, pastoral, this is a vision of culture Williams cites in the chapter on Eliot in *Culture and society* (1958, reprinted 1963, p. 230) and criticises by mobilising against it precisely Eliot's own concept of culture as supposing "the development of...a *whole society*". For even to attempt to represent 'the whole' in the full sense of that term the list would have to include also "steelmaking, touring in motor-cars, mixed farming, the Stock Exchange, coalmining, and London Transport" (p. 230).

Culture and society takes a left-culturalist position. It is socialist in that the theme of the book is to compel recognition for working-class culture in addition to that of the class that might best be termed 'the gentry'; socialist also in its grasp of economic determination (thus, against Eliot and his critique of liberal individualism, Williams is able to argue that Eliot's defence of conservative and elitist culture rests on precisely that economic system of 'free economy' which goes along with the 'atomised', individualist view of society Eliot wishes to attack, pp. 235–8). But the position is culturalist in that its acceptance of the idea of "a whole society" makes it inevitably complicit with traditional liberal

3

notions of the organic unity of society, state and nation in a 'common culture' imagined as transcending class divisions.

Such a domain of transcendence can only be founded in a notion of the individual as somehow constituting an essence and origin finally beyond all structural determinations, economic, social and linguistic (a 'beyond' Williams later in *The long revolution* names by introducing the term "structure of feeling" (1965, pp. 64–5)). Although Williams's text criticises explicitly the "Romantic" tradition and works hard to negotiate an opposing position, it remains committed to a fundamental humanism, as is shown when there is direct confrontation with historical materialism in the chapter on "Marxism and culture". This poses starkly the question of whether art is or is not determined by the economic structure of society and, implicit in this issue, whether the human subject is source or effect, constitutive or constituted.

Williams turns first to the canonical passage in Marx's Preface to the *Critique of political economy* (1859) which argues that according to the epoch of a mode of production people enter social relations which, together with the forces of production, constitute the economic structure of society. This is the base,

> the real foundation, on which rise legal and political superstructures and to which correspond definite forms of social consciousness. The mode of production in material life determines the general character of the social, political and spiritual processes of life. (cited Williams, 1963, p. 259)

And there follows the sentence which, among other things, makes historical materialism a necessary antecedent of the post-structuralist assertion that human consciousness is an effect rather than a source: "It is not people's consciousness that determines their existence, but, on the contrary, their social existence determines their consciousness". The chapter in Williams then enters a fine-print reading of these sentences and the rest of the passage, adding to it the qualification by Engels (from his letter to Bloch, 21 September 1890) that though "the determining element in history is *ultimately* the production and reproduction in real life", account must also be taken of "an interaction" between base and superstructure such that elements of the superstructure, including the arts, exercise an active influence of their own.

Throughout his sympathetic discussion Williams is concerned primarily with literature and the arts, that is, with 'high cultural'

4

aspects of the superstructure rather than the textual productions of modern technology and popular culture (radio, film, television). He pursues the question of how Marxism understands the autonomy of art because it focuses the issue of individual freedom and subjectivity, pressing it through a great deal of Romantic and Arnoldian obfuscation put up by British Marxists in the 1930s towards an inexorable either/or formulated as follows:

> Either the arts are passively dependent on social reality, a proposition which I take to be that of mechanical materialism, or a vulgar misinterpretation of Marx. Or the arts, as the creators of consciousness, determine social reality, the proposition which the Romantic poets sometimes advanced. (p. 266)

If social existence determines consciousness, socialist culture will arise spontaneously from the emancipation of the working class; if, however, socialist culture has to be engineered, planned and fostered, then consciousness determines existence. At what is seen as a polarised impasse — either human individuals act consciously and collectively to shape history or they are passively determined by their position in relation to the mode of production — Williams gives up his engagement, avowing that he writes as "one who is not a Marxist" (p. 269). Yet the argument has reached exactly that point at which the issue of the subject and the problems of relative autonomy are rethought by Althusser's first published essays in France in the early 1960s.

Writing in 1958, Williams is working "almost single-handedly" (Eagleton 1976, p. 23), largely in isolation from any native English socialist culture. The essay really has its home in the 1930s and a pre-war debate, as its list of British Marxists reveals — Rex Warner, Alick West, Christopher Caudwell. It ignores Lenin's articles on Tolstoy of 1908–10 and Trotsky's *Literature and revolution*. More seriously, it does not know of the passage on Greek art and its trans-historical survival apparently above and beyond any given economic base, written by Marx as part of the "Introduction" of the *Grundrisse* (see 1973, pp. 110–11). This was published separately in German in 1939 and in English in 1947, though it was not readily available until it appeared in an edition of the *Introduction to a critique of political economy* in 1971 (see Marx and Engels 1947 and Marx 1971). But this was all later. Georg Lukács's *The historical novel* was not published in English until 1962. Between 1957 and 1964 Brecht's German publisher had been putting out his collected prose, a selection of which appeared in English translation in 1964 as *Brecht on theatre*. These are only some of the older texts re-launched in the changed social and cultural conditions of the 1960s. The years after 1958 saw the ascendency in Britain and elsewhere of the New Left. Its strategy was to transform the whole British Marxist tradition.

The New Left

In October 1964 Labour, led by Harold Wilson, won a narrow victory over the Tories, led by a man who was born the fourteenth Earl of Home (pronounced "Hume"). A smell of old corruption hung over the last months of the Conservative government, a sense of crisis which the newly founded *New Left Review* named and explored in a series of 'manifesto' articles published in 1964. Starting from an analysis of the contemporary conjuncture as a product of British historical experience, they aim to intervene in a present struggle.

For historical materialism the dominant class and the character of an epoch is defined by its mode of production (primitive communism, Asiatic, ancient, feudal, capitalist). In the classic (Oedipal) scenario the oppressed class of one epoch throws out its oppressor to become the ruling class of the next. Thus at the Renaissance the bourgeoisie (aided by the serfs) destroys the feudal nobility and takes its place in charge of a new mode of production which produces the proletariat, who, learning from the bourgeoisie yet exploiting no other class, are uniquely able to overthrow the bourgeoisie and introduce a genuinely democratic, classless society.

Why hasn't this happened yet in England? That is the question addressed by the *New Left Review* in two 1964 essays, Perry Anderson's "Origins of the present crisis" and Tom Nairn's "The English working class". Their answer, which follows Marx closely, is that there has been no working class revolution: (1) because the English bourgeois revolution (also known as the English Civil War) was the first of its kind and happened too early, the English bourgeoisie, unlike the French, never broke fully with the landed aristocracy to establish a separate bourgeois character; (2) because the bourgeoisie had no clear and separate class identity, the working class that emerged in the Industrial Revolution correspondingly could not find a clear class identity to set against it; (3) because the English bourgeoisie developed so early, between 1642 and 1660 rather than after the Enlightenment and 1789, the dominant ideology in Britain, formed in the religious ideas of the seventeenth century, became a form of empiricism rather than a coherent and rationalist world-view.

Accordingly, in a process exacerbated by the success of Empire and sustained by Britain's immunity from defeat or occupation in the Second World War, the British working class was "forced into a *corporative* mode of existence and consciousness, a class in and for itself" (Nairn 1964, p. 52). Cut off from Europe, divorced from rationalism and the Enlightenment, defeated in the early nineteenth century by the joint manœuvres of the landed gentry and the industrial bourgeoisie, the English working class — so Nairn concludes — "immunized against theory like no other class, by its entire historical experience, needed theory like no other". And, he adds, "It still does" (p. 57).

The New Left version of British history and strategy for remaking it was rapidly opposed by the traditional left. Edward Thompson's *The making of the English working class* had been published in 1963 and in fact Nairn's essay is in part a review article on this book. Representing the traditional left, Thompson replied to the New Left account of English history in a long article, "The peculiarities of the English" published in 1965 (and reprinted later in Thompson's anti-Althusserian work, *The poverty of theory*, 1978). To this Anderson in turn replied in "Socialism and pseudo-empiricism" in 1966. Rather than rehearse this debate at the level of content, it may better signal the differences between old and new left Marxism if two passages of text are looked at with attention to the assumptions and style of their discourse.

The first, from the "Conclusion" of *Culture and society*, starts to turn Burke's notorious reference to the working class as "the swinish multitude" against the class Burke speaks for:

> The record of the working-class movement in its attitudes to education, to learning and to art is on the whole a good record. It has sometimes wrongly interpreted, often neglected where it did not know. But it has never sought to destroy the institutions of this kind of culture; it has, on the contrary, pressed for their extension, for their wider social recognition, and, in our own time, for the application of a larger part of our material resources to their maintenance and development.

Such a record will do more than stand comparison with that of the class by which the working class has been most actively and explicitly opposed. This, indeed, is the curious incident of the swine in the night. As the light came, and we could look around, it appeared that the trampling, which we had all heard, did not after all come from them. (Williams 1963, p. 314)

The second, from Anderson's 1964 essay, moves with similarly broad brush-strokes over a large historical perspective:

The distinctive facets of English class structure, as it has evolved over three centuries, can thus be summed up as follows. After a bitter, cathartic revolution, which transformed the structure but not the superstructures of English society, a landed aristocracy, underpinned by a powerful mercantile affinal group, became the first dominant capitalist class in Britain. This dynamic agrarian capitalism expelled the English peasantry from history. Its success was economically the 'floor' and sociologically the 'ceiling' of the rise of the industrial bourgeoisie. Undisturbed by a feudal state, terrified of the French Revolution and its own proletariat, mesmerized by the prestige and authority of the landed class, the bourgeoisie won two modest victories, lost its nerve and ended by losing its identity. The late Victorian era and the high noon of imperialism welded aristocracy and bourgeoisie together in a single social bloc. The working-class fought passionately and unaided against the advent of industrial capitalism; its extreme exhaustion after successive defeats was the measure of its efforts. Henceforward it evolved, separate but subordinate, within the apparently unshakeable structure of British capitalism, unable, despite its great numerical superiority, to transform the fundamental nature of British society. (Anderson 1964, pp. 38–9, original italicised)

The New Left might interrogate the Williams paragraph as follows.

Why the language and tone of the headmaster on speech day ("the record of the working-class movement...is on the whole a good record", "...and will more than stand comparison...")? Why does it seek to justify working-class culture for and to the ruling class and by appealing to what are implicitly its standards? And why is the meaning of the final sentence wrapped up in indirect language and negatives ("did not after all") and a Biblical allusion to the Gadarene swine (Matthew 8: 23–34) when what it is trying to say is that the real aggressor, the real enemy of culture in Britain is the hypocrisy, cruelty, ruthlessness and brutality of the British ruling class, that same class which in the years 1845–1848 ensured that its colony, Ireland, remained a net exporter of food while over one million Irish men, women and children starved slowly to death, that presided over the Belsen-like horrors of poverty described by Engels in his book on Manchester in the 1840s, that holds the world highest figure (not recorded in *Guinness*) for the number of civilians killed in twelve hours (125,000 plus in Dresden on the night of 13 February 1945) and whose true nature is revealed by the magistrates' decision to send mounted horse into the crowd at Peter's Fields on 16 August 1819?

There is a veiled allusion to the Peterloo Massacre in Williams's reference to "trampling" but it is veiled only. Mutedly defensive in tone, the style aims at a magisterial impersonality, illustrated well in the willingness to arbitrate between the classes ("the class by which the working class has been most actively and explicitly opposed") from a point *beyond* the two from which "we" can "look around" in the morning of a kind of Day of Judgement "as the light came" and see everything objectively and as it really is. To occupy this supra-class position we would have to be, like God, a transcendental subject.

The New Left style in contrast shows no hesitation about defining and understanding society in class terms: "the landed aristocracy", "the bourgeoisie", "the proletariat". Confidently aggressive and coldly sardonic in tone, the passage makes no attempt to address itself from a position 'above the struggle'. Explicit, abstract, avoiding Biblical or colloquial language in favour of the precise vocabulary of social science, it aims to set itself at a critical distance from the everyday. Yet it proceeds in the belief that accurate analysis can be at the same time authoritative and committed, objective and partisan, rational and real.

Obviously a difference in generation and conjuncture separates the two paragraphs. Williams is harking back to the 1930s and writing at the height of the 'social democratic' years, of the so-called 'end of ideology', of Eisenhower and Macmillan (who won the General Election of 1959 with the daringly vernacular slogan, "You've never had it so good"). Having behind it a memory only of the post-war period, Anderson's generation speaks out of contempt for the complacency and banal prosperity of the 1950s and anticipates the ever-increasing demands of the 1960s.

But the New Left assurance derives also from its basis in a changed problematic. Eschewing Williams's humanism, it believes social experience to be structured by history in a way susceptible to scientific analysis. The seventeenth-century revolution "transformed the structure but not the superstructures of English society": the New Left is confidently able to separate base and superstructure because it has come to terms with the notion of relative autonomy.

Part of the pessimism of Williams's 1958 text must ensue from the unresolved theoretical dilemma on which it rests and which is brought into the open in the discussion of Marxism and culture. If the Marxist view of base and superstructure is wrong, then trying to be one of "the creators of consciousness" by writing a book on class and culture is merely an individualistic, Romantic enterprise, no better than writing a poem; if, on the other hand, the economy always already determines everything, it's not worth writing at all because it will happen anyway. The New Left escapes this disabling theoretical impasse by means of the Althusserian conception of the relative autonomy of the superstructure (which includes publishing socialist journals). It leads to the conviction that theory matters.

Confronting the national culture

Some of the consequences of this stance are evident in Anderson's essay of 1968, "Components of the national culture". Written in the context of the counter-culture and the activism of the student movement, this extended essay has no hesitation in equating English national culture with academic and theoretical writing (while Nairn, who is Scots, carefully distinguishes between "English" and "British", Anderson does not). "Britain, the most conservative major society in Europe, has a culture in its own image: mediocre and inert" (1968, p. 5): in order to explain this situation the argument begins by excluding the natural sciences and creative arts from its account, and then, in brief, aims to bring together two features (which are neither correspondent nor homogeneous).

One is the absence of a classical sociology in Britain on the model of Durkheim, Pareto or Weber, accounted for, once again, by the failure in the nineteenth century of the English bourgeoisie to define itself antagonistically as a class over against the aristocracy. Instead the hegemonic ideology of England consists of what Anderson refers to as the "aristocratic combination of 'traditionalism' and 'empiricism'" (p. 12). Secondly, England, which in 1900 had "no separate intelligentsia" (p. 14), was forced in the twentieth century to import one, and the one it got, as a consequence of war and revolution in continental Europe, was conservative and attracted to England by its apparent traditionalism and stability — what Anderson calls "a 'White', counter-revolutionary emigration" (p. 17). Each major discipline became dominated by a single, nameable figure.Thus:

	Discipline	*Country of origin*
Wittgenstein	Philosophy	Austria
Malinowski	Anthropology	Poland
Namier	History	Poland
Popper	Social theory	Austria
Berlin	Political theory	Austria
Gombrich	Aesthetics	Austria
Eysenck	Pyschology	Germany
Klein	Psychoanalysis	Austria (p. 16)

On this basis the essay feels able to assess the limitations of each discipline in terms of its failure to totalise its possibilities. Philosophy remains stuck with common sense (pp. 20–2), political theory abstracts the political from the economic (pp. 23–5), history has divorced itself from theory (pp. 26–8), psychology has conceived individual psychology as prior to social determination (pp. 32–3), aesthetics has rested on a psychology of perception (pp. 35–7), while psychoanalysis, a potentially radical discipline, has sealed itself off in a technical enclave (pp. 38–41).

Only two disciplines escape censure: anthropology, an area in which accurate and totalising knowledge was necessary for the survival of Empire, and (though this may comes as a surprise to some readers) the literary criticism of F. R. Leavis. This is seen as a displaced activity but totalising nevertheless for he has "a very specific epistemology" (p. 48), a philosophy of history and an accurate assessment of the cultural situation: "Alone of the thinkers in this survey, he was acutely aware that something had gone wrong in British culture" (p. 51). For Anderson it is no accident that Raymond Williams emerged in the field of literary criticism.

However speculative, Anderson's original and ambitiously comprehensive analysis is intended as a programme for change. It earns its place in this present account for two reasons. It illustrates perfectly the New Left conception of the relative autonomy of intellectual life and its concern with 'struggle at the level of theory'. But it also provides a benchmark by which, in a conclusion, the present study will be able to review developments in English academic culture since 1968.

In the conjuncture of 1974

For a short period the two tendencies of the British left made up a kind of coalition until, in the mid-1970s, hostilities were resumed (as will be discussed in a later chapter). Two texts are symptomatic of this temporary alignment.

In 1973, the same year that he published *The country and the city*, Raymond Williams contributed an essay on "Base and superstructure in Marxist cultural theory" to the *New Left Review* (reprinted in Williams 1980). The title and place of publication tell most of the story. "Either the arts are passively dependent on social reality...Or the arts...determine social reality": what was presented as an intractable either/or in *Culture and society* has now been revised in a way that takes account of newly available and newly produced work by Gramsci, Lukács and Althusser (though Althusser is not mentioned).

At the heart of Williams's revaluation of Marxism is the fact that the social formation is now understood in temporal rather than spatial terms. Thus it is asserted that a stage in the development of production, though it may be made precise by analysis, "is never in practice either uniform or static" so that "we have to say that when we talk of 'the base', we are talking of a process and not a state" (1973, reprinted 1980, p. 34). Accordingly, the notion of determination can lose its connotation of mechanical necessity while the superstructure may acquire relative autonomy:

We have to revalue 'determination' towards the setting of limits and the exertion of pressure, and away from a predicted, prefigured and controlled content. We have to revalue 'superstructure' towards a related range of cultural practices, and away from a reflected, reproduced or specifically dependent content. And, crucially, we have to revalue 'the base' away from the notion of a fixed economic or technological abstraction, and towards the specific activities of men in real social and economic relationships, containing fundamental contradictions and variations and therefore always in a state of dynamic process. (p. 34.)

Without explicit and detailed critical reference back to Althusser's texts and arguments it is hard to be certain exactly what is being conceded in this cagey and relatively informal statement (precisely what "pressures" and "limits" are we talking about? how far "towards" and "away from" and why? and so on). But in this idiosyncratically magisterial style Williams's revised position now discovers and subscribes to a Marxism sufficiently flexible to satisfy a belief in "the specific activities of men", a constitutive subject affirmed in the negative assertion "that no mode of production...no dominant society...no dominant culture, in reality exhausts human practice, human energy, human intention" (p. 43).

On this basis, acknowledging (though not naming) the relative autonomy of 'superstructural' practices, the remainder of the essay can proceed to describe the uneven co-existence at any one time of cultural practice in forms which are either dominant, residual or emergent. The sting, however, is in the tail. For in a kind of supplement or afterthought the essay discriminates between determining structures and constitutive processes, poses them as an either/or and finally throws all its weight on the side of practice.

At first it looks very much like an anti-humanist demystification of high culture and works of art. Noting that aesthetic interest has focused on the consumption of art objects rather on the practices in which they are produced, Williams argues that while sculptures have "specific material existence", texts such as *Hamlet, Wuthering Heights* and Beethoven's Fifth Symphony do not. They are "not objects but *notations*", and what matters is the activity and practice in which they are made accessible "through active perception and interpretation" (p. 47). Therefore we must "break from the notion of isolating an object and then discovering its components" so that "on the contrary" we "discover the nature of a practice and then its conditions" (p. 47).

There are certain difficulties here. It could be asked how a painting or a sculpture is taken to differ from a written or musical text in being an object when both kinds are equally a form of sign or signification. Secondly, the option of analysing the components of a text or attending to the practice of its reproduction is offered as an either/or — we should "look not for the components of a product but for the conditions of a practice" (p. 48). Thus the continuing *relation* between the text as structure and the text as act of reading is collapsed on one side so that the act of reading becomes determining and constitutive. In order for this to happen the materiality of the signifier has been dematerialised into a shadowy simulacrum, "notations", as though writing consisted only of graphic marks on a plain background. Nevertheless, as will be discussed in a later chapter, these two pages from Williams's 1973 essay are the most important. For they inaugurate what will be referred to as 'left deconstruction'.

Myths of power

If this essay from Williams represents the moment of 1974 as a solidarity between two wings of socialist political theory, Terry Eagleton's book on the Brontës, *Myths of power* (1975) may stand for that moment as realised in the mode of literary criticism. Eagleton was Williams's pupil but had been from the early 1970s associated with the *New Left Review* and the politics of the IMG (International Marxist Group) which ran it. It is also fitting that the name of Eagleton, the most important Marxist critic writing in English, should make an early appearance at this point. Although his position is Marxist and not post-structuralist, his work has constantly engaged with post-structuralism. His writings will recur like a red thread through many of the pages that follow.

Myths of power is also remarkable in quite another way. Althusser remarks that when nothing happens this "is also an event" (1977a, p. 126). So far this account of the left and New Left to 1974 has not been compelled by the nature of the discussion to consider the questions raised for Marxist theory by feminism, even though Williams's reference above to "the specific activities of men" now sounds strangely unselfconscious. Eagleton's book begins to open up the question of gender, and, in the period after 1974, it becomes a central issue both in Marxist and post-structuralist theory.

At the level of explicit theory *Myths of power* sidesteps the official British Marxist tradition, which most significantly here includes the account of *Wuthering Heights* written by Arnold Kettle for his *An introduction to the English novel* (1951). In fact *Myths of power* ignores Kettle, and his name does not even appear in the index, possibly because he was for many years a member of the

Executive Committee of the British Communist Party while Eagleton's allegiances were at that time strongly Trotskyist. In this respect *Myths of power* can be read as a work of intended de-Stalinisation.

From the French Marxist critic Lucien Goldmann and his 1967 essay on "The Sociology of literature: status and problems of method", *Myths of power* draws the concept of "categorial structure" as a term to designate ideological structures present both in various different texts and in the social group or class which produces them. It is argued that an ideological structure, specifically a sense of conflict, arising "from the real history of the West Riding in the first half of the nineteenth century" is "imaginatively grasped and transposed in the production of the Brontës' fiction" (1975, p. 4), the conflict being that between the industrial bourgeoisie and the landed gentry. That kind of link had not been asserted with such boldness in literary criticism for 50 years (Kettle is much more reticent).

The concept of categorial structure is meant to negotiate the issue of relative autonomy. On the one hand it tries to maintain a firm sense of the relation between the literary text and the historical formation in which it was produced, the real foundations of a real history (in one of the first allusions to it in English, Macherey's *A theory of literary production*, published in France in 1966 (English 1978), is criticised for treating literature as too distantly separated from its historical origins). On the other hand the notion of categorial structure seeks to preserve an adequate appreciation of the literariness of literature and the degree to which it resists understanding as a reflection of a history which precedes it (in the same footnote on Macherey (p. 138), Goldmann is criticised in turn for conceiving the relation between literature and history as too simple, too transparent).

Yet there is relatively little theory in *Myths of power* and what there is aims to synthesise theoretical Marxism with a traditional left culturalism, with ideas of the author as individual and literature as creation and imagination. The content of the novels is related to "real history" because they are rooted in the lives of the sisters, who lived out an uneven and contradictory position in class terms but also as "socially insecure *women*" (p. 8). But the literary autonomy of the novels is explained by the fact that such experienced history has been "imaginatively grasped and transposed" into a fictionally appropriate form. This relation between 'content' and 'form' becomes rethought by the time of Eagleton's *Criticism and ideology* (1976) but the terms of its phrasing — and conceptualisation — correspond clearly to 1974 and to a coming together of left culturalism and Marxism.

As does something else. *Myths of power* is uncompromisingly subtitled "A Marxist study of the Brontës", and although it was published in 1975 it was written when the miners were on strike in 1974. In addition to a personal inscription, it is dedicated to "the working-class movement of West Yorkshire" and so precisely to those Yorkshire miners, notoriously the most militant, who had led the struggle to topple the Conservative government in the weeks before the book's own acknowledged dating: "April 1974". In this as in its attempt to make cohere culturalist notions of the authorial imagination with a historical materialist conception of economic class the text addresses itself from the moment of British Marxism. The year 1974 is a moment of synthesis but also of transition. If synthesis is achieved in Williams because his Marxism is emerging from a dominant humanism, in Eagleton it is possible because his residual humanism is in transition towards Althusser. Althusserianism is the culture in which British post-structuralism grew, for reasons clearer now than they were at the time.

Relative autonomy and the Althusserian inheritance

Marx, in what must be one of the most frequently interpreted paragraphs outside the Bible, that cited by Williams (p. 4 above), writes of the economic structure of society as "the real foundation" (Marx and Engels 1950, vol. 1, p. 328) on which superstructures rise. This envisages the social formation as a unity in which the apparent and phenomenal existence of the superstructure is determined by the noumenal reality of the base. And for that architecture provides an appropriate metaphor: foundation and superstructure. But the metaphor reveals unequivocally that the conception is of a structure rather than a process. Everything changes once the dimension of time is introduced, as it is by the Althusserian reformulation (see Althusser 1977a, especially the 1962 essay on "Contradiction and overdetermination" and the 1963 essay "On the materialist dialectic").

Althusser redefines the social formation temporally as a number of practices, forms of active *transformation* — economic, political, ideological, theoretical — in each of which a means of production transforms a raw material into a product. Each practice is active in its own *specific effectivity* (materially that's how particular things have to be done) yet each is a necessary condition of existence for the others. Together these practices constitute an uneven and decentred structure but a structure in dominance since economic practice determines the relation of practices at any conjuncture. But even this privileged dominance is qualified by time and so relativised: economic practice determines in the last instance but "the lonely hour of the 'last instance' never comes" (Althusser 1977a, p. 113).

Sustained as it was by the counter-cultural conjunction of workers and students in the late 1960s and early 1970s, the 'work' of reading Althusser in translation advocated in Britain by the New Left seemed to unite in a deeply un-English compound the most exacting and rigorous mode of theoretical discourse with a directly political purpose. In retrospect (for other appraisals, see Benton 1984, Eagleton 1986a, pp. 1–5, James 1987) there is no denying that these Althusserian texts are contaminated with idealism, that (to be very cursory): (1) the account of the social formation as a structure in dominance, however much it recognises the relative autonomy of the various other practices, nevertheless remains grounded in an essentialist understanding of mode of production in the form of economic practice as ultimately corresponding to 'the real' behind the superstructural 'appearances' of ideological and political practice; (2) this 'real' functions for Althusser as a truth effectively given prior to its discursive construction and so able to found a would-be absolute opposition between 'science' and 'ideology'.

Yet the work of Althusser imported into Britain at least three lines of thought, three conceptualisations, which can be validly regarded as post-structuralist: the account of the historical formation as decentred; the assertion that knowledge as proceeding from theoretical practice is discursively constructed; the account of the subject as effect rather than cause.

A decentred structure

Reading Capital brings out firmly how this reworking of historical materialism breaks with its Hegelian residue. In the early Marx all the elements of the whole always co-exist in one and the same time...This means that the structure of the historical existence of the Hegelian social totality allows what I propose to call an *'essential section'* (*coupe d'essence*), i.e., an intellectual operation in which a *vertical break* is made at any moment in historical time, a break in the present such that all the elements of the whole revealed by this section are in an immediate relationship with one another, a relationship that immediately expresses their internal essence. (Althusser and Balibar 1975, p. 94)

For Althusser, it would be as wrong to understand the social formation as a spatial essence as it would be to imagine it as a temporal essence. The notion of absolute, chronological time which we inherit, the "hours, days, months" and "rags of time" which so preoccupy that typically Renaissance figure, John Donne, this, so it's argued, is bourgeois time. The "conception of historical time as continuous and homogeneous and contemporaneous with itself" (p. 96) must give way to recognition that "*there are* different times in history" (p. 96). And so:

it is no longer possible to think the process of the development of the different levels of the whole *in the same historical time*. Each of these different 'levels' does not have the same type of historical existence. On the contrary, we have to assign to each level a *peculiar time*, relatively autonomous and hence relatively independent, even in its dependence, of the 'times' of the other levels. We can and must say: for each mode of production there is a peculiar time and history, punctuated in a specific way by the development of the productive forces; the relations of production have their peculiar time and history, punctuated in a specific way; the political superstructure has its own history...; philosophy has its own time and history...; aesthetic productions have their own time and history...; scientific formations have their own time and history, etc. (p. 99, punctuation original)

And again: "This is the principle on which is based the possibility and necessity of different *histories* corresponding respectively to each of the 'levels'" (p. 100). In *Positions*, citing this argument from Althusser regarding what he summarises as "histories *different* in their type, rhythm, mode of inscription — intervallic, differentiated histories", Derrida adds "I have always subscribed to this" (1981a, p. 58). A conception of the social formation as decentred structure in dominance points towards that of a decentred structure.

Subject and object come into existence together, in a reciprocally situated relation. Althusser is able to show how the Hegelian/early Marxist conception of the social formation unified as an expressive totality presupposes correspondingly Man as its humanist subject. If there is no centre 'inside', there can be no transcendental position 'outside' given in relation to it. The subject is relativised, always already situated, a conception with consequences both for the 'philosophical' or epistemological subject as bearer of knowledge and the empirical subject situated in a lived relation to the rest of social formation.

Epistemology

From this basis Althusser proceeds to denounce what he terms "the ideological scenario" in the production of knowledge according to which the transcendental Subject confronts "the transcendental or absolute Object" (pp. 54–5). Such a scenario is constantly staged by empiricism in such a way as to suppose knowledge of the object is already part of the object itself:

> The whole empiricist process of knowledge lies in fact in an operation of the subject called *abstraction*. To know is to abstract from the real object its essence, the possession of which by the subject is then called knowledge. (pp. 35–6)

Although this account of empiricism would not be readily acknowledged by its defenders it is meant to typify all epistemologies which contrast with that defended as Marxist by Althusser. This conceives knowledge in terms of an active process of construction by which ideology is transformed discursively into science through theoretical practice: "the production of knowledge which is peculiar to theoretical practice constitutes a process that takes place *entirely in thought*" (p. 42). Although technically such knowledge is in part qualified as a 'process without a subject', the distinction between ideology and science cannot be absolute, as Althusser comes to admit (see *Essays in self-criticism*, 1976, especially pp. 106–7). The outcome of this line of analysis, rapidly noticed by some of his English readers, was to 'bracket the real', to defer attention to the truth of a discourse of knowledge in order to stress in the first place its power and effectivity *as a discourse.*

The empirical subject

Again, since object and subject are reciprocal, if the social formation is understood as decentred, unevenly comprised of practices with their own specific effectivity and their own 'time', then the traditional humanist conception of a centred, unified and transcendent subject must be abandoned. The subject must be understood as a dispersed, heterogeneous effect rather than originary cause, as indeed it is in the Marxist tradition from which Althusser takes the concept of the subject as support (*Träger*) for a socially ascribed place or position.

Developing this in the essay "Ideology and ideological state apparatuses", Althusser goes beyond previous Marxist criticism of the bourgeois conception of the subject to a critique which would explain not only the structure of relations determining the position the subject supports but also the internal process by which the subject 'freely' enters that position, both the constituting process *and* how the subject appears to itself as constitutive. Ideology works on subjects so that they "work by themselves" (1977b, p. 169), constructs them through a process of *interpellation*; and this "structure of all ideology, interpellating individuals as subjects...is *speculary*, i.e. a mirror-structure" (p. 168). At this point the Marxist account of how social being determines consciousness is mapped together with Lacan's psychoanalytic account of how the unconscious determines consciousness, how the subject appears as a split between the process of the Other (the Symbolic) and a position of fixity (the Imaginary) in which it misrecognises an identity for itself within that process. This account of the subject is the foundational matrix for British post-structuralism. Since it is the theme of the book it will not be developed further here (a fuller account is given below, pp. 38—42) except to give early warning of a problem regarding the subject which will keep coming up.

The Althusserian subject and post-structuralism

Although Althusser's conception of the subject denies the subject of humanism and in this respect opens a path to post-structuralism, it does so only by means of a functionalism which stands opposed to Marxist notions of social contradiction and class struggle by conceiving the subject *only* as constituted, only as support for an assigned position.

Its account of how the subject is constituted to appear constitutive appeals to the Lacanian conception of subjectivity and thus rests on a psychoanalytic understanding of the subject as unconscious, and therefore as the subject of desire. And while in the Althusserian conception the social formation terminates in the constituted subject, desire is endless. Once the subject has become a subject by entering discourse, its "needs have passed over into the register of desire" (Lacan 1977a, p. 309). For the subject in discourse, no closure can ever be more than a temporary "'anchoring point'" (p. 303) at which meaning closes itself into seeming self-presence, no object of desire ever more than a provisional satisfaction in the constitutively interminable metonomy through which desire always outruns whatever serves as its object, just as the bow-wave of a moving vessel is always sliding away from its bow. In the process of desire the subject is always constitutive though only within the terms of the social formation within which it is constituted, since what may figure as an object of desire is socially and historically discovered, as Lacan constantly stresses — under the system of commodity production, for example, "needs are reduced to exchange values" (p. 252) and objects of desire provided for the subject in the form of capitalist consumption.

Althusser's discussion of the social formation as decentred, of knowledge as a discursive construction and of the subject as effect all directly impinge on British post-structuralism. His work is best regarded now as a structuralism passing over into post-structuralism. Ultimately his account of the subject as ideologically constituted draws upon a psychoanalytic conceptualisation which subverts it. As Hirst and Woolley have convincingly demonstrated by matching and assessing Malinowski's anthropological analysis of incest taboos among the Trobriand Islanders against Freud's *Totem and taboo* (see 1982, pp. 149–60), the order of the social formation and the order of desire are simple *not commensurate*, that is (to borrow from Saussure) while by nature they are theoretically incommensurate they are always brought together in social practices and textual practices.

The issue is not merely of theoretical importance since it is implicated in the political question of the relations between Marxism and feminism, between class politics and the politics of gender (is gender to be understood as a function of economic relations? or does it require analysis in terms of something else — the operation of the unconscious — which cannot be theorised within historical materialism?). Merely asserted here, this theme will recur in the present work; it does so because post-structuralism, it will be argued, is to be defined and distinguished from structuralism because of the recognition it accords to the subject and the subject of desire.

2

Structuralism/Post-structuralism

The symbol manifests itself first of all as the murder of the thing.

Jacques Lacan

As an entry in the Supplement to the *Oxford English Dictionary* well evidences, the now fashionable trope of adding "post-" as a prefix has a venerable history. In the nineteenth century "post-classical" was already familiar and by 1888 there was "post-Christian". In the winter of 1910 in London Roger Fry organised an exhibition of paintings which was called "Manet and the Post-Impressionists", and this was soon followed by "post-Cubist" (1927), "post-Freudian" and "post-Victorian" (both 1938). Leslie Fiedler is credited with "post-modernist" in 1965. Becoming current from 1980, there is as yet no entry for "post-structuralist".

Jonathan Culler's *On deconstruction* says "the distinction between structuralism and post-structuralism is highly unreliable" (1983, p. 30); the purpose of this chapter is to render it less so, first by a review of theories of language, then by working through a specific application of classic structuralism in Umberto Eco's analysis of the James Bond novels (an example which usefully anticipates later discussion of cultural studies). The prefix "post-" is serious not casual for post-structuralism gets its intellectual force by being both *after* structuralism and *because* of it, because of the limitations discovered in structuralism's project.

23

Referent/signified/signifier

With a clarity and familiarity that needs little explanation Hume's *A treatise of human nature* opens as follows:

> All perceptions of the human mind resolve themselves into two distinct kinds, which I shall call *impressions* and *ideas*. The difference betwixt these consists in the degrees of force and liveliness, with which they strike upon the mind, and make their way into our thought or consciousness. Those perceptions which enter with most force and violence, we may name *impressions*...By *ideas*, I mean the faint images of these in thinking and reasoning. (1911, vol. 1, p. 11)

Impressions derive from something out there (the extra-discursive) and ideas derive from impressions. Citing the last two sentences of this passage in 1940 in his book *The imaginary* (translated as *The psychology of the imagination*) Sartre says it shows we have been guilty of a double error:

> We believed...that the image was *in* consciousness and that the object of the image was *in* the image. We pictured consciousness as a place peopled with small likenesses and these likenesses were images. (1963, p. 5).

If we accept the error of Hume's classically empiricist notion that knowledge is derived from reality we are led "to construct the world of the mind out of objects entirely like those of the external world" (p. 7).

Against this Sartre argues that consciousness and the extra-discursive are always separate and that consciousness is *constitutive*, becoming itself in that separation. Taking the usual example of a chair he first affirms that "whether I perceive or imagine that chair of straw on which I am seated, it always remains outside of consciousness" and then denies, against empiricism, that the chair can enter consciousness either as a perception (Hume's impressions) or as an image (Hume's ideas):

> the chair is not in consciousness; not even as an image. What we find here is not a semblance of the chair which suddenly worked its way into consciousness...but a certain type of consciousness, a synthetic organisation. (p. 7)

Sartre is not alone in making this kind of critique of empiricism in the twentieth century. But his argument has a great historical importance. It is the gate through which most French thought passed in the 1940s and 1950s, the gate through which post-structuralism emerges. For the philosophic distinction between the real chair in the extra-discursive and consciousness of the chair coincides with a linguistic distinction between thing and meaning, referent and concept. If we do not construct the world of meaning out of objects derived from the external world, then much greater plausibility can be attributed to Saussure's argument that language is a social institution and that linguistic meaning is a "social fact" (1959, p. 77), not a natural one.

Saussure steps aside from the sense/referent distinction. Rather, his analysis takes the common-sense idea of the "word" and reworks it in terms of a distinction that goes back to the Greek rhetoricians, that between the signifying substance and the matter signified, between the signifier or shaped sound, on the one hand, and the signified, concept or meaning on the other. The signifier "has no natural connection with the signified" (p. 69) though signifier and signified are brought together through convention, the "collective behaviour" of a society (p. 68) and only then take on the positive qualities of being a completed sign. If the signified was derived either immediately or ultimately from the referent, then presumably (such is the implication of Saussure's argument) all words would "have exact equivalents in meaning from one language to the next" (p. 166). They don't. Meanings emerge from the community of meaning and reach out to referents in the extra-discursive (or they may not, since quite a lot of meanings make perfectly good sense to us — 'witch', 'centaur', 'God' etc. — even if they can't be attached to anything at all outside language). It is not the case (to recall Sartre's summary of Hume) that likenesses strike consciousness from the external world; it is the case rather that meaning *issues* from the linguistic system.

The distinction between signifier and signified is a real one. If I am sitting on a bus and overhear two people talking in a language I don't know, I have access to the signifiers of that language but not its signifieds. Music is a mode of signification that apparently consists only of signifiers, shaped and ordered musical sounds without any clear or defined signified meaning. The artificial intelligence of advanced computers can replicate language and the effect of translation because they have been programmed to manipulate the signifiers of one language into an approximate transposition with those of another language, but the machine has no access to meaning, to the signified. I am sure that if the signifier/signified distinction falls, then so does post-structuralism.

Saussure also discriminates language between *langue* and *parole*, between the systematicity of language and any individual act of utterance within it, a distinction which points to the dialectic in all signification between system and event, structure and act, meaning as universal and meaning as particular. For the production of a particular meaning in a context can only take place on grounds that are necessarily shared and intersubjective. Hence Lacan's assertion that "it is in the chain of the signifier that the meaning 'insists' but that none of its elements 'consists' in the signification of which it is at the moment capable" (1977a, p. 153). A word processor may have a facility ("Copy") for storing frequently-used words and phrases (for this section I have "signifier", "signified" and "post-structuralism" copied ready to "Paste"); but in principle *everything* I might want to say, even in my most personal and passionately sincere moments, could be so stored in anticipation. Language consists of elements — words, phrases, sentences — used again and again by different people in different circumstances. The universal condition of language which necessarily betrays the particularity of any individual meaning by the same token guarantees that meaning — a meaning — becomes available to others. Structuralism took up its position firmly on the terrain of the apparently general and universal side of language, post-structuralism recognises in addition its particularity.

A structuralist analysis of James Bond

The conventional framework for the discussion of aesthetic texts, especially in literary criticism, still approaches them primarily as 'works', expressions of the experience and personality of their historical author. In so doing such criticism treats the text as though it were effectively transparent to a meaning or intention supposedly prior to the text and reflected in it. It thus ignores the materiality of a text as a sign, as a meaning produced in the present from a structure or ordering of signifiers. Structuralism, the movement which reached its plateau in the mid-1960s, associated with the work of the structural anthropologist, Claude Lévi-Strauss, broke radically with the conventional critical approach. Founding itself on the Saussurean distinction between signifier and signified it set out to analyse the text as self-sufficient ordering of the signifier of which meaning was an effect. It thus pronounced, in the title of an essay by Roland Barthes, "The death of the author", on the grounds that in a text "it is language which speaks, not the author" (1977, p. 143).

From linguistics structuralism borrowed two main concepts for its model of the text. One is the distinction between *langue* and *parole*, used to argue that any given text was an utterance generated according to the rules of a system of signification of which the text was an instance. In analysing this underlying and invisible system structuralism had recourse to Saussure's account of the way phonemes, the smallest units systematised in a language, are characterised not "by their own positive quality but simply by the fact that they are distinct" and negatively opposed (Saussure 1959, p. 119). Generalising this as a model, structuralism concentrated on disclosing the system of oppositions or opposed features structuring a text.

Umberto Eco's essay on the James Bond novels, "The narrative structure in Fleming", was published in England in 1966 at the height of structuralism's esteem. Though sales have slid since the 1960s, Fleming's *œuvre* remains fairly well known so Eco's analysis has the advantage of being easily accessible. Drawing on the precedent of Vladimir Propp in his *Morphology of the folk tale* (1928), it proceeds on the assumption that the texts have "an objective and conventional structural strategy" (1982, p. 244) which functions to produce their effects and that this structure or "narrating machine" is susceptible to rational, indeed scientific, analysis.

Having defined the corpus for examination — the ten novels from *Casino Royale* (1953) to *You only live twice* (1964) — by excluding *The spy who loved me* (1962), Eco's analysis begins by proposing that the ten texts are generated by a system of permutations from fourteen oppositions or dichotomies:

(a)   Bond/M
(b)   Bond/Villain
(c)   Villain/Woman
(d)   Woman/Bond
(e)   Free World/Soviet Union
(f)   Great Britain/Countries not Anglo-Saxon
(g)   Duty/Sacrifice
(h)   Cupidity/Ideals

(i) Love/Death
(j) Chance/Planning
(k) Luxury/Discomfort
(l) Excess/Moderation
(m) Perversion/Innocence
(n) Loyalty/Disloyalty

These, so Eco claims, will cover "all the narrative ideas of Fleming" (p. 245). The first four, consisting of contrasting characters, are the most important:

(1) *Bond/M*. In the ambivalent love–hate relation of Bond and his chief, M is clearly dominant (and linked to other polarities such as Duty, Country and Order). The narrative machine needs M to start Bond on the road of duty leading to the second opposition.

(2) *Bond/Villain*. Eco has much to say about Fleming's villains, which include Le Chiffre, Mr Big, Seraffino Strang, Hugo Drax, Red Grant, Rosa Klebb and Ernst Blofeld, especially about their sexual and racial ambiguity:

> The Villain is born in an ethnic area that stretches from central Europe to the Slav countries and to the Mediterranean basin: as a rule he is of mixed blood and his origins are complex and obscure; he is asexual or homosexual, or at any rate is not sexually normal. (p. 249)

To the typical qualities of the villain

> are opposed the Bond characteristics, in particular Loyalty to the Service, Anglo-Saxon Moderation opposed to the excess of halfbreeds, the selection of Discomfort and the acceptance of Sacrifice against the ostentatious luxury of the enemy, the stroke of opportunistic genius (Chance?) opposed to the cold Planning which it defeats. (p. 251)

As Bond/M leads to Bond/Villain, so that opposition (which Eco refers to as (i) Love/Death) is "perfected" in the third and fourth opposition:

(3) *Villain/Woman* and (4) *Woman/Bond*. These can be taken together since in the narrative chain the Woman is dominated at first by the Villain and then released by Bond:

The general scheme is (1) the girl is beautiful and good; (2) has been made frigid and unhappy by severe trials suffered in adolescence; (3) this had conditioned her to the service of the Villain; (4) through meeting Bond she appreciates human nature in all its richness ; (5) Bond possesses her but in the end loses her. (p. 252)

These four elements (Bond, M, Villain, Woman) can be paired as opposites in an *ars combinatoria*, a combinatory or set in which each element is permutated with each other to make up what Eco refers to as the "algebra" of the structure (p. 253). It is argued that "the rules" or "game" of the Bond novels leads to an invariable scheme underlying every text:

To sum up, the plot of *each* Fleming is, by and large, like this: Bond is sent to a given place to avert a 'science-fiction' plan by a monstrous individual of uncertain origin and definitely not English who, making use of his organisational or productive activity, not only earns money but helps the cause of the enemies of the West. In facing this monstrous being Bond meets a woman who is dominated by him and frees her from her past, establishing with her an erotic relationship interrupted by capture, on the part of the Villain, and by torture. But Bond defeats the Villain, who dies horribly, and rests from his great efforts in the arms of the woman, though he is destined to lose her. (p. 258)

This account is pretty convincing for anyone the least familiar with Bondiana. The only error I noted was that in *Dr No* Honeychile kills Mander not with a "scorpion" as Eco says (p. 252) but with a black widow spider.

Eco's analysis is intelligent, flexible, useful, and by no means doctrinaire. Minor objections can be made to it. It may work for a group of texts referred to as an "escape machine geared for the entertainment of the masses" (p. 259) but would it work for less obviously formulaic 'high' cultural literary texts? Why must it exclude some texts from its corpus (*The spy who loved me* is ruled out as "quite untypical") (p. 244)? If what's offered is an analysis of a machine or structure why does it hanker after the author and what supposedly "Fleming intends" (p. 260)? Again, if the whole structure leads to Bond winning, then losing, the woman, might not a psychoanalytic reading understand this as a symptom of Bond's excessive submission to M, the symbolic father, which prevents him from ever gaining the bride? A more theoretical question would be to ask what justification there is for analysis founded in a synchronic model of dichotomies or oppositions.

Its legitimacy derives of course from Saussureian linguistics, from the distinction between *langue* and *parole*, from the account of phonemic opposition. Eco's analysis rests secure on — and happily starts from — a set of fourteen oppositions to generate these ten texts because of the powerful demonstration by modern phonetics that Saussure was right. So, beneath the apparent surface of the Bond novels a structuralist analysis uncovers their real source and origin, an essence generated by the permutation of opposed terms, especially the crucial four: Bond, M, Villain, Woman.

What classic structuralism desires is just this essence, a pure 'form' beneath the obvious 'content', something which, like Saussure's phonemic oppositions, has no positive content but which produces an effect simply from the repetition of merely relational oppositions: Bond/M, Bond/Villain, Villain/Woman, Woman/Bond. In fact Eco seems to wish for this essence of an essence when he suggests that his oppositions *themselves* are grounded at a still deeper level in the opposition, "Love/Death" (p. 252). Here a major difficulty becomes apparent. For in theory the narrative consists simply of a sequence in which all the possible oppositions are played out. But how have the synchronic oppositions generated a diachronic *narrative,* especially one in which possible permutations have been suppressed? On this point Eco's high structuralist purity quietly succumbs to Anglo-Saxon moderation and empiricism. For, *in addition* to the four opposites mentioned, a strict combinatory would yield in addition two others, M/Woman and M/Villain. These simply don't fit Fleming's texts (though the Oedipal implications of M/Woman are particularly interesting) and are silently dropped as Eco's account passes forward to a sequencing of events (pp. 254–5) dictated by the Bond texts but not the theory.

Although such structuralism breaks with the commonsensical impressionism of conventional literary criticism, it remains stuck with this notion of a structure which is seemingly in and for itself and which thus "must foreclose the text against history" (Bennett and Woollacott 1987, p. 77). By this very limitation structuralism enables and provokes a move beyond structuralism. The necessity for that move — after and because of — can be summarised in a way which opens up post-structuralism by posing the question of the subject: who is this structure for?

After structuralism

Eco's structure is structured around a centre, a given on which it relies. On this it is liable to Derrida's critique of structuralism, namely that "the structurality of structure" always refers the structure to "a point of presence, a fixed origin" (1978, p. 278). For Eco's Bond that fixed point is located in the old Freudian favourite, Love/Death, Eros and Thanatos. Structuralism claims that "each structure, a monolithic unity, is closed upon itself" (Macherey 1978, p. 145) when in fact the order it professes — and is professed by the analyst — "is merely an imagined order, projected on to disorder, the fictive resolution of ideological conflicts" (p. 155). Eco transforms the Bond texts into a unified order by reducing them to the permutable oppositions — at which juncture disorder returns if we note that Eco's order depends on the repressed oppositions, M/Woman, M/Villain, sharp conflicts indeed. Eco's wished-for structure, hermetic, crystalline, an object closed upon itself, supposes the reader as a corresponding subject.

If we ask "Who is this structure for?", the only answer can be: the reader. While Eco shows very well the historical and ideological meanings attaching to the Villain, he does not rely on these to account for the novels' success. Rather their purpose is inscribed into the list of ahistorical binaries under the fundamental opposition, Love/Death: the novels are timeless archetypes like the fairy story which puts in play good and evil, "primitive and universal forces" (Eco 1982, p. 260). So a reader *is* assumed, a subject identified: eternal human nature.

When the analysis does try to explain the effect of the narrating machine on the reader, its "probable incidence upon the reader's sensitivity" (p. 244), it does so by attempting to fold the effect self-reflexively back into the analysed structure by claiming that this incidence is essentially that of pleasure through "the repetition of a habitual scheme in which the reader can recognise something he [*sic*] has already seen and of which he has grown fond" (p. 258). But these are extemporised adjuncts to the fourteen oppositions and in no way necessarily follow from them. Analysis halts as (according to its own premises) it must, without exploring the many differentiated pleasures available in the Bond texts, pleasures addressed primarily and without hesitation to the *male* reader. In such structuralism the account of the reader and his or her possible positioning is deficient, and it is in the gap opened up by such dissatisfaction that post-structuralism appears.

There is another level at which the question "Who is this structure for?" can be asked. Re-phrased as "Who is this a structure for?" it can be posed to the writer who is writing about the structure. Structuralism elsewhere was often accompanied by claims that the structure was an objective reality which could become the object of scientific knowledge. If each text was an instance of *parole*, an utterance taking place within and on the basis of a system, then that system could be systematically investigated, defined and understood. As Eco argues in *A theory of semiotics*, even in the most magically mysterious and seemingly ineffable work of art there "cannot be a mere 'presence'" since if the text takes place in language it becomes available to people other than its author and so "there must be an underlying system" (1977, p. 271) and this system must be subject to rational, even scientific analysis. Such claims for structuralism were urged by Roland Barthes when in 1966 he wrote:

> We have a history of literature but not a science of literature, no doubt because we have not yet been able fully to recognize the nature of the literary *object*, which is a written object. As soon as one is prepared to allow (and to draw the consequences of the fact) that the work is made from writing, a *certain kind* of literary science is possible. (1972, p. 73).

Here the condition of writing is taken to presuppose a discernible system and this, a matter of 'form' rather than 'content', becomes the knowable reality on which (following the project of the Russian formalists) "a science of literature" is to be founded (five years later Barthes had come to understand the idea of "writing" in a very different way).

Structuralism makes the same assumption about a scientific structuralist's presumed knowledge of a text as it does about the effect of the text on the reader. On the one hand there is the actual reader of a text, presumed by structuralism to be able to realise the structures of the text immediately, transparently, evenly and completely; on the other there is the reader as critic and scientist, a detached observer standing outside the text's structures but superior even to the reader in their access to what a text really is. Both subjects — that of the assumed reader of the novels and that

32

of the writer of the analysis — are presumed to be free-standing and transcendental. The self-sustaining objective structure of the text requires and must correspond to an equally self-sustaining subject. Structuralism becomes transformed into post-structuralism when the structures of the text are seen to be always structures in and for a subject (reader *and* critic). The text of structuralism is intransitive, that of post-structuralism transitive.

Because in Britain post-structuralist writing was taken up within the Althusserian framework the introduction of 'the new criticism' became inseparable from questions of ideology and politics. Within this discursive space post-structuralism developed simultaneously in two directions. Post-structuralist concepts were first adopted in relation to problems of textuality, in an Althusserian analysis of the way readers were positioned by the text. That move takes place earliest and with most influence in the area of film theory, and that will be discussed next together with work in an adjacent area, cultural studies (Chapters 3 and 4). But post-structuralism is also mobilised as a critique of the bourgeois subject, as a means to demonstrate that the supposedly self-sufficient subject was a structure and an effect. In this guise post-structuralism entered the social sciences, history writing and social psychology (Chapters 5, 6 and 7).

3

Film Theory

No one has yet seen a signified without a signifier

Screen 1976

Between 1971 and 1976 the film journal *Screen* drew on theoretical work by Brecht, Althusser, Lacan, Barthes and others for the analysis of film but was able in doing so to extend and develop that basis into a new synthesis. The *Screen* project has radically affected theoretical accounts of film and television throughout the English-speaking world. It also, because of the pre-existing network of Marxist theory connecting different academic disciplines in Britain, spread across disciplines into most areas concerned with aesthetic texts — cultural studies, literary theory, art history, even musicology.

Most previous Marxist writing on art had stressed the historical significance of the obvious 'content' of the work and, with minor exceptions, had seen interest in the formal properties of texts as a formalism which deliberately evaded the social significance of art. From the first *Screen* was committed to an uncompromisingly formalist approach. It was confident that it could show the ideological effect of 'form' and this confidence was increased by the theoretical conjuncture.

Starting from Althusser, the new French critical theory was becoming known in Britain at the time, and each month seemed to discover a new text, a new name. Highly pleasurable films from the everyday cinema could be analysed in terms of difficult, unfamiliar and highly abstract theory — in fact it sometimes seemed as if the more trivial the text, the greater the leverage of theory brought to bear on it. And the Althusserian problematic underwrote and sanctioned the *Screen* project, for it proposed that science was constructed through the theoretical practice by which ideology was transformed through work into knowledge. An active opposition between ideology and science was taken to correspond to the difference between films and the *Screen* analysis of them, and this gave everyone a great deal of confidence that the *work* of theoretical transformation and analysis really mattered.

Althusser defined science as a process without a subject: *Screen* seemed to exemplify this forcefully. It was certainly a process (the theory got clearer, more detailed and more persuasive over the years) and it did not have a subject (the identity of individual contributions to the journal merged into a genuinely impersonal and developing theoretical coherence). Since I have written elsewhere on the diachronic development of *Screen's* problematic (1983b, pp. 121–33), I shall concentrate here on its synchronic accomplishment (for other discussions and criticisms, see McDonnell and Robins 1980, Hall 1980, Willemen 1983, Lapsley and Westlake 1988).

The *Screen* problematic

Avowedly, *Screen* set out to theorise "the encounter of Marxism and psychoanalysis on the terrain of semiotics" (Heath 1981, p. 201). Film was to be understood as a *specific signifying practice*. To quote:

> 'signifying' is the recognition of a language as a systematic articulation of meanings; 'practice' refers to the process of this articulation, to the work of the production of meanings, and in so doing it brings into the argument the problem of the relations of the subject within that work; 'specific' gives the necessity for the analysis of a particular signifying practice in its specific formations. (Heath 1974, p. 128)

The aim is to think together cinema as triply determined: (1) semiologically; (2) ideologically: (3) subjectively, in relation to the subject.

The commitment of historical materialism to *materialism* was exploited by *Screen* when it argued that the semiological determination of film was realised in its specific materiality and that this presented itself at the level of the signifier. "A text is structured primarily at the level of the signifier" since "it is the ordering of the signifier which determines the production of the signifieds" (Wollen 1976, p. 19); and it is a "fundamental axiom of a materialistic aesthetic" that "style is a producer of meaning" (p. 20). The work of the Russian Formalists or Specifiers had shown that the stylistic devices of literature were not mere vehicles for meaning but constituted its very literariness. As applied to the cinema, the semiology of Christian Metz had shown that there were five 'matters of expression' in film: "'phonetic sound, written titles, musical sound, noises, the moving photographic image" (Bellour 1975, p. 23). *Screen* set out to analyse these apparently merely formalist devices of cinema, providing a close and thorough investigation of deep focus, lighting, the point-of-view shot.

Form, the materiality of the signifier, was re-thought in terms of ideology but an Althusserian conception of ideology. The *Screen* problematic understood film not just in terms of the ideological signified, "the province of a traditional 'content analysis'" but through its "ideological *operation*" (Heath in Bennett 1981b, pp. 200–1). Just as each Althusserian practice (economic, political, ideological, theoretical) was a transformation and an act in the present, so film is theorised as signifying *practice*. It is not to be grasped in any sense as a reflection of a meaning which pre-exists it (a view which has considerable centrality in the Marxist tradition, for example in the work of Georg Lukács) but rather as an active transformation or work or operation producing meanings in relation to the reader. The concept of 'signifying practice' explicitly acknowledges its relative autonomy as a practice for which other practices (economic, political) are necessary but not sufficient conditions, a practice historically determined in the last instance by the economic.

Conventional cinema — Hollywood — sells a commodity not in the form of a consumable object (a packet of cigarettes) but as a ticket giving you the right to sit in a seat for a performance. As Metz argued:

> the cinematic institution is not just the cinema industry (which works to fill cinemas, not to empty them), it is also the mental machinery — another industry — which spectators 'accustomed to the cinema' have internalised historically and which has adapted them to the consumption of film. (1975, pp. 18–19)

What people pay for is a pleasure, or, strictly, the expectation of repeating a pleasure. Crucially, then, the need was to understand the nature of conventional cinematic pleasure. It was in theorising the ideological operation of film as subjective, as providing a position for the reader, that *Screen's* problematic developed furthest beyond its Parisian antecedents.

The position of the subject: Althusser on ideology

A starting-point here was Brecht, whose theoretical work had already distanced itself firmly from the reflexive problematic (his essay on "The popular and the realistic" is clearly a critique of Lukács, see 1964, pp. 107–15). Brecht had set out to analyse the commodity structure of art in a capitalist society, not simply in terms of its internal organisation but also its effect on the spectator.

Section 4 of Chapter 1 of *Capital*, "The fetishism of commodities and the secret thereof", had analysed the way commodities appeared "as independent beings endowed with life", self-produced, and concealing the human labour which produced them (Marx 1974, vol 1, p. 77). Analogously, in drama a closed, linear narrative, fixed, consistent characterisation emphasising the inner self and a mimetic style of acting corresponded to art as entertainment and commodity, its realism producing in the spectator empathy and attitudes suitable in the consumer:

Yes, I have felt like that too — Just like me — It's only natural — It'll never change — The sufferings of this man appal me, because they are inescapable — That's great art; it all seems the most obvious thing in the world — I weep when they weep, I laugh when they laugh.

In contrast a non-naturalist theatre, using alienation-effects which revealed the labour that went into the play's production, would effect in the spectator a critical attitude:

I'd never have thought it — That's not the way — That's extraordinary, hardly believable — It's got to stop — The sufferings of this man appal me, because they are unnecessary — That's great art: nothing obvious in it — I laugh when they weep, I weep when they laugh. (Brecht 1964, p. 71)

Whereas realism effected passive identification, non-realist art induced active criticism. This Brechtian analysis of textual effect was worked through by *Screen* and put on to a more substantial footing via psychoanalysis.

Thus a paper on Brecht brings together Marx on commodity fetishism and Freud on fetishism. Freud's example of a fetish comprehends both an object and the way a subject relates to it (by looking at it — what is fetishised is "a glance at the nose"). In the psychoanalytic account the fetish is an effect produced for a male subject as a substitute by the absence of the phallus he imagines in women, and so the fetish is structured by disavowal (*Verleugnung*). The *Screen* paper proposes that in classic (or traditional) realist cinema:

> The structure of representation is a structure of fetishism: the subject is produced in a position of separation from which he is confirmed in an imaginary coherence (the representation is the guarantee of his self-coherence) the condition of which is the ignorance of the structure of his production, of his setting in position. (Heath 1974, p. 106)

Realist cinema provides narcissistic gratification for the ego, the pleasures of scopophilia (*Schaulust*, visual pleasure) and mastery. As will be discussed, this is why those pleasures are appropriately and typically ascribed to a "he" in the sentence just quoted.

But how *can* commodity fetishism be thought together with psychic fetishism, the one an effect of the social formation in terms of political economy, the other an effect of the subject in terms of the unconscious? What conceptual integration can there be between the cinema as economic institution and the cinema as "mental machinery", an institution in the sense that it institutes the subject as seeking the repetition of familiar pleasures? *Screen's* problematic founded itself confidently on the view that a theoretical join had been made between the two terrains in Althusser's essay on "Ideology and ideological state apparatuses" of 1970 (1977b, pp. 121–73).

At issue is the conception of the subject in historical materialism. The classic account is unequivocal. Whether they want to or not, separate individuals have to act according to their class interests so that they find "their position" and personal development "assigned to them by their class" (Marx and Engels 1970, p. 82). Thus the Preface to the first German edition of *Capital* remarks without hesitation that "here individuals are dealt with only insofar as they are the personifications of economic categories, embodiments [German: *Träger*] of particular class-relations" (Marx 1974, pp. 20–1).

And this is the conception underwritten by Althusser when he writes in 1968 that

> the structure of the relations of production determines the *places* and *functions* occupied and adopted by the agents of production, who are never anything more than the occupants of these places, insofar as they are the 'supports' (*Träger*) of these functions. (Althusser and Balibar 1975, p. 180)

Events led Althusser to give much more content to this notion of the subject as support by drawing on Lacan's psychoanalytic account of the subject in the mirror stage. Written and dated "January–April 1969", Althusser's essay on ideology arises in part from a conjunctural need to understand the failure of the French Revolution of 1968, and why, given the circumstances for radical change, most people in France didn't change with the circumstances. The essay is footnoted as introductory and speculative.

A social formation must not only produce but also reproduce itself and the conditions of production (once again, therefore, Althusser begins his analysis by introducing the dimension of time). Capitalism must reproduce labour power, workers with appropriate skills but also with appropriate attitudes, "submission to the ruling ideology" (1977b, p. 128). Antonio Gramsci, the Italian Marxist, introduced the concept of hegemony to specify that a ruling bloc ruled rather in the way of the old Chartist motto: "Peaceably if we can, forcibly if we must". Liberal democracies are characterised by hegemony, the effort to win consent *rather* than use force via the police and the army. Drawing on Gramsci, Althusser argues that submission is obtained both by Repressive State Apparatuses (force) and Ideological State Apparatuses (consent) such as the church, the education system, the family, the trade unions, the media, "Literature, etc." (p. 137). These ISAs *"function 'by ideology'"* (p. 138).

Whereas traditional accounts emphasised ideology as the content of ideas and forms of consciousness, for Althusser ideology is now defined as what constitutes the subject, subject having a contradictory meaning:

(1) a free subjectivity, a centre of initiatives, author of and responsible for its actions; (2) a subjected being, who submits to a higher authority, and is therefore stripped of all freedom except that of freely accepting his [*sic*] submission. (p. 169)

The term means both the subject as determined and passive, as in the sense that a British citizen is a subject of the Queen, and as freely active, as in the sense of the grammatical subject of a sentence. Ideology, then, works on subjects so that they "work by themselves" (p. 169). How can this be? Althusser suggests that social construction is internalised through a process of *interpellation* or hailing, exemplified when someone calls out "Hey, you there!" and the individual addressed turns round recognising that it really is him or her who is meant by the hailing. Through this process subjects are pulled into a position, a social identity, they thus support. This "structure of all ideology, interpellating individuals as subjects...is *speculary,* i.e. a mirror-structure" (p. 168).

Although it is not explicitly dealt with in the essay, Althusser's analysis comes to rest here on Lacan's psychoanalytic account of how an infant identifies itself in the mirror stage (see "The mirror stage", 1977a, pp. 1–7). Looking in a mirror I see that image reflected there as myself ("it's me") when it is never more than my likeness, and so misrecognise my identity in it. Similarly, since I must be somewhere, I live into — and live out — the social roles, identities and likenesses offered by the ideological state apparatuses (family, education, culture). Thus I am constructed to live as a free agent, produced to act as if unproduced. Ideology now comes to be defined effectively as the whole of my lived experience and cultural identity, all that I am beyond what is biologically given, the body.

As stated, Althusser's account of ideology is open to a number of criticisms. Two major objections were put forward by Paul Q. Hirst (1979). The first is that Althusser writes of the subject as interpellated through the specularity of the mirror stage in a mechanism of *recognition*. But as Hirst acutely remarks, "the dual-mirror relation only works if the subject...who recognises already has the attributes of a knowing subject" for recognition "presupposes a point of cognition prior to the recognition" (p. 65). It therefore presupposes what it seeks to explain. Recognition must be conceptualised rather in terms of misrecognition. This misappropriation of psychoanalysis and the Lacanian conception, by treating the subject as conscious rather than unconscious, seeks to elide that incoherence in Althusser's account which supposes it can integrate the subject in ideology with the subject of the unconscious.

A second and related issue concerns the functionalism of Althusser's account, that it corresponds to classical sociological notions exemplified by Talcott Parsons of the social formation as a harmonious order such that every aspect of it, including the lived experience of the individual, contributes to the orderly functioning of the whole. Hirst points out that Althusser "resolves the problem of 'the reproduction of the relations of production' into the distribution of agents suitably equipped as 'supports' for the 'places' of the social division of labour", and so, "the 'places' are thus provided with subjectivities adequate and appropriate to them" (Hirst 1979, p. 46). If "the subject acts insofar as he or she is acted" by the system (Althusser 1977b, p. 159), if capital reproduces itself through ideological apparatuses which reproduce submissive subjects, it is hard to see how radical social change might come about.

It is necessary therefore to stress that subjects can never be evenly and passively reproduced since they are always produced in a *contradictory* process, not recognising themselves but caught up in temporary and alterable structures of *misrecognition*, never fully present in the identity they assume, always exceeding it. This process of contradiction within the subject can be understood variously: as the contradiction between conscious and repressed unconscious; between the subject's imaginary fixity and the operation of the symbolic order which grounds this fixity; between the place of the subject's identity apparently reflected back to it by texts and the means of representation which produces them (and it); between signified and signifier.

Thus: texts interpellate readers. They may work on them so they misrecognise themselves as free individuals, returning to them an apparently coherent and full identity. For example, the male spectator of a film will be invited to identify himself with a handsome and successful hero in the cinema, treating the screen as a mirror which reflects an image of himself as he would like to be. This notion of the structuring of the ego in imaginary coherence calls on Lacan's distinction between the imaginary and the symbolic. In the realm of the imaginary, language is understood "in terms of some full relation between word and meaning" (MacCabe 1985, p. 65, an essay first published in *Screen* in 1976) while in the symbolic it is understood in terms of the syntagmatic and paradigmatic chains by whose operation the signifier makes meaning possible. And so:

> as speaking subjects we constantly oscillate between the symbolic and the imaginary — constantly imagining ourselves granting some full meaning to the words we speak, and constantly being surprised to find them determined by relations outside our control. (p. 65)

The drama of the subject is defined by the absence opened in the subject by the non-semantic materiality of the signifier:

> the imaginary is then the consistence of the subject images set up to fill the lack; the symbolic is made of gaps, divides, and effects — 'causes' — the subject in that division. (Heath 1976, p. 55)

(This is reproduced exactly as printed with certain terms deliberately sliding between being nouns and being verbs).

Screen's analysis draws several implications from the Lacanian conception of subjectivity. One is that the subject does not exist outside or prior to discourse but is constituted as an effect within discourse through a particular stitching together or suturing of imaginary and symbolic. Another is that since there can be no signified without a signifier, there can be no imaginary coherence for the subject without an operation of the signifier in the symbolic to bring about that coherence. And a third is that a textual institution such as classic realism works to disavow the signifier, so producing a position of imaginary coherence in and for the reader by means of the various strategies through which the signifier is disclaimed. This corresponds to Althusser's understanding of ideology as producing submissive subjects, subjects who submit precisely in misrecognising their subordination as freedom. Much of subsequent work in *Screen* is devoted to analysing these textual strategies in detail and to bringing the project into closer connection with the politics of feminism as well as with an understanding of history.

One further comment must be introduced before proceeding. In its account of the effect of filmic texts on their readers, *Screen* draws on Kristeva's concept of the subject and its *position* (*Screen* also mobilises the idea of signifying practice from Kristeva, see for example the essay "Signifying practice and mode of production", first published in English in *Edinburgh Magazine '76*, an issue edited by *Screen* personnel, Kristeva 1976, pp. 60–75). Kristeva, notably in *Revolution in poetic language* (1984, published in France in 1974), working from a basis in Lacan, posits the introduction of the subject in terms of the *semiotic*, a primary realm of drives and their articulations exemplified by sound and rhythm, and the *symbolic*, the domain of communicated meaning in which the speaking subject identifies itself as a subject by proposing an object it refers to.

For Kristeva this "realm of signification" is always "a realm of *positions*...establishing the identification of the subject" (1984, p. 44) (the analysis then goes on to discuss the structuring of such identification in terms of the mirror stage and lack). Subsequently turning to the historical formation, *Revolution in poetic language* discusses the avant-garde work of Mallarmé and Lautréamont as potentially radical because it promises to break the unity of the subject individualised in the symbolic through the irruption of the semiotic. Important as it is for the *Screen* problematic, the work of Kristeva points in a separate direction. For *Screen* joins the concept of position to Althusser's account of interpellation, at the same time reintroducing the Lacanian conception of the subject as structured between the imaginary and the symbolic (it is to be stressed that Lacan's 'symbolic' is *not* the same as Kristeva's). While Kristeva provides essentially a history of literary texts defined in terms of subject and position, the work of *Screen* in contrast defines a relation between text and reader as the way a textual structure offers a position to its reader. A sense of the detail and effectiveness of this analysis can be gained by considering three essays that were first published in *Screen* between 1974 and 1976.

MacCabe on realism

In a wonderfully compact and suggestive essay, "Realism and the cinema: notes on some Brechtian theses", published in *Screen* in 1974, Colin MacCabe drew on the Brechtian opposition between 'Aristotelian' and 'Epic' cinema as well as the Althusserian account of ideology to give a firmly formalist critique of realism, both novelistic and cinematic.

MacCabe's analysis aims to theorise the structure of what it calls "the classic realist text" as this is exemplified in both the nineteenth-century novel and traditional Hollywood. The term is thus designed to exclude from account texts such as the novels of Dickens or the Hollywood musical, whose realism is controversial. While most Marxist discussions of realism are reflexive in turning on the supposed adequacy between realist text and reality, this essay starts from the notion of the text as a signifying practice, a form which produces rather than reflects meanings. As such the novelistic text is materially constituted at the level of the signifier as writing and, in all but the shortest texts, as a bundle of different discourses (manifestly the case in a modernist text such as Joyce's *Ulysses*). These discourses are organised by the classic realist text in a way which seeks to deny the signifier by closing on truth:

> A classic realist text may be defined as one in which there is
> a hierarchy amongst the discourses which compose the text
> and this hierarchy is defined in terms of an empirical notion
> of truth. (MacCabe 1985, p. 34)

This hierarchy corresponds to that between a metalanguage and an object language.

Object language and metalanguage, a distinction drawn in the area of formal logic by Alfred Tarski (see 1949), separates what is said in a sentence of a language — how a language is *used* — from a higher order or metalanguage in which the object language is mentioned or discussed. Thus, if I write in Navajo Indian about Modern English, then Modern English is the object language and Navajo Indian is the metalanguage, placed outside and beyond English, and taking it as an object of study. If however the same language is drawn on for both object language and metalanguage their relation is more obviously relative and must be indicated by (for example) quotation marks so that terms in the object language appear within quotation marks in the metalanguage while the metalanguage itself does not. MacCabe's essay proposes that the discourses of the classic realist text are hierarchised between object language and metalanguage.

As illustration the essay picks up the use of inverted commas in a passage from George Eliot's *Middlemarch* as "perhaps the easiest way to understand" the object/metalanguage effect in classic realism. What the characters 'in' the novel say to each other constitutes an object language, as it were, and is bracketed off in quotation marks according to the usual typographical convention; in contrast, the passages without inverted commas, the narration, seems to stand outside and beyond the dialogue as a metalanguage in which it is cited and explained in a way it cannot explain itself:

> While those sections in the text which are contained in inverted commas may cause a certain difficulty for the reader — a certain confusion vis-à-vis what really is the case — this difficulty is abolished by the unspoken (or more accurately the unwritten) prose that surrounds them. In the classical realist novel the narrative prose functions as a metalanguage that can state all the truths in the object language — those words held in inverted commas — and can also explain the relation of this object language to the real. (pp. 34–5)

Conventional literary criticism acknowledges the force of realism when it treats the narrative prose — the metalanguage — as the voice of the author, attributing authority to it in such phrases as "George Eliot knows..." etc., colluding with the effect rather than criticising it. MacCabe's analysis seeks to show how it works. At the crux is a *relation* between two forms of discourse and its effect on the reader. In so far as the object language is shown to be partial and inadequate, the metalanguage appears complete and perfect. Our sense of adequacy and inadequacy is defined in terms of two things: knowledge, the materiality of discourse.

To the extent that the represented characters are shown to be ignorant and lacking in knowledge — of their own motives, their situation, even their presence within a fictional narrative — to that extent the metalanguage of the narration is confirmed to be a discourse of knowledge. By reference to a version of the real it can explain both what the characters are partially aware of ("all the truths in the object language") and what they do not know ("the relation of this object language to the real").

Although texts such as *Middlemarch* are of course fictional and not read as having a referent, this analysis asserts they are structured in accord with an empiricist notion of truth. In doing so it follows Ian Watt's 1957 book *The rise of the novel* which noted how empiricism and the novel support each other in the seventeenth and early eighteenth century. More importantly, it derives from Althusser's critique of the empiricist conception of knowledge as abstracting an essence "from the real" (Althusser and Balibar 1975, pp. 35–6). This process consists in separating the apparent from the real, the inessential from the essential, so that, "as the husk is removed from the nut, the peel from the fruit" and "the veil from the girl" (p. 37) (Althusser points up the unconscious charge in the empiricist enterprise), truth already present in the object is revealed as accessible without mediation to the knowing subject. Similarly, the classic realist text, through its deployment of object language and metalanguage, advances a claim "that the narrative prose has direct access to a final reality" comprised of the timeless "truths of human nature" (MacCabe 1985, p. 37).

But the same strategy aims to conceal the materiality of the signifier (this in its turn being a condition of possibility for the empiricist conception of the knowledge process). To the extent that the object language is drawn to attention as material (characters' speech being marked as idiomatic or determined by their situation — in the passage cited from *Middlemarch*, for example, one of the speakers is drunk), then the metalanguage can present itself to the reader as immaterial and unwritten, a signified without a signifier. The effect is for the narration to seem transparent in the sense that signifier and material means of representation are "dematerialised to achieve perfect representation — to let the identity of things shine through the window of words" (p. 35).

Here MacCabe's essay brings Derrida's story of the Western metaphysics of being as presence and truth together with Lacan's discussion of enunciation and enounced (see Lacan 1977b, especially pp. 138–42) to argue that "the problem that has troubled western thought since the pre-Socratics" has been that of the "separation between what was said and the act of saying", between the enounced (what is represented in discourse as the signified or meaning or statement) and the act of enunciation (the material process of the signifier of which meaning is an effect): "The problem is that in the moment that we say a sentence the meaning (what is said) seems fixed and evident but what is said does not exist solely for the moment and is open to further interpretations" (MacCabe 1985, p. 35). Viewed from this perspective, one developed by Derrida in *Dissemination*, classic realism aims to close off the process of enunciation by concealing the signifier, precisely that which persists across different interpretations and renders the text open to further and different readings.

This combined effect from the enactment of an empiricist sense of the knowledge process and from the effacement of the signifier provides a position for the reader of the realist text. This position is that of "pure specularity" (p. 39) permitting the subject to identify itself in a mirror image as though it were *fully* present to itself: "Freud's insight is that the unproblematic taking up of the position of the subject entails the repression of the whole mechanism of the subject's construction" (pp. 45–6). If the mechanisms which produce this misrecognition are disavowed, as they are through the effacement of the means of representation in the realist novel, then the subject as reader of the text apparently has direct access to the real. Since as an object the real is represented as apparently self-sufficient and timeless, the subject will be interpellated into a secure position of dominant specularity, placed as though outside and looking in:

> These features imply two essential features of the classic realist text:
> 1. The classic realist text cannot deal with the real as contradictory.
> 2. In a reciprocal movement the classic realist text ensures the position of the subject in a relation of dominant specularity. (p. 39)

By introducing the idea of contradiction here — derived ultimately from an account of history as class conflict — the analysis finds a link back to traditional Marxism. Realism compels us to treat as natural and always already pre-given that which is humanly constructed, in a contradictory process, and therefore alterable. In realism "the real is not articulated — it is" (p. 39).

MacCabe's style is densely packed so a diagram and an illustration may help.

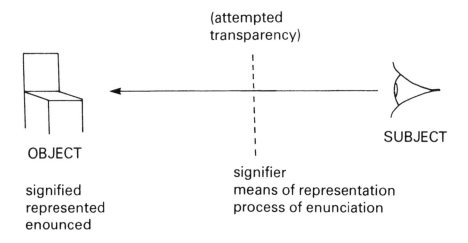

(attempted transparency)

OBJECT   SUBJECT

signified   signifier
represented   means of representation
enounced   process of enunciation

47

Dominant specularity can be compared to the experience of flying and sitting by the window. The experience derives from two effects. On the one hand I can find extraordinary pleasure on a clear day looking at the world from a position *sub specie aeternitatis* — there it is in all its textured variety — and here I am correspondingly like the Masonic eye of God, master of its fullness and visual plenitude. On the other hand I am situated by a double contingency: inside an aluminium cylinder 5 metres wide and 70 metres long, travelling at unimaginable velocity over 6 miles of empty air through which, if dropped, I would fall at a speed of 120 miles per hour to the unyielding earth. My gaze captured by the sight from the window, I am able to disavow these contingencies because I seem to be fixed and static. But the dependence of this position on what operates to produce it can easily interrupt my misrecognition of self-sufficiency and mastery — to undermine my imaginary satisfaction, to resituate me in relation to my contingency, it only takes a little turbulence, a few puffs of wind, and the plane quivers like a ship at sea except there is no sea, only a million buckets of air.

Realism gives you the view from the window, modernism is like the turbulence which reminds you where you are.

The classic realist text: comment

MacCabe's analysis has been attacked by David Lodge in an essay on "*Middlemarch* and the idea of the classic realist text". This neatly sidesteps the distinction on which MacCabe's essay rests when it dismisses the signifier/signified opposition as merely methodological; it evades the force of the object language/metalanguage distinction by recasting it as the ancient, Platonic contrast between mimesis and diegesis. Drawing on the critical commonplace that the narrator in George Eliot's novels is not reliable, Lodge's essay goes on to argue that "the diegetic element is much more problematic" than MacCabe's account admits (1981, p. 225). Lodge's essay is widely understood by conventional literary criticism to have seen off the theory of classic realism. Lodge's critique and its reception reproduce precisely a classic ideological manœuvre within the British empiricist tradition: no attempt is made to come to terms with the theoretical analysis — instead one fact is taken to refute a whole theory of novel and film and to justify dismissing the challenge (including the political challenge) offered by that theory.

Middlemarch was after all introduced by MacCabe's essay as an *illustration*, as "the easiest way to understand" the theory. A much more cogent objection would pick up the way the theory envisages the position of dominant specularity brought about by the relation of object and metalanguage as a moment of static perception rather than a *continuing* effect of the narration. If object language and metalanguage are re-thought as appearance and reality (in a way hinted at for example by de Man's analysis of the Wordsworth poem in the essay "The rhetoric of temporality", 1983), then it can be understood that dominant specularity is constantly at risk and constantly restored in the unfolding of the classic realist narrative until the attempted closure of the conclusion.

Consider this incident from Chapter 4 of Dashiell Hammett's *The Maltese falcon* when Brigid O'Shaughnessy (if that is her real name) is asking help from Sam Spade:

> She went down on her knees at his knees. She held her face up to him. Her face was wan, taut, and fearful over tight-clasped hands. "I haven't lived a good life," she cried. "I've been bad — worse than you could know — but I'm not all bad. Look at me, Mr Spade. You know I'm not all bad, don't you? You can see that, can't you? Then can't you trust me a little? Oh, I'm so alone and afraid, and I've got nobody to help me if you won't help me."

After some more of this, Spade's response is reported as follows:

> Spade, who had held his breath through much of this speech, now emptied his lungs with a long sighing exhalation between pursed lips and said: "You won't need much of anybody's help. You're good. You're very good. It's chiefly your eyes, I think, and that throb you get into your voice when you say things like, 'Be generous, Mr Spade'". (1964, p. 31)

The effect of object language and metalanguage here cannot be simply distributed between direct and indirect speech. Even though Spade's response is sanctioned by the narration — the sigh and the pursed lips signify his disbelief — it is his direct speech which relatively offers itself as metalanguage.

Playing on the two senses of the word "good" (she says she isn't morally good, he says she's good all right, as an actress and *femme fatale*) and on vision (she ask him to look at her and he sees through her), the exchange clearly positions the reader in identification with Spade's dominant specularity. Spade as the knower of truth (he digs it up?) is privileged in exactly the way proposed by MacCabe's account of the detective in *Klute*. The woman presents an appearance behind which he discerns reality. Critically deconstructing her performance, he not only knows how it works ("It's chiefly your eyes") but masters it by citing it in quotation marks, "'Be generous, Mr Spade'". We should recognise not simply a *spatial* hierarchy in which object language appears subordinate to metalanguage but a *temporal* effect in which the realist narrative continually produces the reader as bearer of knowledge in a passage from falsehood to truth.

MacCabe's analysis develops from work on the novel in France that had preceded it, particularly the extended deconstruction of a Balzac short story by Roland Barthes in *S/Z* of 1970. But MacCabe's work is precisely a *development*, clarifying and evidencing ideas sketched out by Barthes. In the run-up to *S/Z* Barthes owed more to Derrida and the concept of writing than to Lacan and the conception of the subject. "The death of the author" of 1968 attacked the notion of authorship on the Derridean grounds that "writing is the destruction of every voice, of every point of origin" (1977, p. 142). And the distinction drawn in *S/Z*, between the 'readerly' text concealing the operation of the signifier and the 'writerly' text displaying it, discriminates two kinds of text — and implicitly two modes of reading — rather than theorising the effect of the text in positioning the reader.

In its account of the five codes that govern the text *S/Z* names the hermeneutic code as "The Voice of Truth", which is indeed how MacCabe describes the effect of the narrative metalanguage. And the philosophic distinction between object language and metalanguage held a consistent place in Barthes's conceptual framework. Referred to in the analysis of myth in *Mythologies* (1953 French, 1972 English, see 1973, pp. 156, 158), it is the subject of an essay in the *Critical essays* of 1964 (English 1972) and of section IV. 3 in *Elements of semiology* (1967). *S/Z* argues that writing functions "to annul the power" of one language over another, "*to dissolve metalanguage* as soon as it is constituted" (1975, p. 98). It also notes that a multivalent text can subvert the opposition between true and false "if it fails to attribute quotations"

(p. 45) — MacCabe's illustration of classic realism turns exactly on the careful differentiation between quotation — dialogue — and unmarked narrative prose. *S/Z* further notices at one point that the readerly, that is the realist, text aims for internal solidarity and "is controlled by the principle of non-contradiction" (p. 156), an assertion developed in MacCabe's account of how realism acts to exclude contradiction.

All these details are successfully integrated in the British development. But they are now held together much more coherently because they are grounded in the notion of the subject. On the one hand they can be put forward in a confident association with Marxism and political radicalism (following Althusser the realist text can be exposed as having not merely an ideological meaning but a directly ideological operation in encouraging subjects to think they "work by themselves"). On the other hand they are re-founded in the psychoanalysis of Lacan — the readerly text offers the subject a position of dominant specularity. Between *S/Z* and *Screen* from 1974 on there is a shift of problematic, from a structuralism (the effect of the text) to a post-structuralism (the positioning of the reading subject). This shift, in opening the issue of the subject and his or her unconscious pleasures, inevitably posed the question of gender.

Mulvey and the politics of the look

In the late 1940s Karl Popper helped to shape the contemporary components of the national culture with a series of lectures and writings defining science by means of a criterion (falsifiability) which seems specifically designed to exclude and marginalise the two most radical discourses of our time: historical materialism and psychoanalysis. One consequence of Althusser's work was to reinstate psychoanalysis through the essay of 1964, "Freud and Lacan", and again more cogently with the essay on Ideological State Apparatuses (ISAs) of 1970. In the conjuncture of 1974 a text was published in Britain (though written by a New Zealander) which can claim to be one of the most original and influential contributions to the human sciences since the 1930s: Juliet Mitchell's *Psychoanalysis and feminism*. Within a year of its first printing the book was made massively available in a Penguin paperback (at the same time, from 1973, the Penguin Freud Library began to put out the first issue of the complete standard edition in paperback). Almost alone, by linking it to radical politics, Mitchell's text put psychoanalysis on the agenda of feminism.

Psychoanalysis and feminism sets out from Lacan's re-reading of Freud, that is, from Lacan's avowed project of "turning the meaning of Freud's work away from the biological basis he would have wished for it towards the cultural references with which it is shot through" (1977a, p. 106). So, for instance, it argued that in the case of 'penis-envy' "we are talking not about an anatomical organ but about the ideas of it that people hold and live by within the general culture" (Mitchell 1975, p. xvi). In the section "The making of a lady" Freud's two essays of the 1930s on female sexuality (which had been largely discounted by feminists) are mobilised to argue that both little girl and little boy start off as equally active in desiring the mother.

On this basis (it is the emphasis introduced by Althusser) psychoanalysis becomes a means to analyse the ideologies at work in maintaining women's oppression — ideologies lived as they are promoted by men and submitted to by women — back to their roots in the unconscious: "the unconscious that Freud analysed could thus be described as the domain of the reproduction of culture or ideology" (p. 413). Writers on gender and feminism (de Beauvoir, Friedan, Greer, Firestone, Millett; see Part II, section 2) who have failed to grasp the concept of the unconscious are mercilessly criticised (Greer, for example, is dismissed with the remark that when she repeats erroneous interpretations "the very vivacity of her arguments seems to be based on a contempt for understanding them" (p. 342)). Those who refuse to take psychoanalysis on board as a way to confront the reproduction of patriarchy are seen as responsible for perpetuating it. Freud returns with a radical difference: psychoanalysis "is not a recommendation *for* a patriarchal society, but an analysis *of* one" (p. xv).

Laura Mulvey's work in *Screen* on the representation of women in the cinema forms part of this project. On the one hand it willingly appropriates psychoanalytic theory as a political weapon because "it faces us with the ultimate challenge: how to fight the unconscious" (1975, p. 7), on the other it enlarges the *Screen* analysis of how mainstream cinema offers its viewer a position of dominant specularity by arguing that this is in fact a masculine position. Appearing in *Screen* in the year after MacCabe's essay on realism, Mulvey's essay on "Visual pleasure and narrative cinema" has become a classic of feminist analysis (reprinted in 1981a, though not in a complete version). Marrying theory to practice,

Mulvey has gone on with Peter Wollen to direct a number of films, including *Penthesilia, Riddles of the Sphinx* and *Amy*.

Just as evolutionary theory divided the instincts of species into self-preservation and reproduction, so psychoanalysis mainly distinguishes between narcissism or ego libido and sexual drive. Work in *Screen* had already considered the magic of Hollywood in terms of "its skilled and satisfying manipulation of visual pleasure" (Mulvey 1981a, p. 206), the darkness of the auditorium, for example, contrasting with "the brilliance of the shifting patterns of light and shade on the screen" (p. 207). Drawing both on Freud and on Lacan's account of vision and the ego (1977b, pp. 67–119), the essay analyses this visual pleasure or scopophilia in relation to narcissism and eroticism. Conventional cinema invites the pleasure of "using another person as an object of sexual stimulation through sight" (1981a, p. 208) but this erotic pleasure is always developed in the direction of narcissism and the possibility of identification. The viewer can treat the image of the person on the screen as though it were an idealised reflection of themselves, a flattering misrecognition encouraged for example by the star system.

Visual pleasure discloses both possibilities but conventional cinema organises them — and so the viewer — into a particular structure:

> In a world ordered by sexual imbalance, pleasure in looking has been split between active/male and passive/female. The determining male gaze projects its phantasy on to the female figure which is styled accordingly. In their traditional exhibitionist role women are simultaneously looked at and displayed, with their appearance coded for strong visual and erotic impact so that they can be said to connote *to-be-looked-at-ness*. Woman displayed as sexual object is the leit-motif of erotic spectacle: from pin-ups to strip-tease, from Ziegfeld to Busby Berkeley, she holds the look, plays to and signifies male desire. (p. 209)

Mulvey's side-heading is succinct: "Woman as image, man as bearer of the look".

If the present asymmetry of gender relations enacted in the cinema aligns the terms "active", "male", and "sexual looking" on the one side and "passive", "female" and "identification" on the other, this will explain why a man is reluctant to gaze at an image of a man styled to be looked at. But it also explains the narrative forms of conventional cinema in which there is a "split between spectacle and narrative" supporting "the man's role as the active one of forwarding the story, making things happen" (p. 210). That masculinised look, however, though "pleasurable in form, can be threatening in content" (p. 209) either through being looked back at or through the threat of castration (always implied by the figure of woman within the phallocentric system). Woman is dealt with by Hollywood narrative in a double strategy: either mastery by "investigating the woman, demystifying her mystery" (1975, p. 13) or fetishistic scopophilia which "builds up the physical beauty of the object, transforming it into something satisfying in itself" (p. 14). Hence classic realist cinema works through: (1) a plot which uncovers knowledge of the truth (exemplified in Mulvey by the films of Hitchcock); (2) a visual plenitude which disavows its own production (the films of von Sternberg). Both effects presuppose illusionistic narrative film and the camera as a "mechanism for producing an illusion of Renaissance space" (p. 18).

The first thing to be said about this theoretical analysis — which goes well beyond the discussion of sexed looking in John Berger's *Ways of seeing* (1972) — is that the empirical support for it is overwhelming. For example the sentence "Woman as image, man as bearer of the look" (1981a, p. 209) perfectly characterises the thirty-odd photographs in any issue of a popular tabloid such as the *Sun*, for these split neatly into images of men looking past the camera with a commanding gaze and images of women returning the look of the camera with an invitingly submissive smile. What it leaves untheorised is the question of the female spectator, a criticism entered by Bennett and Woollacott, for example, when they point out that Mulvey "tends to pay little attention to the way in which women viewers or audiences view films" (1987, p. 213).

In a later article Mulvey takes up the question she has been asked so often since the 1975 paper: "what about the women in the audience?" (1981b, p. 12). While maintaining the assertion that in the visual codes of mainstream cinema "the in-built patterns of pleasure and identification seemed to impose masculinity as a 'point of view'" (p. 12), Mulvey argues that while some actual women spectators will be unable to occupy the masculinised position, others will, or will to some degree. If so the reason lies in human bisexuality though this weighs unevenly on men and women under patriarchy: "for women (from childhood onwards) trans-sex identification is a *habit* that very easily becomes *second Nature*" (p. 13) and so they can take up the masculinised point of view. Men, it is implied, are not required to make this kind of shift and are not so easily habituated to it (this indication of how the dominant mode of masculinity can be analysed as seeking to be masculine and only masculine has been taken up elsewhere; see Easthope 1986).

Screen's project in film theory thus continued to extend its scope and depth. While MacCabe's analysis of classic realism in terms of subject position and dominant specularity was able to link an understanding of cinema to historical materialism and radical politics, Mulvey's account added a politics of gender while simultaneously adding to the detailed analysis of film. Her essay can be considered thoroughly Althusserian in that it refuses to treat 'men' as humanist subjects, source of agency (and of women's oppression); instead the essay persists in attacking a structure, patriarchy. A question remains here, and one to which discussion returns: does the concept of patriarchy as an unconscious system integrate satisfactorily with the conceptions of economic determination and class struggle required if the perspective of historical materialism is to be retained?

Mulvey's essay gives prominence to the issues of narrative and the history of illusionist Renaissance space. In a long essay published in *Screen* Stephen Heath took up these questions in a way which strengthens the historical basis of the whole project.

Heath on 'narrative space'

Here the stock terms demonstate what is at stake: the motion pictures, the movies, the flicks; it is the threat of motion, of displacement that is in question, but this threat is overcome from the start. (MacCabe 1985, p. 68, an essay first published in *Screen* in 1976)

In scope, in depth, in subtlety of detailed analysis of the object cinema, Heath's essay on narrative space (*Screen*, 1976, reprinted in Heath 1981) may well mark the peak of *Screen's* achievements in the area of film theory. It brings together in the closest theoretical and evidenced coherence three conceptual frameworks: the sign, ideology and the subject. It does so by constantly working out a related opposition between fixity and process, similarity and difference, continuity and discontinuity, presence and absence. The ideological operation of Hollywood — what Godard in *Wind from the east* calls 'Nixon–Paramount' and *Screen* termed 'classic realism' — is analysed back to its beginnings in painting and Quattrocento space and forward through manuals of painting to manuals of cinematic technique. Here only enough detail will be given to illustrate the project's grasp on the formal specificity of painting, of film. The essay situates the Western visual tradition and so anticipates and enables other work on the history of painting discussed in Chapter 8.

Heath's essay analyses classical cinema as a specific signifying practice. It is a specific in that it stitches together the single photographic shot and a moving *sequence* of shots, the frozen moment of Renaissance space with the temporal concatenation of narrative, but specific also in that this dominant mode of film ('entertainment') was constructed historically and could be otherwise (as the work of certain avant-garde directors discloses). And it is a signifying *practice* since it works actively to contain the excess of meaning necessarily produced by a still image, to hold the spectator in a certain position.

Such cinema, grounded as it is in the photograph, presupposes Quattrocento space. Introduced in the West in the fifteenth century, these codes of representation rely on a perspective system organised around central projection. Heath cites the art historians:

> It is the art of depicting three-dimensional objects upon a plane surface in such a manner that the picture *may* affect the eye of the observer in the same way as the natural objects themselves...A perfectly deceptive illusion can be obtained only on *two conditions*: (a) the spectator shall use only one eye, (b) this eye has to be placed in the central point of the perspective. (G. Ten Doesschate, *Perspective: fundamentals, controversials, history* (1964), cited Heath, p. 28)

The scientific basis for linear, monocular perspective is not in doubt (an objection made to Heath's argument in Carroll 1982, see esp. pp. 109–17) but in the Quattrocento tradition it becomes used for art and pleasure rather than to increase knowledge. Renaissance space was *constructed* historically and for "five centuries men and women exist at ease in that space" (Heath 1981, p. 29) with its commitment to central perspective images. Cinema continues to repeat this "monocular perspective, the positioning of the spectator-subject in an identification with the camera as the point of a sure and centrally embracing view" (p. 30).

Cinema, however, is 'moving pictures'. Movement, especially that of human figures, implies process, an excess which already the art tradition tries to fix through composition within the frame. With moving pictures the represented figures constantly risk moving out of the frame, moving left, moving right, coming and going. According to its particular economy the more they move the more they must be held — through a *narrativisation* which "contains the mobility that could threaten the clarity of vision in a constant renewal of perspective" (p. 36). Hence narrative space: "The transitions thus effected pose acutely the problem of the filmic construction of space, of achieving a coherence of place and positioning the spectator as the unified and unifying subject of its vision" (p. 38). In detail this economy explains the procedures advised by the film manuals: the use of master-shot, the 180-degree rule, the 30-degree rule, matching on action, eyeline matching, field/reverse field, avoidance of 'impossible' angles, integration of the point-of-view shot, sound track subservient to the image-track (voice-over limited to memory sequences, for example). Hence conventional film manuals: "Making a smooth cut means joining two shots in such a way that the transition does not create a noticeable jerk and the spectator's illusion of seeing a continuous piece of action is not interrupted" (from *The technique of film editing*, K. Reisz and G. Millar, cited Heath, p. 42).

MacCabe's account of 'classic realism' endangers itself by referring to the problematic issue of realism — Heath steps round such pitfalls by writing consistently about 'classical cinema'. Further — it is a good example of the collectivity of *Screen's* project — while MacCabe had claimed in his essay of 1974 that realism is "transparent" in the sense that its metalanguage is "not regarded as material" (1985, p. 35), Heath argues that narrative space acts through "the holding of signifier on signified" (1981, p. 37), that transparency is "impossible — no one has yet seen a signified without a signifier" (p. 44), and that classical cinema does not efface the signs of production but rather "contains them" through narrativisation (p. 51). Seemingly slight and technical the qualification is in fact radical. MacCabe's classic realism is analysed with essential emphasis on formal structure and textual effect in what remains largely a structuralism: Heath's account of classical cinema is more fully post-structuralist since it is founded in a conception of process which narrative space seeks to fix and contain. This process is the process of the subject.

For Lacan the symbol manifests itself "as the murder of the thing" it stands in for (1977a, p. 104). Following Freud's discussion (in *Beyond the pleasure principle*) of his grandson's entry into language though playing the 'Fort–Da' game, Lacan proposes that the completed sign, signifier held on to signified meaning, is "a presence made of absence" (1977a, p. 65) and that the infant in entering discourse to become a child encounters at the edge of its being a lack or loss or absence which it tries to fill: "absence itself gives itself a name in that moment of origin" (p. 65). But this origin, perpetually recreated in the subject, *creates* the subject, *is* the subject. Lack and absence must be actively denied and disavowed in the process by which the subject extemporises a fixity or presence for itself — *as* itself. The subject must win an imaginary identity from the symbolic order out of which it emerges and on whose grounds it takes its place as an 'I'.

Fixity for process, presence for absence, imaginary for symbolic: the first term privileges itself over the other on which it depends and stands in for it in an act of denial of what's inside (Freud's *Verneinung*) and disavowal of what's outside (Freud's *Verleugnung*). Lacan names this joining together as *suture* or stitching up, and it is drawn on by Heath to understand how narrative space finds a coherence for the spectator in the absences round which it is structured, absences such as that opened up, for example, by the off-screen space:

> In its movement, its framings, its cuts, its intermittences, the film ceaselessly poses an absence, a lack, which is ceaselessly recaptured for — one needs to be able to say 'forin' — the film, that process binding the spectator as subject in the realization of the film's space. (Heath 1981, p. 52)

Thus "the suturing operation is in the process, the give and take of absence and presence, the play of negativity and negation, flow and bind" (p. 54). Classical cinema contains the process which produces it by offering a position of imaginary coherence to the spectator. In contrast, avant-garde cinema, by exhibiting and reworking the codes of narrative space, constitutes the possibility of a radical cinema (Heath's example — from Oshima's *Death by hanging* — is the sequence with the cat).

"How to make sense in film if not through vision, film with its founding ideology of vision as truth?" Heath asks (p. 44) and answers by showing that

Cinema is not simply and specifically ideological 'in itself';
but it is developed in the context of concrete and specific
ideological determinations which inform as well the
'technical' as the 'commercial' or 'artistic' sides of that
development...Film is dominantly articulated in the interests
of the 'theatrical cinema'. (p. 33)

Narrative space is a specific historical construction, one that might
well be defined as a form of bourgeois space. To this point Heath
cites the art historian, Pierre Francastel:

Spaces are born and die like societies; they live, they have a
history. In the fifteenth century, the human societies of
Western Europe organized, in the material and intellectual
senses of the term, a space completely different from that of
the preceding generations; with their technical superiority,
they progressively imposed that space over the planet. (Cited
Heath, p. 29)

On this showing, the cinema of narrative space, resting as it does
on Renaissance space, is equally an historical construction. The
very fact that *Screen* can criticise that discursive practice from a
point outside it may itself be evidence of a crisis, arguably terminal,
for that space.

The politics of *Screen*

Whereas the Marxist tradition had generally supported realism and
'critical realism' against modernism, the film theory of *Screen*
criticised the realist tradition and followed Brecht in regarding
modernist techniques as a necessary condition for radical art. In
fact, *Screen* went further than this. If the realist text, seeking to
close itself off in the way of a commodity, sought to hold its
audience within the confines of 'entertainment' (from the French
entretenir, which includes the meaning of 'to trap'), the modernist
text, by compelling the audience into a more distanced and critical
stance, could begin to educate, thus threatening to subvert the
conventional opposition between leisure and work, pleasure and
instruction. Further still, following Althusser, the modernist text
might interpellate the reader according to a different mode of
subjectivity. "Socialist emulation forms individuals in a different

way and produces different individuals" (Brecht, cited MacCabe 1985, p. 50): thus the modernist text, displaying rather than concealing its own textuality, denying the reader a position of seeming autonomy and coherence, might actually "work on and transform the very form of ideology — to change the position of the subject within ideology" (p. 53).

A re-drawing of the received Left wisdom about realism versus modernism had been undertaken in France, in work by Kristeva, Barthes and others associated with the journal *Tel Quel*. Coming after — and because of this intervention — the *Screen* project was much more thoroughly grounded in the Lacanian conception of the subject prioritised in Althusser's 1970 essay on ideology. It therefore felt entitled to claim it had gone beyond the position taken up by Barthes, for example, in *The pleasure of the text* (French 1973, English 1976) with its preference for those passages in which 'the text of bliss' (implicitly modernist) unveiled a *jouissance* not made available by 'the text of pleasure' (implicitly realist). Against "Roland Barthes and the *Tel Quel* group" MacCabe's essay argues that "over and above these *moments* of subversion, however, there are what one might call *strategies* of subversion" (p. 48) by which the revolutionary text might not simply transgress but transform classic realism.

In its own less forthright style "Narrative space" documents a similar distinction. Certain texts from contemporary independent cinema are criticised because they try to *break* with Hollywood narrative by avoiding narrative altogether, this leading to work on "'film as film'" and "an aesthetics of transgression" (Heath 1981, p. 64). In contrast other texts (for example, Oshima's *Death by hanging*) "work less on 'codes' than on the operations of narrativization" (p. 64), not evading but transforming narrative space. Explicitly, *Screen's* development had brought it to a point where it felt confidently able to condemn aestheticism, formalism and libertarian transgression, and instead advocate another possibility for radical cinema. In this it had introduced an important distinction within the overbroad category of modernism, one which can now be re-read as a contrast between post-modernism and modernism. Thus, the libertarian text, in a post-modernism of fragmentation and dispersal, would deny altogether any coherent position to the subject while the radical text is modernist in aiming to re-work and relativise the subject's coherent identification.

None of this passed without challenge, particularly from writers on the Left, especially Terry Eagleton and Stuart Hall. Discussion focused on three questions: does this theory of film still keep in touch with a sense of history? does the theory still count as Marxist and uphold the principles of relative autonomy and economic determination of the superstructure? is this how real as distinct from notional readers are affected by the text? The debate points to the answers "Yes", "Maybe" and "No".

Screen and history

The issue of history came up in a particular way. *Screen* did not generally print reviews and so it was all the more surprising when out of the blue the issue of Spring 1977 carried a patronising and unsympathetic review of Terry Eagleton's *Criticism and ideology*. Publication of this is hard to explain except on sectarian grounds. Some of the main contributors to *Screen* were at the time members of the British Communist Party (including the then editor, who wrote the review) while Eagleton was identified with the Trotskyists who dominated the *New Left Review*. As part of a longer article Eagleton attacked *Screen* in a 1978 issue of *NLR* (Eagleton 1978, pp. 21–34) (a reply was published in *NLR* no. 110).

Eagleton dismisses *Screen* for its "formalism" (p. 23), for imagining "that films which draw your attention to the camera thereby impel you out inexorably onto the picket lines" (p. 24) (this is repeated in Fredric Jameson's *The political unconscious*, which defines the *Screen* approach as confining its work to individual texts (1983, p. 283) and, though slighting, is almost the only notice North America has taken of *Screen's* work outside film journals). Like the other heretical 'isms' of the Left (economism, theoreticism), the term 'formalism' implies the error of overtotalising and so an *excessive* concern with form as central or exclusive determinant. While paying full attention to formal features precisely because it was able to make them visible as *ideological* features, *Screen* explicitly opposed formalism — as was argued above and as for example when an essay of 1976 refers to the notion that "the breaking of the imaginary relationship can constitute a political goal in itself" — as "the ultra-leftish fantasy of the surrealists" (MacCabe 1985, p. 73). And *Screen* was consistently concerned, not with single texts, but, with a whole regime of representation (the narrative space of classic realism). It is this, "the mental machinery" (in Metz's phrase), which is seen to demand political analysis and transformation.

But Eagleton's main charge is that *Screen's* formalism evaporates history, that "the historical specificity of the ideological codes upon which texts labour is dwindled to the merest gesture" (1978, p. 23). For this argument two senses of 'the historical' need to be distinguished. There is history as period and conjuncture, the narrower dimension usually understood in terms of years and decades, but there is also a wider scale of history understood particularly in the Marxist conception of the *epoch,* the era of a mode of production. *Capital,* for example, analyses the structure of the capitalist mode of production but, besides footnotes and instances, is historical only in the sense that it characterises the mode of production of an epoch.

As Raymond Williams notes, "some of the best Marxist cultural analysis" is "very much more at home in what one might call *epochal* questions" (1980, p. 38). *Screen* is not attempting to investigate the historical as determined by conjuncture; it is certainly concerned to analyse the dependence of narrative space on what might be termed the epochal space of the Renaissance. It is also concerned to work in an historical framework by analysing film "in a specific signifying practice in a given socio-historical situation" (Heath 1981, p. 64), above all the practice of Hollywood and so Hollywood realism as a 'machine' of representations instituted both ideologically and industrially. Cinematic realism, with its origins rooted back in that space in which "for five centuries men and women exist at ease" (Heath 1981, p. 29), corresponds to the past, a bourgeois past, while modernism at the least symptomatises a crisis in the forms of that past and at best foresees a socialist future.

Screen and relative autonomy

The topic of history brings the discussion right up against the issue of economic determinism and base/superstructure relations in Marxist theory. If there are aspects of the *Screen* problematic — with its attention to discursive formations, subjects and the *power* of a discourse (such as that defined as narrative space) to produce subjects as its effect — which now might seem to owe more to Foucault than to Althusser, this was hardly apparent at the time (indeed Foucault did not clearly emerge in the *Screen* scenario until "What is an author?" was reprinted in the issue of Spring 1979). Yet in retrospect *Screen* seems often to herald the arguments of the later Foucault.

From its inception the *Screen* problematic was governed by the distinction between signifier and signified. Conceived in terms of Althusserian relative autonomy, the cinema was seen as both a *signifying* practice, actively producing meaning in its own specific autonomy, and a practice relatively determined by the others of the social formation (Hollywood as economic institution, for example). Subsequent to the work during the mid-1970s of two Althusserian sociologists, Barry Hindess and.Paul Q. Hirst (discussed further in Chapters 5 and 6) these Althusserian questions — and answers — became increasingly fraught.

"No one has yet seen a signified without a signifier": introducing the notion of the signifier in connection with Althusser and the relative autonomy of ideological practice, Paul Q. Hirst poses the ineluctable alternative: *either* a "represented exists outside of the process of representation" (in which case that process may reflect it with a greater or lesser degree of distortion); *or* "the represented exists as an effect of a process of signification" and "has no existence beyond the process which represents it" (in which case it is "not an origin to which we may return to question the truth of the reflection") (1979, p. 68). The concept of ideology supposes a relation of correspondence/non-correspondence between ideology and an ulterior reality it 'reflects' (for example, the signifying practice of Hollywood cinema seen as commodity fetishism corresponds to Hollywood as capitalist producer of commodities). Even if ideological practice is considered as relatively autonomous, there is partial correspondence and so a relation of correspondence/non-correspondence. But there can be no such relation once the instance of the signifier is recognised as operating according to its own diacritical system. So, Hirst argues, "if there is any determining action of the means of representation in constituting what is 'represented' by them then these forms of correspondence/non-correspondence are shattered" (p. 72). There is. And they are.

The debate over relative autonomy broke out in *Screen* in 1977 when Rosalind Coward attacked some work on subcultures from the Birmingham Centre for Contemporary Cultural Studies (then led by Stuart Hall). Taking off from the problematic issue that language cannot confidently be ascribed to either base or superstructure, her paper criticises the work for its commitment to a conception of the social formation "in terms of an essential division between capital and labour which is directly reflected in economic classes, which themselves are reflected at the level of culture and ideology" (Coward 1977, p. 90). Hirst's argument about "the determining action of the means of representation" (p. 92) is drawn on to undermine this notion of reflection. Regarding signification, it is proposed that "it is never a question of what class produces what form or what content of a signifying practice, but rather how systems of representation inscribe (ideological) positions" (p. 95).

In the issue of Winter 1977/78 Stuart Hall and others replied, the nub of their argument being to enforce Hirst's either/or and demand a clear response to the question: is signifying practice relatively autonomous, determined in the last instance by the economic (what they refer to as a "limit-position" *within* Marxism)? or must we recognise "the *absolute autonomy* of signifying practice" (a position outside Marxism) (Hall *et al.* 1977, p. 115)?

Coward, herself a former student at the Birmingham Centre, replies to the reply in a way which reveals what is politically at issue in the debate and a main reason why it took on such importance when it did. Quite simply, feminism will not theorise within the classic Marxist account of base and superstructure. It is a fine paragraph, lucid, angry and to the point:

Mao's and Lenin's writings would have been dismissed as being outside their contemporary 'limit-positions'. The contemporary implications of this notion are also clear: members of the women's movement are to crawl back into their corners suitably reproved for attempting to theorise those things which Marx never bothered with. The centrality of the conception of class is very clearly problematic for feminism since it is difficult to accept either the idea of women as a class since economic class divisions cut across women as much as men; neither is it helpful to conclude that just because marxist theorisation is inadequate, we should relegate questions of the positions of women to secondary positions of class. Questions such as the organisation of sexuality do arise. And marxism has as yet nothing to say about them. Socialist–feminist theory has been exploring areas that have not been developed by traditional marxism. For any marxist grouping to dismiss these as not corresponding to 'limit-positions' can only be destructive. (Coward 1977/8, p. 122)

Coward's polemic makes explicit a difficulty implicit in Mulvey's analysis of gendered spectatorship: how can patriarchy and class struggle be mapped on to each other, integrated into a grand theory? Coward's solution does not resolve the crisis. It may be a heresy for Marxism (or it may not) but the issue is clear: if classic Marxism is in conflict with a valid form of political radicalism, specifically feminism, then classic marxism must give way; a new theorisation must be found. This was indeed close at hand.

It would be very hard (to return to Hall *et al.* and their critique of Coward) to guess what the absolute autonomy of a signifying practice would look like in contrast to its relative autonomy. In fact, the two questions both come up within the same essentially spatial problematic, that is, one assuming "the primary existence of a central point" (the economic) "from which secondary and descendant forms would emanate" (ideological practice, signifying practice) or not. In contrast, in the different and essentially temporal paradigm envisaged by Foucault (and Coward who has just been cited) every local site is a point of origin and a source:

> power...is produced from one moment to the next, at every point, or rather in every relation from one point to another. Power is everywhere; not because it embraces everything but because it comes from everywhere. (Foucault 1981, p. 93)

The line of argument Coward draws out from Hirst heads in just this direction with its emphasis not on representation as effect of a cause but as cause of an effect, "how systems of representation inscribe (ideological) positions" (1977, p. 95).

Ideology and the subject of the film

If as suggested *Screen* is already by 1977 moving away from a fully Althusserian position (priority accorded to the determining power of economic practice 'in the last instance') and towards acknowledgement that every aspect of the social formation is to be understood primarily in terms of its specific effectivity and as a local site actively working to inscribe the subject in a position, then a central feature in the theoretical background of the *Screen* problematic becomes exposed for critique: the Althusserian conception of ideology. There are two aspects to this critique.

The first concerns Althusser's assertion in the essay on ideology — quite apparent from the particular ideologies of particular social formations — that it was possible to define the form and function of "ideology *in general*" (1977b, p. 150, italics original). As such ideology has no history because it "*is eternal*, exactly like the unconscious" (p. 152, italics original). Effectively, Althusser has defined ideology as the ego itself.

Now clearly in every human society individuals have needed some sense of their individual existence as an 'I'. This is well argued in an important essay by Marcel Mauss, "A category of the human mind: the nature of person, the nature of 'self'", which notes that there has never been a language in which "the word 'je-moi'...did not exist" and "there has never been a human being without the sense not only of his [*sic*] body, but also his simultaneously mental and physical individuality" (1970, p. 61). This, however, does not exclude the possibility that the precise shape, force and meaning of the ego will differ in different cultures so that, to take the most pressing example, post-Renaissance Western culture has clearly tried to put to work a conception of the ego as wholly self-acting and self-produced.

Screen, committed to the possibility that radical cinema, in denying a transcendental position to its spectator, could intervene in the direction of social change, necessarily therefore had to oppose explicitly the Althusserian account of the eternally unchanging subject of 'ideology in general' and deny Althusser's "thesis that ideology has no history" (MacCabe 1985, p. 53). But, at the very point of making this movement, the *Screen* problematic tries to retain sufficient purchase on the notion of ideology in general to argue that cinema can act on ideology *outside the cinema*. For this it is rightly taken to task by Stuart Hall, both outside the pages of the journal (see Hall 1980) and within when the criticism of Coward's position affirmed that the Althusserian/Lacanian conception of the subject as underwritten by *Screen* "seems to leave us at the level of Language-in-general, ideology-in-general — a form of abstraction" (Hall *et al.* 1977, p. 116).

Published in 1976 a second essay on realism by Colin Macabe tries to gather up some of the theoretical debris which had accumulated around the issue of realism in the previous two years. Yet when this and the 1974 essay are read in series it can be seen that they continue to rely on a notion of contradiction in general. Thus they run together: (1) contradiction as class struggle (1985, p.

49); (2) the contradiction between active production and passive consumption (p. 54); (3) the contradiction in ideology "which produces a position for the viewer but denies that production" (p. 69) and "the contradiction between narrative and discourse" in a text (p. 69). Adherence to a conception of ideology on the Althusserian model as ideology in general is overtly stated when it is argued that art and forms of radical cinema may have the "ability actually to work on and transform the very form of ideology — to change the position of the subject within ideology" (p. 53). It is harder to detect such a move in the work of Heath though it is surely present for example in a paragraph which moves without hesitation from reference to "ideological representation" and the process of the subject to "the functions of suture in image, frame, narrative" (Heath 1981, p. 53), functions which undeniably concern the operations of film and text.

The objection to this theoretical assumption — an objection that derives from the formulations introduced by Coward and these as they correspond to the work of Foucault — is that it elides into a single, essentialist notion of ideology in general, the *differentia specifica* of a social formation, its different 'times'. One elision is that between 'life' and 'art', between the ideological effect, on the one side, of the whole range of economic and political practices in which signification is not dominant, and on the other of ideological practices such as the cinema in which signification *is* dominant.

A second elision is that made between different areas of the discursive formation. Within any discursive ensemble any number of different discourses operate with their own weight and effectivity. For example, the texts of mainstream cinema as forms of fictional narrative do not have the same weighting and significance as those of television news (though both can equally be analysed in terms of realism and providing the viewer with a position of dominant specularity). If accepted, this argument in no way disables the *Screen* project but it would set a limit on the supposed effect of cinema on ideology in general. It would not weaken — would in fact strengthen — arguments for the political necessity of engaging with cinema as a specific site, film as film.

Readers implied and actual, text as structure and act

This issue of ideology and a willingness to solder together 'life' and 'art' leads directly to another problem in this theorisation of film, that of the relation between implied and real spectators (or readers). The difficulty is radical and reaches far beyond the immediate concerns of *Screen* into questions opened up around text and reader by post-structuralism and deconstruction generally.

Screen proceeded on the assumption that a systematic understanding of film could be reached by considering how a position for the reader was "inscribed in the film" (MacCabe 1975, p. 61). 'Subject position' was theoretical, not actual: "*in themselves* the cinematic codes implied in the film text are not capable of producing an unambiguous reader" (Brewster 1977, p. 160); at stake was only "the implicit reader", "an ideal reader, one who completely conforms to the supposed intentions of the text" (p. 162).

Part of the purpose of MacCabe's second essay on realism is to undertake a holding action on the problem. The first essay, that on classic realism is accused retrospectively of being "contaminated by formalism", "by a structuralism that it claimed to have left behind" (1985, p. 77):

> Traditional criticism holds text and author/reader separate...my article made the subject the effect of the structure (the subject is simply the sum of positions allocated to it) but it preserved the inviolability and separateness of the text...But the text has no such separate existence. (pp. 77–8)

One solution is to "dissolve the reader into the text" by regarding the text in terms of identification and subjectivity (p. 78). This does not solve the problem, for, as with "Narrative space" (published in the same issue as MacCabe's revisionist argument), dissolving reader into text amounts to nothing but a more thoroughly integrated use of psychoanalytic concepts and terminology in relation to the formal properties of film. Worse is to come.

In 1978 *Screen* published an essay by Paul Willemen (see also Willemen 1983) that, in the course of an extended analysis, pointed out with brutal frankness what had always been known but disavowed:

> there remains an unbridgeable gap between 'real' readers/authors and inscribed ones, constructed or marked in and by the text. Real readers are subjects in history, living in given social formations, rather than mere subjects of a single text. The two types of subject are not commensurate. But for

the purposes of formalism real readers are supposed to coincide with the constructed readers. (1978, p. 48)

Inscribed readers, then, all read a text the same way; real readers all read it differently.

To this a subsequent essay responded by saying that "to hold that a given text is 'different for everybody' is as much the end of any consequent political analysis and practice as to hold that it is 'the same for everybody'" (Heath 1978, p. 104), correctly implying that the two positions are united in a relation of specular reciprocity since common to both is the either/or assumption that *if* a text is not the same for everyone, it must be different for everyone. Asserting that subject and object come into existence together, conceding that "everyone is the possibility of difference in reading, reception, response", the essay goes on to claim that nevertheless "the film is the same", that is, "offers something of a common terrain on which meanings are made and remade" (p. 107). This argument, while accepting the actual variability of reader's response, nevertheless reinstates the *Screen* problematic. It is possible and necessary to carry through the analysis of texts in terms of the position of the subject as an effect of the text even while acknowledging that this position cannot be supposed as more than one *offered* to or *provided* for the reader (in fact this verbal concession was generally made in *Screen*'s practice and followed from the Althusserian conception of hailing or interpellation).

This has been a long chapter, necessarily so. *Screen* introduced post-structuralist arguments into British culture within the context of an explicitly political commitment by underwriting the Althusserian conception of ideology. But, as exemplified particularly by the work of Mulvey and Coward, it was able to extend that radicalism into the politics of gender (in fact from the early 1980s it emerged effectively as an exclusively feminist intervention). Thus *Screen* exercised a determining influence by exploring and evidencing in the specific area of cinema a critique and deconstruction of the subject, the supposedly autonomous and implicitly bourgeois 'individual'. This work was picked up and developed elsewhere.

In addition, however, *Screen* provided an exemplary intervention in relation to aesthetic texts. Because it kept such a firm grip on the specificity of cinema as a signifying practice, it demonstrated the power of the Althusserian/Lacanian conception of the subject to integrate and make sense of their formal properties.

On this it is important to distinguish a *hermeneutics* of interpretation from a *poetics* of the text. If the first is concerned mainly with the level of signified meaning at which the text is open to interpretation as it is engaged with by readers and in readings, the second is aimed at an analysis of the text as an organisation of the signifier. A camera movement or cut in a film, a metrical regularity or rhyme in a poem are invariable material properties of a text in a way signified meaning is not. *Screen* worked on precisely those features that traditional Marxist criticism had been unable to theorise and so had tended to dismiss as *merely* formal. Theory was able to enter this arena and argue that forms were always ideological, an understanding which was soon taken over into other disciplines which directed analysis at the aesthetic text in terms of the effect of the text in positioning the subject.

Screen, while beginning from a structuralism centred on the properties of the text, develops, through a process of auto-critique, towards a post-structuralist recognition that the reader reads the text as much as the text reads the reader. This issue, the necessary and ineluctable dialectic between text as structure and text as act, left till last in the preceding account, will recur and will be given fuller attention again in the last chapter.

Another major issue is also left over. From the first *Screen* proceeded on the assumed basis of an Althusserian distinction between ideology and science, between cinematic texts and those texts analysed as ideological practice from the metalinguistic position of a theoretical practice able to comprehend them as they did not understand themselves. In this the film theory held itself back from the full import of post-structuralism, though undoubtedly the weakening of resolve evident in various *Screen* essays from around 1977 reflected this crisis. It was provoked by the work of Hindess and Hirst, and discussion of it will be deferred till Chapter 5. It will make for a better order of exposition if we consider first an area of theoretical inquiry close to film theory and one into which the *Screen* intervention became rapidly transplanted: the field of media or cultural studies.

4

Cultural Studies

What does the proletariat expect of its intellectuals? That they disintegrate bourgeois ideology.

Bertolt Brecht

Cultural studies, media studies, work on television and film, the teaching of communication — all these in Britain bear the imprint of the work of Raymond Williams. That work has been widely promoted by the Birmingham Centre for Contemporary Cultural Studies led for many years by Stuart Hall. During the 1970s the Centre published its research particularly in the form of annual *Working Papers in Cultural Studies*, nos 1 to 11, and these break a path in re-thinking the analysis of culture in terms of various theoretical advances as these came to attention — Lukács, the Frankfurt school, Enzensberger (whose "Constituents of a theory of the media" had been published in *New Left Review* no. 64 in 1970).

The founding model, however, was Marxist and throughout the period hardly an article in *Working Papers* was complete without a diagram with double-headed arrows to show the interaction of base and superstructure and the way economic forces were mediated on the terrain of culture. Although for example *Working Papers* no. 10 of 1977 contains two articles on subjectivity and individuality, the Centre's project continued primarily Marxist in terms of the 'limit position' laid down by Hall and others in their controversy with Coward and *Screen*. The intervention of post-structuralism in cultural studies came elsewhere, for example in the work of Roz Coward and John Ellis.

Language and materialism, subtitled "Developments in semiology and the theory of the subject", written by Coward and

71

Ellis, was published in 1977. Covering most of the writers in French who contribute to post-structuralism — with chapters on Saussure and structuralism, Barthes and *S/Z*, Althusserian Marxism, the conception of language and subjectivity in Lacan and Kristeva — the book in essence records "the encounter of psychoanalysis and Marxism on the terrain of language" (p. 156), that is, it follows very much the line of British post-structuralism marked out by *Screen*. Attacking humanist assumptions of an originary subject, *Language and materialism* argues that the subject is an effect constituted in the process of the unconscious, of discourse and of the relatively autonomous practices of the social formation. As a theoretical exposition whose theory is not applied or illustrated in relation to any body of work, it is the kind of book that makes library cataloguers despair for it fits no conventional classification, not even particularly that accorded it here under 'cultural studies'. However, Coward's later book, *Female desire*, undertakes a fine analysis of versions of women's sexuality as staged in popular culture.

Judith Williamson's *Decoding advertisements* (1978) is a direct intervention in the field and one of the best books written on advertisements as texts. It consists of detailed analysis of 116 visual and verbal texts. In the main, advertisements are read in terms of ideological theme under four categorisations: science and cooking, nature, magic, narrative and history. Post-structuralism is mobilised in the form of the Althusserian/Lacanian conception of the subject as (textual) effect.

An advertisement's mode of address, it is argued, interpellates or hails the reader "as a certain kind of person" (p. 51): "Your Pentax becomes part of you"; "'farouche' — The perfume created by NINA RICCI, Paris, for all the women you are." And Lacan's account of the mirror stage as the way that the infant comes to identify itself in the imaginary unity of the ideal ego is said to be "very similar to the process of advertising which offers us an image of ourselves that we may aspire to but never achieve" (p. 64). Examples here include an advertisement for "Glow 5" showing a woman full-face in a mirror smiling at the viewer and the words, "When did your skin last smile back at you?" Williamson comments that

this mirror image involves a separation — between you, 'not happy with your skin', and the version of you with perfect skin, shown actually *in* the mirror within the ad: a situation where your skin smiles back *at* you indicates a gulf between *you* and *your skin*. (p. 67)

The advertisement acts to anneal the gap it has opened up — between your perfect self and you — by inviting the viewer to merge with the image in the represented mirror: separation is recuperated on condition that the viewer becomes a "Glow 5" woman.

Williamson's work gives an innovative turn to the concepts of interpellation and identification. *Screen*'s post-structuralism aimed to understand the terms of the positioning of the subject by a textual relation between signifier and signified, the formal structuring by which a filmic means of representation placed the spectator in alignment with the reality represented. This study of advertising gives more stress to the signified *content* of the text — who it thinks you are, who it calls you to identify with. Farouche offers you a single, unified individuality made up from "all the women you are", Glow 5 flatters you with the misrecognition of yourself in the beautiful young face that smiles at you from the mirror in the advertisement. This is an emphasis which appears in later versions of cultural studies.

U203: the Open University course on popular culture

The Open University provides degree courses mainly for mature students who have no previous qualifications and who study at home. Between 1982 and 1987 it offered a one-year interdisciplinary or 'U' course in cultural studies open to students in their second year or above. U203, "Popular Culture", has been taken by over 5,000 students, more than graduated in that period from all the other media and cultural studies courses in the country. It formed an institutional link between intellectuals who had been involved in *Screen* reading groups, members of the British Film Institute, academics in polytechnics and universities and film and television practitioners, thus, quite apart from students, performing a re-education for several hundred teachers besides an uncounted number of the general public who eavesdropped on its television transmissions. The course was intended to run and run but as an interdisciplinary course it had no empire to defend it within the University bureaucracy and so, in a time of cut-backs, it was terminated in October 1987 (see Cubitt 1986).

Written by a team of twenty-six, including sociologists, anthropologists, historians and lecturers in media studies, and led by Tony Bennett (now Senior Lecturer at Griffith University in Brisbane), the course was assessed by Raymond Williams and Terry Eagleton among others. It has been the most ambitious, serious and comprehensive intervention in cultural studies in Britain, and, apart from the work of the Birmingham Centre, the most important. Students were taught by means of: thirty-two course units written for the course; three books of selected material or readers; republished offprints from books and essays; sixteen television programmes as well as radio broadcasts transmitted nationally by the BBC; tape cassettes sent to students; regular seminars held across the country; an intensive one-week summer school held at Preston so students could study Blackpool, the popular seaside resort on the Lancashire coast. Though the course units are in effect lecture notes, as with all Open University courses, the risk has been taken of publishing them and I shall not hesitate about referring to them here.

U203: course content

The course intends to have a radical purpose, to encourage its students to see Britain as if they were visitors from abroad or another planet and "interrogate critically the part that popular culture plays within your life" (Course Guide, p. 5). So, since the course began just after Christmas, it began with a study of Christmas as a form of popular culture. 'Popular' was in distinction from 'high' culture as an area which could be seen *both* as active and passive, both an expression of the creative impulses of people and a consumption over which the broad mass of people have little control (see Bennett 1981a, p. 83). This negotiation itself the course analysed through Gramsci's concept of hegemony: the ruling bloc rules by winning consent rather than using force, admitting dissent so long as it is expressed on the grounds of consensus defined according to the long-term interests of the ruling bloc.

The state of the art in cultural studies prior to the Open University course was signalled by Stuart Hall's 1980 essay, "Cultural studies: two paradigms" (reprinted in the course reader, *Culture, ideology and social process*, Bennett *et al.* 1981c, pp. 19–37). The two paradigms are represented by the view on the one hand that subjects, individual and collective, are constitutive, culturally expressive, and on the other, that all such expression is determined in advance by structures which are both social and signifying. U203 turns to the concept of hegemony as a means to transcend this opposition, because the concept of hegemony specifies "a *negotiated version*" of relations between the bourgeoisie and the ruling class, between the imposed 'structures' of the dominant ideology and the cultural expression of the working class, as Bennett explains in a retrospective account of the course :

> Gramsci argues that the bourgeoisie can become a hegemonic, leading class only to the degree that bourgeois ideology is able to accommodate, to find some space for, opposing class cultures and values. A bourgeois hegemony is secured not via the obliteration of working class culture, but via its *articulation to* bourgeois culture and ideology so that, in being associated with and expressed in the forms of the latter, its political affiliations are altered in the process. (1986, pp. xiv–xv)

With a long section of one of the readers given to Gramsci, hegemony becomes the centring concept of the course, constantly referred to in the units.

Limited unfortunately to British history, the syllabus covers a period from around 1800 with an increasing concentration as it reaches the present day. Popular culture is understood to comprehend both practices and texts, practices as forms of 'lived experience' in which signification is not dominant and texts as forms of signifying practice in which it is. Among the popular cultural practices considered are the traditional country pastime of throwing at cocks (you tether a cockerel to a peg and throw things at it until it is dead), the eating of 'kets' (children's sweets designed to nauseate the adult, see James 1982) and package holidays in Benidorm. The structuralist and post-structuralist input into the course comes in units 13–17 which study form and meaning, and are later illustrated by the analysis of such texts as The Who's "Generation", television crime series and soap opera, Fleming's *Dr No* (Bennett and Woollacott have followed through this work on Fleming in *Bond and beyond*, 1987).

Anthologies prepared for the course (Bennett *et al.* 1981b, Bennett *et al.* 1981c, Waites *et al.* 1982) make available to students a number of texts of classic structuralism, including Eco on Bond and Barthes's "Introduction to the structural analysis of narratives".

And *Popular film and television* (Bennett *et al.* 1981b) reprints a lot of material from *Screen* including MacCabe on realism and Mulvey on gendered viewing. In the course units on 'Form and meaning' students are introduced to the ideas of interpellation, the subject as construction, position as an effect of the text.

Students of U203 have already been confronted with a critique of the humanist notion of the 'individual' via the Althusserian account of ideology, as that which works 'behind our backs' in the way "individuals 'live' their relationship to the material conditions of their social existence" (Bennett 1981a, p. 82). So when the syllabus turns from practices to texts they are already prepared for the assertion that the reader does not simply bring himself or herself to the text but finds identity in the text:

> texts 'read' their readers rather than the other way about. In order to *be* read, the text imposes a specific identity on the reader/viewer/listener and in that sense 'creates' her or him...in reading ourselves into a text, we take on a temporary identity ... (Martin 1981, p. 8)

A passage from a Hardy short story is drawn on to show how a text can "position us" in terms of gender (a man is looking and a woman is being looked at) and education (the reader is "expected to be a fairly experienced person, with wide knowledge of what London contains", p. 27). Thus the story "pulls the reader" into a relationship with its narrated events and characters. These notions of pulling and positioning the reader rely on the Althusserian concept of interpellation which the course elsewhere makes explicit, for example listing and defining the term in its Concepts Glossary.

On this basis the course defines post-structuralism and discriminates it from structuralism as follows:

> Although it would object to the notion of the human subject as transcendent (that is, existing outside the structure and operating it), post-structuralism marks itself off from its classical forerunner by its dynamic rather than static character. More precisely, it does not just see the subject as existing within the structure and dependent on it, but rather sees the subject as produced by the structure, the play of signifiers. (Bourne 1981, p. 46)

This relatively innocent definition precisely accords with the British version of post-structuralism. Its application is carried through in the analysis of a number of advertisements, of narrative (with reference to Barthes and *S/Z*,) of problems surrounding realism and, most significantly, in a sustained discussion of popular culture and *pleasure*.

U203 works with two related but distinct assumptions about text, reader and position. Firstly, and mainly, textual positioning is understood as a way to answer the question, "Who does this text think you are?" Position is defined in terms of content, of "assumptions, tastes, values" (as the Concepts Glossary says) very much in the way it is used in Williamson's *Decoding advertisements*. But secondly, though less stress is given to this, position means what it meant in the *Screen* problematic: the process in which signifier and signified operate to constitute the subject. Thus in the discussion of realism appeal is made to MacCabe's account of dominant specularity and, with reference to the cinematic techniques discussed by Heath's "Narrative space", it is affirmed that "they all centre on the position of the spectator as a position of intelligibility" (Donald and Mercer 1981, p. 83).

However, the notes on realism open up a wider account of it, specifically by proposing some characteristics especially suitable for the signified content of realism, that it should be historical rather than supernatural or mythical, if possible contemporary, and democratic in the sense of representing the world of ordinary people rather than aristocrats. They also repeat the criticism that the analysis of classic realism errs on the side of formalism by failing to account for "the interaction of particular texts with particular subjects at particular historical moments" (Donald and Mercer 1981, p. 85).

The rest of the course follows this through by re-inserting texts into their historical situations and actual readerships by discussing, for example, the Bond novels in relation to the attitudes of the later 1950s and early 1960s, and the past thirty years of crime series on British television (from *Dixon of Dock Green* via *Z Cars* to *The Professionals*) in relation to developing contemporary ideologies of law and order. Clearly this attends to though does not resolve the problem of what the text brings to the reader and the reader to the text, of text as structure versus text as act. It solves it, in fact, rather by collapsing structure into act so that the trans-historical persistence of text-as-structure is denied by the privileging of text-as-act within history. Texts come to be dematerialised, treated as merely transparent vehicles between a historical intention and an historical reading. Contemporary readings are privileged as original — and originary (though the capacity of the texts to be re-read without final end is demonstrated by the analytic texts themselves, the course units and notes, as they advance this reading of those texts, a reading from the early 1980s hardly possible for the 'original' audience).

The pleasures of popular culture

In "Popular culture: the pleasure and the pain" (1982), John O. Thompson gives a witty, quirky and extremely provocative critique of U203 based on the three anthologies published in conjunction with the course. A prime criticism is that the course follows the traditional, moralising and puritanical left dismissal of popular culture as the opium of the masses, a capitalist con, ignoring the fact that many of the products of popular culture are deeply pleasurable. The article recognises that assessing the course outside its "full teaching context is not really sensible" (p. 43) and in fact one of the units *is* devoted to a discussion of pleasure. In this also the course enlists post-structuralist ideas.

Unit 17, entitled simply "Pleasure", never really clarifies whether it is addressed at pleasure as text or pleasure as practice. But it is post-structuralist in deploying the argument that pleasure, though seemingly pre-eminently natural, spontaneous and *obvious*, is always constructed in and for the subject. After arguing initially that how a society delimits 'good' and 'bad' pleasures is always historical, the account goes on to assert that "particular forms and mechanisms of pleasure are actually constituted by and within the social" (Mercer 1981, p. 49). Brecht on 'Dramatic' versus 'Epic' theatre, Mulvey on cinematic scopophilia as masculine pleasure, the *Screen* analysis of dominant specularity as a means of deriving visual pleasure from post-Renaissance perspective are all called in evidence.

And so is narrative and its possible pleasures. At this point psychoanalysis seriously begins to enter the argument. The unit cites Steve Neale's work on genre (1980), which takes as its basis the Lacanian conception of repetition and difference to propose that all 'classic' narratives exert a tension,

the tension between process (with its threat of incoherence, of
the loss of mastery) and position (with its threat of stasis,
fixity or of compulsive repetition, which is the same thing in
another form). This tension, which informs all semiotic
systems in so far as they are grounded in desire, realises itself
in two distinct forms of pleasure: firstly, the potential
'boredom' of stasis; and, secondly, pleasure in position in the
face of the anxieties potentially attendant on unlimited
process. (Neale 1980, p. 26, cited Mercer 1981, p. 63)

Narcissistic pleasure, the pleasure of mastery, consciousness and
fixity, a repetition in which the ego constitutes itself as the same
from one moment in the process of time to another, marks one pole
of a continuum of which the other is desire, loss of certainty, entry
into a process which is unconscious, difference amid which the ego
holds itself together only around a temporary anchoring point. One
depends on the other: "fixity can only be pleasurable if there is a
promise of movement or a potential for movement: the pleasure of
movement can only be pleasurable if there is a 'promise' of
eventual stability" (Mercer 1981, p. 64). Thus, the pleasures of
familiarity (which need novelty if they are not to pile up into
boredom) are joined in a dialectical process with the pleasures of
novelty (which need familiarity if they are not to slide away into an
excessive disruption).

From here it is a single move, which the course unit makes, to
the distinction Barthes introduces in 1973 between the "text of
pleasure" that "contents, fills, grants euphoria...linked to a
comfortable practice of reading" and the "text of bliss" that
"imposes a state of loss" and "discomforts" by bringing to a crisis
the reader's relation with language (cited Mercer, p. 64). Having
got to this point, the discussion has no choice but to support it by
bringing forward what it has assumed — psychoanalytic theories of
the constitution of the subject in Freud and Lacan. Towards the end
there is a tactical attempt to shepherd these theoretical accounts of
pleasure back into the fold of historical materialism via Bakhtin
(alias Voloshinov) on Freud and on language. But in default of a
unified theoretical perspective able to contain both psychoanalysis
and historical materialism, both the subject in the unconscious and
the subject in ideology, the discussion stops rather than concludes.

Students of U203 "Popular Culture" learn to ask of texts —
Dallas, a Sherlock Holmes short story — whether they are more
like a text of pleasure or a text of bliss. Post-structuralism enters the

course in a *teachable* mode, as a publicly acknowledged theoretical framework to be learned, mastered and applied. In this respect the course presupposes its own pedagogical subject, one for whom its theoretical basis (in Gramsci's Marxism) provides a position of dominant specularity before whom popular culture, both as text and practice, signifying practice and historical situation, are laid out in a seeming unity (and so texts can read off against a pre-existing historical model). This subjectivity the course enforces but does not interrogate (though it is interrogated elsewhere, see Easthope, forthcoming).

Yet post-structuralism remains to undercut the rest of the Open University course in at least two respects. While its overall tendency aims to domesticate psychoanalysis by making use of it for the particular task of textual analysis (and not elsewhere, to understand the 'lived' experience, for example, of people going on package holidays, Unit 11), psychoanalysis has a powerful capacity to resist this containment, unsettling and counterposing it. Secondly, while the official doctrine of hegemony must consign popular culture ultimately to the category of a false consciousness which betrays the revolution, the issue of pleasure resists this condemnation by endorsing and even celebrating the pleasures of popular culture, from watching soap opera to throwing at cocks (a Foucauldian possibility?). At the risk of a certain inappropriate authoritarianism — 'Ve haf ways of making you analyse pleasure' — this enclave of work effects a pleasurable disruption in the otherwise consistent theoretical coherence.

5

The Social Sciences

the dangerous tool of reason

Perry Anderson

Regarding any structure post-structuralism asks the question, "Who is this structure for?" But that question leads in two directions, as was already mentioned with reference to Eco's structuralism: firstly to the conception of subject and subject position as effects of the text; and secondly towards the epistemological question of how reality can be known to a subject. How can anyone, situated as they must be within discourse, come to have a knowledge of reality since that knowledge can only be constructed in and through discourse? Such questions about the foundations of scientific truth have been debated at many junctures in Western twentieth-century philosophy but they emerge once more with particular force in post-structuralism.

Whereas in American deconstruction the topic of epistemology came up via the work of Derrida — and especially his essay on the anthropology of Lévi-Strauss — in British post-structuralism it was posed particularly in the area of social sciences, in the writings of Barry Hindess and Paul Q. Hirst, teaching in the Departments of Sociology at Liverpool and London Universities respectively. They, with certain contributors to *Screen*, were members of an informal grouping in London (thus MacCabe's paper "On discourse" was first read in 1976 at a seminar on Social Relations and Discourse organised by Hirst and Sami Zubaida, see MacCabe 1985, p. 109). Once again, because of the British context, the issue of epistemology was pulled into the orbit of Marxism and pursued in consequence of the work of Althusser.

For reasons Marx explored in *The German ideology*, the dominant culture in France has a rationalist, in Britain an empiricist tradition. James Boswell in his *Life of Dr Johnson* records that one day in 1763, after coming out of church, he and Johnson

> stood talking for some time together of Bishop Berkeley's ingenious sophistry to prove the non-existence of matter, and that every thing in the universe is merely ideal. I observed, that though we are satisfied his doctrine is not true, it is impossible to refute it. I never shall forget the alacrity with which Johnson answered, striking his foot with mighty force against a large stone, till he rebounded from it, "I refute it *thus.*" (1945, p.130)

It would be hard to invent a little narrative which better revealed the neurotic basis for an obsession with the real. Boswell was right and, as Catherine Belsey has pointed out, all Johnson did was hurt his big toe. An action does not refute an argument, only another argument does; but Johnson's boot has the weight of the English tradition behind it.

Translated into an empiricist culture, French rationalist modes can become shocking and potentially radical. The first book by Hindess and Hirst came from the press with smoke still rising from remarks such as "Our constructions and our arguments are theoretical and cannot be refuted by an empiricist recourse to the supposed 'facts' of history" (1975, p. 3). For the Johnsonian heritage such polemical remarks are a scandal; yet the weight of that heritage makes itself felt in the frequency with which Hindess and Hirst have to explain that they believe tables exist, that their theoretical position does not "cause us intellectual discomfort when we refrain from walking out of the top windows of high buildings" (1977, p. 8). And tradition insists symptomatically in the very phenomenon of the British intellectual Left in the late 1970s agonising over how there might be a knowledge of the real.

A Marxist epistemology

An epistemology always aims to establish a relation of knowledge between an object and a subject of that knowledge. Writing in the Introduction to the *Grundrisse* Marx defines his account of 'The method of political economy' by contrasting his own work with that of the classical economists (such as Adam Smith and Ricardo) (1973, pp. 100–2). For understanding political economy it seems obvious and correct to begin with "the real and the concrete" such as population, the nation, states. Far from being self-evident, such conceptions turn out to require analysis into more simple concepts so that starting from the supposedly concrete in fact leads to the discovery of "a small number of determinant, abstract, general relations" (e.g. division of labour, money, value) (and from a conceptual basis in these, the classical economists could not but justify the capitalist mode of production as natural — a better understanding of political economy requires, in the subtitle to the German edition of *Capital*, 'A critique of political economy' from a position which envisages its transformation).

Therefore it is crucial to move in the other direction. Beginning from such abstractions as labour and money, *already* worked up by classical economics, this advances to categories such as the state, international exchange and the world market. While the first method moves from concrete to abstract, the second ("the scientifically correct method") conducts back towards the concrete totality. On one side, then, reality remains (as Marx puts it bluntly) "outside the head" (objective), and on the other, theoretical understanding is "a totality of thoughts...a product of thinking" (subjective); but such understanding brings object and subject together because it "appropriates the concrete" and "reproduces it as the concrete in the mind". So: reality retains its independence outside discourse but knowledge of reality is constructed through the discursive transformation of perceptions, concepts, categories so that they become enabled to reproduce the real.

"We must completely reorganise the idea we have of knowledge, we must abandon the mirror myths of immediate vision and reading, and conceive knowledge as production" (Althusser and Balibar 1975, p. 24): having already criticised epistemology under the name of empiricism for assuming that knowledge "is already *really* present in the real object it has to know" (p. 38), Althusser goes on to argue that though Marx frequently used phrasing implying that knowledge revealed the 'real' beneath the 'apparent' he understood knowledge not as revelation but an effect consequent upon a discursive process. In two long passages (1977a, pp. 182–93 and 1975, especially pp. 86–90) Althusser comments on 'The method of political economy' as described in the *Grundrisse*. While *For Marx* has as its precedents the work of Bachelard and, implicitly, Kuhn's *The structure of scientific revolutions*, *Reading*

Capital is also able to draw on the early Foucault, in particular *Madness and civilisation* and *Birth of the clinic*.

Against empiricist epistemologies, Althusser affirms that "theoretical work presupposes a given raw material and some 'means of production'" which results in a product (1977a, p. 173). Stressing knowledge as a never finished process of active transformation he names these as Generalities I, II, and III.

Generality I is of an ideological nature, the material *already* conceptualised on which a theoretical practice sets to work; Generality II, the instruments of theoretical production, is "the 'theory' of the science at the (historical) moment under consideration" (1977a, p. 184) able to transform Generality I into Generality III, the finished product, the knowledge effected within an authentic science. Althusser proposes that the Marxism of Marx was the theoretical product ($G'III$) resulting when Ricardo and French socialism ($G'I$) was transformed by means of a version (strictly inversion) of Hegel ($G'II$) (and similarly that the Marx–Hegel relationship ($G'I$) has been transformed by means of Marxism ($G'II$) into *Reading capital* ($G'III$); see Althusser 1972, pp. 168ff).

Affirming with Marx both the independence of the extra-discursive (the real) and the discursive construction of knowledge through theoretical practice (thought about the real), Althusser concludes "there is a relation between *thought*-about-the-real and this *real*, but it is a relation of *knowledge*, a relation of adequacy or inadequacy of knowledge" (1975, p. 87, italics original). In the process of the construction of knowledge (or science) "it is not a question of *guarantees*" (p. 55). Knowledge cannot be referred 'up' or 'out' to a truth existing *outside* the very process of its construction. This entails substitution of "the question of the *mechanism*" for that "of *guarantees* of the possibility of knowledge" (p. 56). Instead of knowledge as generally understood, truth achieved once and for all and guaranteed by an epistemology, we must think instead of a process leading to "the '*knowledge effect*'" (p. 62).

Marxist epistemology, as re-worked in Althusser, appears immune to the simplistic claim that there cannot be knowledge because you cannot have a signified without a signifier so that all science depends upon discourse. It positively affirms that knowledge is a process of transformation, an intervention with its own force of which knowledge is a dependent effect, posing subject and object in reciprocity. The crucial object analysed by the theoretical practice of Marxism is the economic mode of production. This is the object with which Hindess and Hirst test out the Althusserian account in *Pre-capitalist modes of production* (or *PCMP*, 1975), a book which led to an acrimonious controversy to which the two writers reply in *Mode of production and social formation* (or *MPSF*, 1977) (subtitled "An auto-critique of *PCMP*"). It is only via the detours and difficulties of the first book that the second reaches an important critique of epistemology.

Pre-capitalist modes of production

A section of the *Grundrisse* develops a history of the various epochs, each characterised by their distinct mode of production, which precede capitalism (see Marx 1973, pp. 471ff). Though the chapter headings of *PCMP* ("Primitive communism", "The ancient mode of production", "The feudal mode of production") invite us to read it as an empirical study of historical formations, we would be mistaken to do so for it is rather, as it claims, "a work of Marxist scientific theory" (1975, p. 3), an intervention within theoretical practice. Accordingly, its avowed position forcefully rejects empiricism:

> Concepts are formed and have their existence within knowledge. They are not reducible to or derivable from any set of 'given', 'real' conditions. The concept of the feudal mode of production, for example, is not the product of a generalisation from a specific set of historically 'given' feudal societies...On the contrary, the concept of the feudal, or any other, mode of production is the product of theoretical work. Its theoretical status and validity can be determined only within the field of concepts which specify the general definition of mode of production. (1975, pp. 1–2)

For these reasons they say "their arguments are theoretical" and cannot be refuted by any "empiricist recourse to the supposed 'facts' of history" (p. 3).

In the wake of Althusser and Balibar *PCMP* sets out to analyse the "theoretical means for the production of knowledge of concrete social formations" (p. 9). Against *Reading capital* Hindess and Hirst deny that there can be a general theory of modes of production because this would be to "represent each particular mode as a particular variant of a single general structure" (p. 7), so assuming history as an expressive totality, a single essence unfolding itself first in one mode of production and then in another (in a word, Hegel). Though there can be no such general *theory* this "does not mean there can be no general concepts" (p. 8) through which to interrogate the conditions of existence of a mode of production, particularly the conditions set by the relations of production and the forces of production. On this theoretical basis, then, Hindess and Hirst claim that:

> For each of the pre-capitalist modes of production briefly indicated in the works of Marx and Engels we may pose the following question: "Is it possible to construct the rigorous concept of that mode of production as a distinct and determinate articulated combination of relations and forces of production?" (p. 18)

They do feel able to construct a coherent conception of the ancient and the feudal modes of production but can find no determinate concept for the 'Asiatic' mode of production.

With this same post-structuralist insistence that knowledge depends on discourse the conclusion of *PCMP* aggressively confronts the widely held belief that Marxism is based above all in the study of history. Hindess and Hirst affirm that "Marxism is not a 'science of history' and Marxist theoretical work has no necessary connection with the practice of the historian" (p. 308). They do so on the grounds that "by definition, all that is past does not exist" (p. 309) and that "the object of history is whatever is *represented* as having hitherto existed" so that the object of history "does not exist except in the modality of its current existence, as representations" (p. 309). This leads on to the claim, deeply shocking to traditional British Marxists (and surely meant to be), that "the study of history is not only scientifically but also politically valueless" (p. 312).

These assertions that in historical study there is nothing outside the text are made in a book whose bibliography mentions neither Derrida nor Hayden White:

> Artefacts, washing lists, court rolls, kitchen middens, memoirs, are converted into *texts* — representations through which the real may be read...Far from working on the *past*, the ostensible object of history, historical knowledge works on a body of *texts*...History is a potentially infinite text, constantly

doubling back on itself, constantly being re-written. Marxist
history in no sense escapes these limitations. (p. 311)

Derridean as this sounds, it owes less to Derrida than to Althusser
and Lacan — to the Althusser who describes the construction of
knowledge as a form of theoretical practice, to the Lacan who
insists on the insistence of the signifier, that "the symbol manifests
itself first of all as the murder of the thing" (1977a, p. 104) and that,
since there is no Other of the Other, "no metalanguage can be
spoken" (p. 311) from a position of knowledge outside the process
of signification and the social formation.

Instead of history what must be worked on is theory because,
since that theory depends on its "current existence" in
representations in the present, such theory is able to act on the
present when linked to a Marxist political practice: "All Marxist
theory...exists to make possible the analysis of the current
situation" (1975, p. 312). Conventional history writing cannot do
this because it is empiricist and therefore merely ideological (a
claim vehemently opposed by other Marxist historians and
discussed in the following chapter).

So far Hindess and Hirst have been given a clear run to see where
they get to. What they do is to re-deploy Althusser's Generalities I,
II and III against Althusser. Thus, Marx's *Grundrisse* account of
pre-capitalist economic formations constitutes G^{I} for which
Reading Capital's analysis of mode of production in terms of
conditions of existence provides G^{II}, the means of theoretical
production; G^{III}, the product, is a critique of the epistemological
and ontological assumptions of Althusser and Balibar. Althusser,
and in his company, Hindess and Hirst, depart from the
epistemology Marx describes as 'The method of political economy'
because they assume in Generality I an opposition between
'concepts' and 'facts'. While it is certainly the case that referents
are extra-discursive but signified meanings occur only within
discourse, it is clear that the inadequate and ideologically
contaminated political economy of Adam Smith and Ricardo — the
starting point or equivalent of G^{I} in Marx's proposed method —
nevertheless has a purchase on empirical reality; and, at the same
time, its 'facts' only really count as facts within the theoretical
framework of its 'concepts'. So even G^{I} resists the rationalist
categorisation imposed by the either/or of 'concepts' versus 'facts',
and in his criticism of Althusser (one which encompasses Hindess
and Hirst) Edward Thompson makes great play of exposing this

mistake (though he only does so by confusing 'facts' with 'experience', see 1978, pp. 201–17).

However, Althusser does concur with Marx in asserting that $G^{|}III$, the product of theoretical practice, appropriates the real since there is a relation between thought about the real and the real, "a relation of adequacy or inadequacy of knowledge" (1975, p. 87). On this Hindess and Hirst part company with Marx, Althusser and Balibar: a discourse of knowledge, at least in the example of the study of history, does not refer to a reality ('the past') but exists *only* as a set of present representations and so *only* as a form of intervention. It would have been all right if they had argued that history, as a discourse of knowledge, is a discursive intervention before it subsequently and contingently refers to a specific, real object — instead they advance an unnecessary either/or. For many of their readers Hindess and Hirst seem to forfeit all claim to serious attention at this point. And yet perhaps their road of excess does lead to some wisdom, for *PCMP* makes way for the auto-critique of *MPSF*.

Mode of production and social formation

PCMP supposes that a conceptual organisation can work on the concept of mode of production. In so far as the supposition itself presupposes a relation of knowledge and a correspondence between the organisation (subject) and mode of production (object), it can be seen to rest on the base of an epistemology. In their auto-critique, *MPSF* (1977), Hindess and Hirst set out to eradicate this last vestige of empiricism. They also attempt to confront their own rationalism.

MPSF begins by intervening once again in the debate over base and superstructure in Marxist theory. Whereas such theory has traditionally treated the economic basis as "the real foundation" for the superstructure, Althusser had insisted that the social formation was a decentred structure in dominance determined in the last instance by economic practice. And, in a smaller compass, whereas *PCMP* had followed Althusser in according priority to the concept of mode of production, *MPSF* is concerned specifically to deny this privilege: "There is no general priority to the economic over other levels of the social formation" (p. 5). Besides the theoretical reason given for this move — that "there are no privileged 'basic concepts' of marxism or of any other field of theoretical discourse" (p. 30) — two other things are needed to explain it. One, given in the text, is the political necessity to regard all aspects of the social formation as sites for intervention, not simply struggle at the level of the economy; the other, not given, is the rapid growth during the late 1970s of the recognised importance of the women's movement, a recognition which went along with the difficulty of theorising feminism in relation to Marxism, gender in relation to mode of production.

Hindess and Hirst now reject mode of production as a privileged concept; and they reject privileged concepts because they have now come to regard their former project as contaminated with epistemology, that is, with supposing a relation of appropriation or correspondence between an object (mode of production) and the discursive construction of that object. This critique becomes possible from the new position worked through to in *MPSF*, which is a rejection of epistemology altogether.

Epistemology conceives of the relation between discursive knowledge and reality in terms of both a distinction and a correlation (a difference within epistemology being that empiricist epistemologies conceive the correlation between knowledge and reality as effected through experience while rationalist epistemologies — such as that supposed by *PCMP* — conceived both as deriving in different ways from rational order). To distinguish between reality and knowledge and then to define knowledge as knowledge of a correlation between the two *must* assume there are "uniquely privileged levels and forms of discourse" so able to distinguish and correlate. But how can these levels and forms themselves be validated?

They can't:

> The circularity and ultimate dogmatism of all epistemological conceptions should be evident since there can be no demonstration that such-and-such forms of discourse are indeed privileged except by means of forms of discourse that are themselves held to be privileged. (pp. 13–14)

If we know, how can we know that we know (get a "demonstration") without the new knowledge itself being subject to interrogation...and so on? In consequence, though they deny again and again that people can walk through walls, Hindess and Hirst reject all epistemology, meaning by that a knowable relation (of distinction and correlation) between reality and knowledge:

> *To deny epistemology is to deny that correlation. It is not to*
> *deny forms of existence outside of discourse but it is to deny*
> *that existence takes the form of objects representable in*
> *discourse.* The rejection of epistemology implies a rejection
> of the epistemological conception of knowledge as involving
> a more or less adequate representation or appropriation of
> some independently existing reality. (p. 21, italics original)

No knowledge outside representation, no epistemology. As before
there is an argument from the inescapable dependence of signified
upon signifier, knowledge upon discursive construction. But in
addition there is the argument that adequacy or correspondence
assumes a standard, terms, or *criteria* by which that correspondence
can itself be judged and these in turn require further justification in
infinite regress. As Lyotard remarks succinctly, "what proof is there
that my proof is true?" (1983 p. 24).

Although Hindess and Hirst (in an aside) deny their position is
sceptical (since scepticism is a position within epistemological
discourse, p. 8), the position sounds very like scepticism. As such
it goes back at least to Hume's argument that rationality itself
cannot be rationally justified. In other forms it is endemic in
twentieth-century Anglo-American philosophy, notably in
Wittgenstein's attack on the unsatisfiable "craving for generality"
(1958, p. 17) which seeks, for example, some common property to
justify the application of a general term to what are taken to be
particular instances of that generality.The argument, then, is not
fully original, though it is deployed with considerable vigour and
confidence. Its interest here is rather that it forms a parallel to
arguments about epistemology and knowledge advanced in other
post-structuralist texts, especially certain ones from Derrida.

A post-structuralist epistemology

Invited to the famous Baltimore conference in 1966, Derrida took
with him some work in progress. Published out of sequence in
Macksey and Donato's anthology in 1970, "Structure, sign and play
in the discourse of the human sciences" rapidly acquired in the
United States, as Lentricchia says, "the status of a sacred essay"
(1980, p. 168), because it demonstrated that discourse was busy
everywhere turning metalanguage, knowledge, and the real into
impossible concepts.

"Empiricism is the matrix of all faults menacing a discourse which continues...to consider itself scientific" (1978, p. 288): Derrida's critique of what is taken to be the epistemology of science under the name of empiricism follows Althusser closely (the papers for *Reading Capital* were delivered in 1965). The essay enforces an either/or. A discourse of knowledge can be understood in terms of: *either* "fixed origin", "point of presence", "centre" (p. 278), "transcendental signified" (p. 280), "truth", "objective significations" (p. 284); *or* "play" (p. 278), "system of differences" (p. 280), "infinite substitutions" (p. 289), "the element of discourse" (p. 282). Though of course these terms are not equivalent, they do fall clearly on one or other side of the fence and are meant to:

> There are thus two interpretations of interpretation, of structure, of sign, of play. The one seeks to decipher, dreams of deciphering a truth or an origin which escapes play and the order of the sign...The other, which is no longer turned toward the origin, affirms play. (p. 292)

Deriving from linguistics, the argument is that since signified depends on signifier and since from Saussure we learn that signifiers are negatively differentiated, no signified can hold an absolute or transcendental or automatically privileged position above the order of discourse producing it.

The essay has been widely taken up within American deconstruction to imply two diverse things: (1) the dependence of a discourse of knowledge on discourse makes knowledge impossible; (2) no discourse of knowledge can refer to reality and this makes knowledge impossible. The first view is incorrect, the second is not even broached in "Structure, sign and play".

The first view indeed corresponds to a foundational opposition within the essay: either truth is centred in a transcendental signified outside all process or signification or there is play and only play. The opposition posed is as questionable as its absolutist presupposition. Absolute truth on one side of the *aut* is mirrored by absolute play excluding all truth on the other; the absolutist certainties of 'empiricism' have been re-founded in the opposition intended to refute them (since the absolute truth claimed by empiricism is impossible, there is absolutely no truth but only play).

While this is an attack on empiricist epistemology (one which could hardly come as a surprise to a reader of *Reading Capital*) it would certainly not be a satisfactory response to the account of epistemology in the Marxist tradition, which has from the first accorded full weight to the process of the discursive construction of knowledge, to the process by which knowledge is said to be "a product of thinking" (Marx), a theoretical practice whose "mechanism" can seek no (absolute) guarantees but is rather a transformative act resulting in "the knowledge effect" (Althusser). To this Hindess and Hirst add a critique of even the Althusserian notion of adequacy because it claims general grounds for epistemology, grounds which cannot be validated outside the discourse of knowledge itself. As *MPSF* says in a phrasing which marks the proximity of its chosen position to that of Derrida's essay, "the entities specified in discourse must be referred to solely in and through the forms of discourse, theoretical, political, etc., in which they are constituted" (p. 18).

However, Hindess and Hirst are doing much more than repeat the tautology that signifieds are signifieds and objects of discourse are objects of discourse, as can be understood if the second kind of appropriation of Derrida's essay is considered, that which assumes it denies the possibility of reference. While *MPSF* accepts that all discourses, including scientific ones, cannot escape the play by which they *are* constituted as discourses, it does not derive from this the view that there can be no discourse of knowledge.

For a discourse to refer to reality supposes a relation between what is signified within the discourse and a referent or group of referents in the extra-discursive. Although it proves convincingly that there can be no transcendental signified, "Signature, sign and play" has nothing to say about *reference* and a possible relation between signified and referent which would help to constitute a discourse of knowledge (though elsewhere Derrida has confronted the question of correspondence/non-correspondence between signified and referent; see, for example, the extended footnote in *Positions*, 1981a, p. 105 on the necessity of science and the inescapability of truth). Hindess and Hirst have pursued the argument about adequacy, correspondence, and the possible *general* relation between signified and referent claimed by a discourse of knowledge and shown why no such general relation can be maintained. For the reasons given, there can be not merely no guarantees for it, but no demonstration.

However, if the infinite regression by which an object language seeks to validate itself in a metalanguage which only turns out to be another object language requiring further validation, if the movement upwards (as it were) to ever higher levels of abstraction and generality is endless, there may still be a movement back towards the concrete. This has been suggested by Hirst as follows:

> There are no general criteria of adequacy or truth...We would argue that discourses and practices *do* employ the criteria of appropriateness or adequacy (not of epistemological validity) but these are specific to the objectives of definite bodies of discourse and practice. None will pass muster as a general criterion of validity, but there is no knowledge process *in general* and, therefore, no necessity for such a criterion. Techniques of criticism of Biblical texts are of no use in garage mechanics. Questions of priority and relation in the Gospels, of the state of wear of a gearbox elicit different types of tests and disputes about them. The referents and constructs, Gospels, motor cars, depend on conditions which differ, so do criteria and tests. (1979, p. 21)

From this position Hirst draws the conclusion that "in the absence of a privileged level ('experience', or 'reason' which imposes form on discourse)" one has "to accept the *difference* of the referents of discourse, the potential infinity of referents" (p. 19).

This argument restores adequacy between discourse and referent as a criterion of knowledge but only in a way which might be qualified as follows: the good news is that, after all, discourses of knowledge do refer, the bad news is that there can be no demonstration of this beyond the specific and local methods by which each such discourse constructs a knowledge of its referents.

Consequences

Advocating an essentially post-structuralist position on epistemology, the arguments of Hindess and Hirst were very painful to some of the New Left (as registered in their nickname, Hinders and Hurts). The Althusserian Marxists of the *New Left Review* failed to engage with the arguments and stayed content to dismiss them in a footnote (see Anderson 1976, p. 110) or a phrase ("weightless iconoclasm", 1980, p. 126). Hirst in particular has lamented the lack of comradely exchange (1986, Preface and pp. 1–7), which only becomes more explicable if not excusable when its sectarian context is recalled, Hindess and Hirst associated with the Communist party, *NLR* with the International Marxist Group

(IMG). Even in 1986 *NLR* could still publish a long, vituperative and moralistic account of "The Odyssey of Paul Hirst" which limits its critical engagement to the statement "Hirst has long since parted with Marx" (Elliott 1986, p. 104).

Even in *Screen* the influence of the two sociologists, though huge, was subterranean and only symptomatically apparent, as for example in Paul Willemen's footnote remark denying any equation between ideology and the Lacanian imaginary on the grounds that "there is no 'pure' imaginary to be opposed to the symbolic (or in Althusserian terms: science)" (1978, p. 63). If the Althusserian concept of ideology is being defined in Lacanian terms as the imaginary and his science as the symbolic, it is clear that any possibility of a discourse of knowledge has been thoroughly relativised in terms of the situation of the subject.

The consequence of the debate is of course to render untenable the Althusserian opposition between science and ideology, a position from which Althusser himself had meantime retreated. As he writes in *Elements of self-criticism*, his account of Marx's development from works of ideology to works of science (historical materialism) across a 'break' observable from 1845 onwards, had been guilty of a theoreticist error in "contrasting *truth* and *error* in the form of the speculative distinction between *science* and *ideology*, in the singular and in general" (1976, p. 106). There is, then, no *absolute* distinction between ideology and science of the kind error/truth. In Britain this necessary acknowledgement had a number of consequences.

One was quite simply a loss of confidence, as Colin MacCabe has recalled (1985, pp. 13–14). To the extent that, say, the work of *Screen* had grounded itself in the Althusserian problematic — cinema was the 'lived experience' in ideological practice which the theoretical practice of the film journal could analyse and understand as it could not understand itself — to that extent the project suffered (though there are several other reasons for *Screen*'s change of direction in the late 1970s). Another has to be described as a form of disavowal: *NLR*, which led the whole intellectual movement in the 1960s, shut its eyes and sailed on regardless, earning reproof for this from Terry Eagleton (see "Marxism, structuralism and post-structuralism", 1986a, pp. 89–98).

A third consequence was not noted at the time. The intervention of Hindess and Hirst over the question of epistemology — which is surely an intervention *within* Marxism and certainly within the Althusserian problematic — left British post-structuralism impervious to the scepticism of American deconstruction. As published in *The structuralist controversy*, "Structure, sign and play" was read as just another essay, often by readers more interested in the work of Lacan that collection made available. Because of Hindess and Hirst British post-structuralism worked through on the terrain of a political discourse (whether Marxist or not) the argument that "the entities specified in discourse must be referred to solely in and through the forms of discourse, theoretical, political, etc., in which they are constituted."

Although the effects of this position carry through into other areas, especially literary theory, Hindess and Hirst have had their greatest impact in the social sciences where the claims to be a discourse of knowledge are put forward most strongly. In one particular area British post-structuralism intervened again precisely over the question of the subject, to argue that empiricism supposed a transcendental subject and such a subject was impossible. Over the conception of the individual — as person or subject — post-structuralism enters the arena of historical studies.

6

Historical Studies

the superabundance of 'life' and 'concreteness', of the
superiority of the world's imagination and the green leaves
of action over the poverty of grey theory ...

Louis Althusser

The year 1963 saw publication of Edward Thompson's massively detailed, vividly written and passionately argued account of the development of British society between 1800 and 1830, *The making of the English working class.* As previously mentioned, Thompson's intellectual and political position led him into controversy with the Althusserian Marxists. His essay on "The peculiarities of the English" attacked the *New Left Review* position in 1965. And this, together with a new 200-page polemic, was published in 1978 as *The poverty of theory.* Much of this is an argument within Marxism, and much also — especially the debate over epistemology, history and empiricism — covers terrain already discussed in the previous chapter. Here I will look at just enough to give a context for the argument over structure and the nature of the subject which took place between Thompson and Paul Hirst and which succeeded in introducing post-structuralism into the field of historical studies. First it is necessary to consider the contrasted style and language by which the debate was sustained on each side.

Green leaves and grey theory

The post-structuralist stylistic of the Althusserians, whether in *New Left Review* or *Screen* or *Pre-capitalist modes of production*, aims for a rationalist rigour, consistency in the use of technical terms, scrupulous impersonality and a high degree of abstraction. It aims in fact to correspond to the conception of theoretical practice and the knowledge process as a 'process without a subject'. Struggling for detachment from the idiom and warmth of everyday life, the vocabulary and sentence structure of Althusserian and would-be Althusserian discourse prefers "the poverty of grey theory" over "the green leaves of action", a phrasing whose ironic dismissal of humanist sentimentality (Althusser and Balibar 1975, p. 117) is robbed of its irony when borrowed by Thompson for his title. And his own style is very different.

Thompson writes in the first person in a language pestered with allusion, digression, caricature, humour, personal abuse, metaphor, joke, irony — in sum, the well-known English commonsensical knock-about bequeathed by Dryden and the Augustans. There are pages with comic pictures, including a fine illustration of an eighteenth-century orrery, which is in fact a mechanical model of the planetary system but which Thompson passes off as a model of Althusser's structure in dominance, adding a note that the machine "may be simply rotated by turning the handle of theoretical practice" but that it is also possible "to replace the handle with a motor: see next plate" (the next plate shows a nineteenth-century self-regulating machine of some sort but is labelled, "The Motor of History: Class Struggle") (pp. 292–3). The author himself appears on the back cover, his eyes hidden because his head is buried in his hands while perched on his shoulder a tabby cat stares at the camera in a feline version of dominant specularity. Whereas the Althusserian stylistic situates itself in its material existence as writing, Thompson's language wishes to be a *voice speaking*. Discursively, Thompson's text presents itself on the grounds of consensus and common sense; the risk therefore is that instead of offering a critique of everyday life, it will partake of it. Over the issue of the subject, this danger is not avoided.

Conceding blithely as a truism the view that "everything that we think takes place in thought" (p. 207), Thompson nevertheless proposes that the active appropriation of reality by thought takes place *"not on any terms which thought prescribes* but in ways which are determined by the properties of the real object" (p. 209, italics original). Reality is seen to be available for the experience of the subject, and this experience is an experience of history as process rather than structure. What's wrong with Althusser and the Althusserians is that they seek to reduce "process" to "structure" (the terms are Thompson's, see pp. 249–95, *passim*). They are guilty of a "categorial stasis" (p. 253 and again p. 301), one which substitutes for the open experience of process the closed conceptualisation of structures: "Althusser's constructions of the 'theory of history' afford no terms for *experience*, nor for process when considered as human practice" (p. 290). And this is Stalinism, for regarding people as "the bearers of structures" is how Stalin treated the kulaks and killed three million of them (p. 332). But people are not bearers of structures — they are free individuals.

To refute the Althusserian view *The poverty of theory* invents a fictional character and tells the story (pp. 342–3) of a woman who is a wife, a mistress, a mother, a clothing worker, a shop steward, a Labour party member, an occasional violinist, and a member of the Church of England. She is indeed a "bearer" *(Träger)* or support for many determinations which the text lists, a point at which "relations, structures, roles, expectations, norms and functions *intersect*". But, so it is asserted, "not one of these definitions affect the fact that she remains a woman", and as such she may turn round on a putative Althusserian and shout out: "'I'm not a bloody THING!'" (p. 343). The example is meant to bear something of the force and weight of Boswell's story of how Johnson refuted Berkeley.

'The necessity of theory'

All these criticisms put forward by *The poverty of theory* are replied to in Paul Q. Hirst's review essay on the book, entitled "The necessity of theory" (reprinted 1986). His account begins by citing a fantasy of Thompson's, one whose language mixes in equal measure the timeless simplicities of the King James Version of the Bible, castration anxiety and an ideological privileging of British national culture:

A cloud no bigger than a man's hand crosses the English Channel from Paris, and then, in an instant, the trees, the orchard, the hedgerows, the field of wheat, are black with locusts. When at length they rise to fly on to the next parish, the boughs are bared of all culture, the fields have been stripped of every green blade of human aspiration: and in those skeletal forms and that blackened landscape, theoretical practice announces its 'discovery': the mode of production. (Thompson, pp. 358–9, cited Hirst 1986, p. 59)

Hirst comments:

Thus Thompson the squire of Empirica Parva (p. 188) beset by a foreign pestilence, alien in essence to British life. Thompson assures us he has great respect for the right kind of French intellectuals (*Annales*, and Pierre Bourdieu, for example). But this is the metaphorics of xenophobia — and there are numerous other instances. What Thompson reveals here is the depth of his belief that there is a characteristic British tradition and culture. I think this notion of a fundamental national culture orientation is a myth. (p. 59)

Playing off against Thompson's native English, Hirst's review is written in a style with a new edge, its theoretical rigour sharpened into tones of sardonic anger and contempt that recall the stylistic of Marx. More is at stake than the content of ideas, however important these may be. Denying Thompson's belief that British national culture is an essence resting on a fundamental orientation that cannot be altered, Hirst's text seeks to intervene through its form as well as its argument in re-making the national culture.

At issue once again are the former topics: the nature of history and historical study; epistemology; Marxist politics. Hirst's text argues: that Thompson's essential strategy is to mount a theoretical argument which aims to disable theoretical argument by arbitrarily setting limits to it (giving it an inside and an outside); that knowledge of history is not derived from 'facts' but constructed; that there can be no epistemology; that Thompson in the name of Marxism surrenders the analysis of capitalism to an abstracted notion of 'history' ("*Capital* is a mountainous inconsistency...its laws cannot be verified, and its 'predictions' were wrong", Thompson, p. 257, cited Hirst p. 63). But the crux of the controversy is the nature of the subject. Whereas Thompson's critique of Althusser is founded on a concept of the subject as transcendental, Hirst proposes a deconstruction of the subject that is post-structuralist.

Access to the reality of history, above and beyond the 'imposed' structuralist categories of Althusser is made possible for Thompson via 'experience' ("a category which, however imperfect it may be, is indispensable to the historian", Thompson, p. 199, cited Hirst, p. 71). But the notion of experience, writes Hirst, however much it accepts mediations between subject and object (and Thompson does, for example, on p. 111 in acknowledging that the relation between thought and its object becomes "exceedingly complex and mediated"), must presuppose "a means of unifying the external world as object to the subject of knowledge and of explaining its mode of presentation to the subject" (Hirst, p. 71). Thus Thompson:

> Thought and being inhabit a single space, which space is ourselves. Even as we think we also hunger and hate, we sicken or we love, and consciousness is intermixed with being; even as we contemplate the 'real' we experience our own palpable reality. (p. 210, cited Hirst, p. 72)

At which Hirst exclaims in a furious parody of a pre-Darwinian bishop deducing a benign creator from the natural order: "How convenient! How providential that reality should make the world in empiricism's image and give us confirmation of the fact" (p. 72). Thompson's category of 'experience' assumes that knowledge and its object "are united in the knowing subject", located within the "single space which is Man". And it is this same "Man", universal and unchanging — though unmistakably British in Thompson's conception — who forwards history and makes it intelligible.

The subject of history

Hirst's critique consists of three assertions. The first is to deny the humanist conception, and is made with a force that requires citation of a whole paragraph:

> The locus of this epistemological doctrine *manqué* is the category of the human, of Man. It is Man beyond any category, the 'reality' of humanity and our 'palpable' experience of ourselves, that we are referred to. But who is this stranger we are supposed to recognise in ourselves? Real men? But they come in many guises, from the Gas Board to the Gestapo. They say and do things which have no parallel,

things which to Thompson's "rational mind" form "the greater part of the history of ideas" which is "a history of freaks" (p. 195). Are these "freaks" practitioners of 'reason'? If so that reason is at once reasonable and freakish. Or is reason a matter of the right values? Thompson waxes lyrical about the practical knowledges of ordinary men, "the sailor 'knows' his seas" (p. 199). Of course sailors do, but they also know where not to go in order to avoid the sea monsters and they know the fate that awaits the poor fool who sets out into the Atlantic to sail to Cathay. These things form a single 'knowledge', confirmed a hundred times over by 'experience'. Likewise, witch hunters 'know' their witches, they can smell them a mile off and can search out their palpable marks with unerring accuracy. (pp. 72–3)

There can be no universal human subject such as Thompson supposes, able to be a bearer of knowledge acceded to *through* experience — the variety of beliefs, all confirmed by experience, evidences this. As Hirst adds, "the one piece of knowledge I feel any certainty about is that men can say *anything* and consider it reasonable" (p. 73).

And women? Thompson has constructed his narrative of a woman shown to be determined in social and gender relations in order to appeal to some essence of her humanity which is beyond all social structuring and historical determination: "she remains a woman". Not to hold this humanist viewpoint is to be a Stalinist or a Dalek, a science fiction monster who cries *"Exterminate"* (Thompson, p. 337) at the sight of the human.

It is not hard for Hirst to expose the astonishing sleight of hand which conflates categories here so that a *theoretical* viewpoint about historical determination can be equated — *tout court* — with a *moral* decision. Thompson is like someone who says doctors are cannibals because analysing the structures of the human body is the same as eating it. What Hirst does not remark — though he reasonably might — is the phallocentric assumption in Thompsonianism at this juncture. The appeal to an essence of woman ("she remains...") repeats the traditional ideological image of Woman as Man's other, secret, ineffable, darkly transcending (yet thus guaranteeing) his universalising rationality. The rhetoric of the paragraph would collapse if it were re-phrased to conclude "he remains a man".

Having denied the universality of the subject, Hirst, in a second line of argument, denies its unity. Thompson's notion of experience supposes the subject "as a unitary self-experience, presence-to-self in the single and continuous space of consciousness" (p. 74), a stable point or platform on which experience can become aware of itself. But the subject is not like that, or only like that.

Invoking Freud, Lacan and the concept of the unconscious, Hirst argues that the conscious ego, aware of its own experience, is not the only form of self but is merely part of a divided subject split in a dynamic relation between conscious and unconscious. The unconscious constantly returns to demonstrate the limits of the ego's sense of itself as centre of meaning, for example when "unconscious thoughts and desires interrupt centred speech" (p. 74). The subject "is not an originary unity but a *trace*, a construction in language". In writing this Hirst is not alluding to the Derridean trace but to a sentence from Lacan often cited in the pages of *Screen*: "The unconscious *is* a concept forged on the trace of what operates to constitute the subject" (1966, p. 830, cited Heath 1977, p. 49). That is: the psychoanalytic understanding of the unconscious takes as its object something than can never be directly observed but only evidenced in its effects or traces (verbal slips, memories of dreams, hysterical symptoms, and so on).

Hirst's third argument develops from the other two, and concerns essentially the transparency — or rather non-transparency — of discourse. To Thompson's assumption of an intelligible totality in the real must correspond a knowing subject with access to that unified intelligibility. However, experience depends upon discourse (there can be no signified without a signifier) and discourse offers no transparency through which "definite statements about observables" may be able to pass unchanged like rays of light through a window pane. Hirst argues that 'experience' must rest on "the possibility of a pure 'observation language'" and no such discourse exists — "the problem is the notion of a *language* of observables, of its grammar and syntax" (p. 75).

So, no universal subject for experience, no subject which is not split between an 'I' who thinks and another 'I' of the unconscious which 'thinks' where the conscious ego is not, no discourse whose forms can be a merely incidental vehicle for the transfer of experience. And so:

Without the support of a stable presence-to-itself of consciousness, 'experience' is threatened with dispersion.

Once we attach a question to the 'I', posing it as an effect by no means singular or stable (although by no means without effects), then the solidity of "experience" as a something *of* the subject becomes in turn problematic. (p. 75)

Hirst's 'structuralism' undermines Thompson's 'culturalism'. Yet it does so in fact by means of a post-structuralist account of the subject as constructed within structures — social, psychic, linguistic — and as the effect of discourse rather than its unconditioned source and origin.

Is this the end of any conception of individual human agency? It would be hard to imagine a social formation in which there was no attribution of identity to the individual subject through the ascription of distinct personal names or one in which there were no discourses of individual moral responsibility construing the subject as responsible for his or her actions, as Mauss observes (1970). Hirst's position does not deny agency. Taking up Thompson's humanist affirmation that the motor of the historical process is human agency, "*E pur' si muove!*" (Thompson, p. 300), Hirst qualifies it as follows:

Yes, Edward Thompson, it does move. But the movement towards socialism involves more than 'human agency' *per se*: it involves definite forms of organisation, specific practices, policies which are no mere derivation of values, and so on. (p. 85)

Theoretical differences — as they always do — turn out to involve political differences, an assessement of where, how and with what aims a political commitment should be made.

The return of the real

The debate over post-structuralism and historical studies has continued, and is being fuelled by the publication of *Post-structuralism and the question of history*, (1987), edited by Derek Attridge, Geoff Bennington and Robert Young. Hirst's review of *The poverty of theory* was first published in *Economy and Society* in November 1979. In December 1979 at Ruskin College, Oxford, over a thousand people took part in the meeting of English left historians organised by the History Workshop, a meeting which included a debate between Stuart Hall, Richard Johnson (of the Birmingham Centre for Contemporary Cultural Studies) and Edward Thompson himself (see Samuel 1981, pp. 375–408). This discussion develops on in Johnson's essay "Culture and the historians" (1982) and is well summed up in Gregor McLennan's "History and theory: contemporary debates and directions" (1984).

Perhaps because it had only just appeared, Hirst's review was not mentioned in the History Workshop debate. Hall, in his intervention, makes the simplest and most unequivocal condemnation of Thompson's position when he states that to Thompson "history presents itself as a complex 'lived' whole" and so "any conceptualisation of it must be a reduction of the 'evidence'" and that this amounts "to saying that 'the evidence' speaks its meaning transitively, without the mediation of concepts" (Samuel 1981, p. 382). His view gets lost, partly because of the particularly English *tone* of the debate, which is carried on always with a view to reasonable compromise, to assimilating those 'aspects' of 'structuralism' that are 'rightly' drawn to attention while rejecting its 'modishness'.

How little headway Hall's argument could make against the prevailing terms of debate can be measured from Raphael Samuel's editorial preface to the History Workshop volume, which inevitably presents itself as final arbiter of the two sides of the controversy ('on the one hand...on the other...'). It does so, as in this following passage, in terms defending Marxism through a classically English identification of Marxism with the real:

> The starting point of the structuralist critique, that theoretical propositions can't be derived from empirical evidence, is a correct one. But it by no means follows that the inverse of this is true, i.e. that the construction of new theoretical concepts can proceed by a purely deductive process of reasoning without reference to empirical work. For Marxists, theoretical work has always generated propositions designed to explain and understand the real world, and to interpret concrete situations even if they cannot be verified by reference to empirical enquiry alone. Theory-building cannot be an alternative to the attempt to explain real phenomena, but is, rather, a way of self-consciously defining the field of enquiry, clarifying and exposing to self-criticism the explanatory concepts used, and marking the limits of empirical investigation. (pp. xlviii–xlix)

Even if the second sentence does follow from the first, there is no coherent resolution between the avowed acceptance in the first sentence that theory cannot be derived from the empirical and the role of 'useful handmaiden' for tidying up concepts granted to "theory-building" in the last sentence — no resolution, that is, except the presumed *opposition* between theory and the real in which the real naturally assumes priority.

A conclusion to this chapter must err towards pessimism. Post-structuralist arguments such as that so well advanced by Hirst remain a thorn in the side of history writing in Britain. Their effect is to throw in question the whole enterprise of conventional empiricist history (including much Marxist history). Yet the History Workshop discussion, typical as it is of the prevailing debate in English historiography, suggests that the traditional settlement will continue to live — though perhaps not at ease — with this kind of 'alien' intervention. More than any other academic discourse, the writing of history is the one most contaminated by unexamined Englishness and its ideology of the real.

7

Psychology

I would rather be: (a) a bishop, (b) a colonel.

Question from the 16PF psychometry test

When Perry Anderson in 1968 reported on the contemporary state of psychology he found it committed to "belief in a fundamental psyche which is prior to societal determinations" (p. 31). To some degree this was challenged by work from a Marxist perspective such as the essays edited in 1974 by Nigel Armistead as *Reconstructing social psychology*. In the same period, however, the insistence on positivist science in psychology increased just as the residual influence of psychoanalysis on psychology declined. This is the context within which *Changing the subject* (1984) has intervened.

Changing the subject

Subtitled "Psychology, social regulation and subjectivity", the book was written as a collective text by Julian Henriques, Wendy Hollway, Cathy Urwin, Couze Venn and Valerie Walkerdine, three of whom (Henriques, Venn, Walkerdine) were on the editorial committee of the journal *Ideology and Consciousness* (1977–9). Among the English texts which contributed to the project, *Changing the subject* mentions *Screen* (1984, pp. 204, 218), the journal *m/f* and the work of Coward and Ellis (1977). Yet in drawing on these as offering what it terms "materialist theories of ideology" and the subject (p. 214), the book seeks to interpose itself firmly within the discipline of psychology (and so comes complete

106

with the social science trope of saying what an argument will do, doing it and then saying it has been done). Designed in three sections, each of which begins with introductory theory followed by two applications within the field, the book is 150,000 words long and only the theoretical framework can be discussed here.

Changing the subject means to change the subject of academic psychology. Explicitly naming its project as "post-structuralist" in virtue of directly "addressing the question of the constitution of subjects" (Henriques *et al.* 1984, p. 92), the text aims to deconstruct the individual conceived and presented as "the transcendental unitary subject" (p. 195), the autonomous and ahistorical self naturalised by conventional psychology. As a social science, psychology is a discourse with strong claims to be a discourse of knowledge but it is also, through its deployment in such areas as child development, schooling, welfare agencies, medicine, occupational psychology and job analysis, a practice of manifest social power which "regulates, classifies and administers" (p. 1).

The text intervenes therefore in two ways: in terms of an object and in terms of the discourse and practice of psychology in which that object is produced. The object of psychology, the abstracted individual, is submitted to critique from two directions, one showing its social and historical construction, another arguing its constitution by processes which are irrational as well as rational (this leads to a reinstatement and revalidation of psychoanalysis within psychology).

At the same time *Changing the subject* enters a strong critique of the epistemological status of conventional psychology from a Foucauldian position; it is intent on challenging the discourse and practice of psychology as a deployment of power/knowledge. To make the point more insistently, the book claims the term 'deconstruction' for itself within a particular definition. In analysing the history and imbricated genealogy of discourses Foucault shows that the statements of a discourse invisibly depend on those of other discourses which are pulled into it. *Changing the subject* therefore defines "deconstruction" as a strategy of critique which "retraces the system of 'dependencies' of a discourse" (p. 104 but see also p. 125 and the index entry for the term).

The purpose of changing the subject of psychology works through three stages — critique, deconstruction, reconstruction — and the first begins by attacking the transcendental subject of psychology as it is reproduced by the social/individual dualism. Much contemporary theory relies on a notion of the social construction of the self through the 'internalisation' of social roles. *Changing the subject* argues that such socio-cognitive theory is achieved by reducing "the social to the intersubjective" on the assumption "that individual and society are commensurate as theoretical notions" (p. 24). But this fails to solve the problem of dualism, for thus collapsing 'role' and 'self' together does not explain, for example, why "boys and girls take up different positions" in the social domain (p. 20).

In the area of occupational psychology dualism is represented by an object (the job) and a subject (the worker). Job evaluation or job analysis tries by various methods to give an objective definition of a job. Occupational psychology then aims to fit the right person to a job on the basis of an abstract definition of "the core characteristics of a person" (p. 32) through such protocols as the 16PF (16 Personality Factor) and the EPI (Eysenck Personality Inventory). The 16PF claims to measure 'general personality' by means of a questionnaire. The presuppositions inscribed in this are well exposed when it is answered by the writer of this section, Wendy Hollway, who finds herself confronted with questions such as "I would rather be (a) a bishop, (b) a colonel" and who convincingly argues that for many of the questions the only answer "would be 'it depends'" (pp. 46–7). She also cites work revealing that people who want to get jobs give different answers to the 16PF from those who've already got them. When this effect due to the actual situatedness of the personality being tested is dismissed as 'motivational distortion', the term "demonstrates the assumption of a true self" (p. 49) made by such psychometry as the 16PF.

Assuming a dualism between job as object and worker as subject conventional psychology poses "the two categories as fixed entities" (p. 43) and cannot begin to analyse the *relation* of a worker to his or her work in a specific historically determined situation. It further enforces this dualism through its own power as a discourse of knowledge, adhering to a positivist science, taking the personality of the assessee as its object and therefore positioning the assessor as a scientist, "a neutral instrument for gathering 'facts'" (p. 51). Recent evidence is quoted which shows that liking someone in an interview has a real effect and has proved "difficult to stamp out" (p. 51). From a basis in this critique of social/individual dualism *Changing the subject* feels able to move forward to a deconstruction of psychology both in terms of its epistemology and the object, Man, it presumes.

A Foucauldian epistemology

Arguments about discourse and knowledge move across five topics: from the anti-humanist work of Althusser proposing that the subject is constituted as an effect, to the topics of signification, discourse, power, and, in the specific meaning given to the term by Foucault, genealogy. The position on epistemology taken by *Changing the subject* derives from Foucault but also from Hindess and Hirst and can be summarised by four statements:

(1) The real exists extra-discursively; the writers deny that everything is determined by discourse and are concerned to insist that "we have not thrown out the real" (p. 100).

(2) In discourse, even in a discourse of knowledge, meanings are produced from meanings, concepts from concepts; thus

> discourse does not start out as a system of statements and a set of questions about the 'real'...it is caught in a materiality which is a historical product; its specific questions arise from there, where the instruments of its construction are to be found. (p. 113)

It is crucial therefore to deconstruct a discourse of knowledge by inquiring after its dependencies, that is the assumptions it carries within in from its relation to other discourses.

(3) There is a relation between knowledge and the real but no general epistemology can guarantee that relation, for "the relation of knowledge to the 'real', then, is a question tied to the specificity of a given conjuncture of events and is not a general epistemological question concerning guarantees, rules and logical procedures, etc." (p. 114). Knowledge "is always a historical question" (p. 144) because the adequacy of a discourse to the facts it claims to specify is always involved in arguments about what counts as evidence, what calculations of effect are made and what other discourses are allowed to participate in the statements of a discourse.

(4) The production of knowledge is always open to the effect of politics, as is implicit in the previous assertions: "The point of view we are developing starts out from the proposition that all knowledges are productive in the specific sense that they have definite effects on the objects one seeks to know" (p. 92). This is the case in all the social sciences, but especially so in psychology

with its intimate connection to practices of administration and regulation (a good instance being the 16PF assessement).

As a major task in its deconstruction of the discourse of psychology *Changing the subject* sets out to uncover the historical construction of the subject of psychology, since it is only this which ensures the discipline's conceptual coherence. It does this in two ways. First it recalls the birth of the subject as post-Renaissance Man, "the unitary, rational subject which begins to appear in western culture from the seventeenth century" (p. 121), this self-guaranteeing, non-contradictory subject combining the subject of reason (and science) with the abstract legal subject.

Second, it tracks the discursive production of the subject of psychology — modelled on the bourgeois subject — in the late nineteenth century, especially after Darwin. Two effects are crucial. Darwinism promoted a distinction between normal and abnormal functions of the mind, and from this subsequently ensued psychology's ejection of psychoanalysis, a science predicated on the normality of irrational drives. And also after Darwin "the human subject is biologised" (p. 145), mind reduced "to the same material status as the body" (p. 135). This becomes the subject of modern psychology, the subject covertly assumed as "the male European rational individual" (p. 130); by concealing from itself the fact and history of its own construction psychology is able to ignore "the historically specific character of what it takes to be its pre-given object" (p. 140). (Then, in an extended critique of Piaget, *Changing the subject* exemplifies this argument by showing that developmental psychology is premised on an abstracted and dehistoricised conception of the subject as location of "certain capacities within 'the child'" (p. 154), capacities the practices of development psychology in schools actually help to create.)

The subject of Changing the subject

Critique, deconstruction, reconstruction: in its third section the text advocates a transformed psychology. Instead of the individual or even the subject it formally proposes to replace such terms with a conception of "the way discursive practices provide subject *positions*" (p. 203, italics original), a conception linking its argument closely with the concerns of British post-structuralism.

To give content to this notion of subject position the book turns to psychoanalysis, for four reasons. In contrast to the rational subject of psychology, psychoanalysis "gives space to our fundamental irrationality" (p. 205); by introducing the concept of a subject split between conscious and unconscious processes, it undercuts the assumption of a unitary subject; while psychology divides cognition from affect, in psychoanalysis these processes are viewed as intertwined; it provides an account of the continuity of the subject in ways which do not reduce to social or biological determinisms (for which psychology was earlier criticised). From here *Changing the subject* develops an account of psychoanalysis in Freud and especially Lacan with two particular concerns: to make room within it for a feminist politics (as anticipated by Juliet Mitchell); to re-work the subject of psychoanalysis away from an account of a universal subject towards an account of one historically situated.

A critique and re-conceptualisation of the subject is fundamental to *Changing the subject*. It governs the text's perspective on Marxism, and this in two respects. On the one side, repeating though not naming Hirst's discussion, it criticises Althusserian social theory once again for its functionalism, for sharing with structuralism assumptions of "the monolithic, unitary character of power and the social domain" (p. 92): in contrast to this the work of Foucault, by introducing the question of the subject, promises to make links between "a diverse and contradictory social domain and the multiple and contradictory subject" (p. 92). By the same token, the book's commitment to feminism (marking it symptomatically as a text of the 1980s rather than the 1970s and explicitly recognised in the section "Feminism: liberation and beyond" at the beginning, pp. 7–8) gives it reasons to surpass the traditional base/superstructure model with its prior commitment to oppression in terms of class rather than gender. The book's feminist concern is carried through in the final two illustrations, Wendy Hollway on "Gender difference and the production of subjectivity", Cathy Urwin on "Power relations and the emergence of language".

The text makes clear that its focus of attention on the subject is analytic, not ontological. The subject is not presumed to be of greater importance than social relations but attention to it is because the subject is the locus of power, contradiction and resistance, because, in Foucault's argument from "The subject and power" (1982) as summarised in *Changing the subject*, "power works through subjects' actions" (p. 117). Process, the coexistence of the

111

old and the new, results in "contradictions in our positioning, desires and practices — and thus in our subjectivities", contradictions articulated in every relation and every practice which thus become "a site of potential change as much as it is a site of reproduction" (p. 260).

The subject is privileged because it is the opening to politics. Because academic psychology has helped "to constitute the very form of modern individuality" through its conjunction with various social practices, to seek to re-think the subject of psychology "implies a different politics of transformations" (p. 1). Hence the title. Hence also the critique of conventional psychology's scientism, its presumed objectivity, which only acts to deploy the power of its discourse more authoritatively and insidiously. And hence the epistemological position staked out by *Changing the subject* according to which the effect of a discourse as knowledge, though undeniably gaining purchase on the real, must be seen as subordinate to its political effects.

"Is the subject constitutive or constituted?" (p. 95): *Changing the subject* does not finally offer a satisfactory answer to its own question. It follows Althusser in arguing consistently that the subject is constituted as an effect but it also notes that "the post-structuralist displacement of the unitary subject...elides the specificity of the construction of actual subjectivities in the domain of discursive practices" (p. 204). In practice, in introducing its own analysis, in the chapter on gender difference, the book seeks to bridge this gap (which is in fact a disjunction between the subject of the unconscious and the subject of ideology) in two ways.

One suggestion is to adopt the concept of 'investment' (p. 238), which, it is argued, is a mechanism at the level of the psyche enabling the subject to take up a position of social power. This however disregards the psychoanalytic principle that *all* positions are invested, those of both oppressor and victim, sadist and masochist. A second proposal is even more unsettling, for it is suggested that a man's vulnerability is due to his "'desire for the Other'" (p. 247), a desire which is said to illustrate "Lacan's slogan, 'the desire for the Other is the desire for the mother'" (p. 249). There is however no such slogan in Lacan though there is certainly something else, the repeated assertion (or slogan) that "desire is the *désir de L'Autre* (the desire of the Other)" (1977a, p. 312), desire which is of (or from) the Other in that "the first object of desire is to be recognised by the other" (p. 58). The consequence of reducing Lacan's desire *of* into desire *for* is not slight, for it gives precedence to the subject's imaginary unity as locus and origin of desire rather than the intersubjectivity of the Other.

This in turn is quite consistent with the rest of the argument, which can be accused of trying to define subject position by synthesising unconscious drive with forms of social power, a synthesis which overbalances to the side of the conscious self (which misrecognises itself as the source of desire) and also a premature synthesis failing to recognise the position correctly underwritten elsewhere when *Changing the subject* denies that "individual and society are commensurate as theoretical notions" (1984, p. 24). While arguably no theorisation of the social formation and of the unconscious can be made to cohere, in practice the subject is always a subject in ideology and simultaneously a subject of desire. Instead of seeking to elide the two, *Changing the subject* might better have acknowledged that the subject is constituted relative to the available objects of desire which its desire constitutively exceeds.

Psychology in Britain continues to be predominantly cognitive, with research agendas set by what is going on in the United States. In most areas psychologists have proceeded as before on the assumption that there is "a fundamental psyche which is prior to societal determinations" — only within social psychology has *Changing the subject* been effective and only in the somewhat marginal position of a 'radical perspective'. The book, nevertheless, has succeeded in making an intervention there, one achieved by mobilising conceptions of the subject and subject position given a central focus by post-structuralism in Britain, as well as concomitant arguments about epistemology. This and the two previous chapters have pursued the critique of the subject in terms of the empirical or social subject in areas of the human sciences. In the following chapters discussion will turn to discourses analysing the aesthetic and how the conception of text as offering a position to the subject is put to work in these.

113

8

Art History

While the last three or so decades have witnessed extraordinary and fertile change in the study of literature, of history, of anthropology, in the discipline of art history there has reigned a stagnant peace.

Norman Bryson

In the late 1970s various attempts were made to break the closed circle of traditional art history in Britain: by feminism, for example in *Old mistresses* (1981) by Rozsika Parker and Griselda Pollock; by Marxism, for example in Tim Clark's essay on Manet's "Olympia" first published in *Screen* in 1980. This chapter need make no apology for concerning itself with a single text, Norman Bryson's *Vision and painting: the logic of the gaze*, published in 1983. Almost alone this intervention has contrived to dislodge the book which, since its publication in 1960, had constituted the foundation for mainstream art history in Britain, Ernst Gombrich's *Art and illusion: a study in the psychology of pictorial representation.*

Vision and painting is a text of great subtlety and force of analysis. If certain sections of it seem a bit laboured and heavy going to the reader familiar with post-structuralism this is accounted for by the book's step-by-step uphill struggle against the dead weight of the inherited discourse of art history. The book is often sustained in this task by drawing on previous work in British post-structuralism. Although the debt to *Screen* is not admitted except in footnotes (e.g. p. 179, fn. 13) and the adoption of the term 'signifying practice' (pp. 16, 50, 85, 122), the work of Colin MacCabe and Stephen Heath (specifically in the essay on

"Narrative space" of 1976) is acknowledged, not least because the work appears in a series they co-edit, 'Language, Discourse, Society'. As far as possible the account here will avoid detailed engagement with the history of painting and concentrate on the theoretical perspective deployed.

In essence *Vision and painting* makes four moves. First, it attacks the particular form of the naturalist fallacy prevalent in its specific area, in fact naming the view that art is a copy of nature as "the Natural Attitude" (p. 12). Then in its place it develops an account of realism not dependent on a reflexive problematic and the idea of art as copy of nature. In a third excursus it analyses the different kinds of subject position provided historically by painting from Giotto to Vermeer. And in a fourth turn *Vision and painting* shows that the visual text, always interacting with the world outside it, is always taken up and lived into by a subject placed within the process of the social formation so that any position offered is always in fact exceeded.

'The Natural Attitude'

Vision and painting begins from the assumption that painting is "the most material of all the signifying practices" (p. 85), grounded as it is in the physical materiality of the iconic sign which is produced through labour and the body. However, in the West (and the book makes frequent contrasting reference to Chinese art) the traditional doctrine of painting as mimetic, as an 'Essential Copy', extending at least as far back as Pliny's first-century record of how Zeuxis could paint grapes so life-like that birds tried to eat them, has increasingly in the twentieth century run up against the fact of cultural relativism, that is, that different historical periods favour entirely different modes and schemes of visual representation. This challenge is met and the naturalist fallacy has been most recently revitalised in Gombrich's *Art and illusion*, which draws on the scientific epistemology of Karl Popper. Because induction depends upon observation and since in the passage of time observation can never be complete, as the test of scientific truth Popper would displace *verification* with *falsification*:

While no number of observations of white swans enables the derivation of the universal statement that "all swans are white", one single observation of a black swan is sufficient to produce the derived and universally valid statement that "not all swans are white" (Bryson 1983, p. 19).

Gombrich adapts this distinction to what Bryson calls "the hypothesis-theory of perception" (p. 29). Undeniably the modes of painting change across historical time but Gombrich is able to relegate this feature into what he calls a "schema" by equating it with the Popperian hypothesis. He then seeks to account for advance in the history of visual representation by claiming innovation derives from an act of cognition ('what we see') which reveals the inadequacy of a prevailing schema ('what we know') just as in Popper the single, falsifying instance refutes any hypothesis. Here, as Bryson indicates, access to a world of the real *beyond* any schema is "essential if the false start is to be distinguished from advance" (p. 35).

And so, as Bryson explains, in Gombrich's account

> certain sign-systems are claimed as naturally closer to the anterior reality they are said to reproduce, while others are formed at a distance from nature, as purely artificial conventions. The problem is this: to prove the validity of the sliding scale, it is necessary to appeal beyond the sign to a world disclosed to consciousness directly and without mediation, against which the different systems are then compared; and this raises the whole set of objections already levelled against the natural attitude. (p. 53)

Just as there cannot be a signified without a signifier, so there can be no transcendent and unmediated access to the real outside historically variable systems of representation within which that real is constructed. Gombrich's revisionism accepts the historical relativity of schemes of visual representation only in an attempt to recuperate this fact by making it a condition for an act of cognition supposed as unmediated contact between consciousness and the world outside any 'schema' at all. In the possibility of that act the natural attitude and idea of art as the essential copy is once again perpetuated.

The effect of the real and the position of the subject

Suppose however that the naturalist fallacy is rejected, how can realist visual representation in the Quattrocento tradition be understood solely as "the effect of the real" (p. 65)? With reference to the greater realism of Giotto's "The Betrayal" compared to Duccio's, Bryson asks: "considering *vraisemblance* only as a *rhetoric* of persuasion, how may we account for the Giotto's persistent persuasiveness?" (p. 55). Asserting that realism depends on attempted effacement of the signifier in favour of the signified, *Vision and painting* answers first in relation to the signified meanings Giotto's text foregrounds.

"Judas — kisses — Christ": the inherited schema of 'the betrayal' is simple, and both the Duccio and the Giotto recognisably reproduce the same. But the Giotto is "marked by a dramatic excess of information over and beyond that quantity required for us to recognise the scene" (p. 56). If the schema is a form of denotation, this excess of detailed information serves as connotation. Since the image of the kiss between Judas and Jesus can be easily grasped without illustration and since at this point the analysis is perhaps most brilliantly specific, it is worth citing at length Bryson's account of how in the crucial detail in Giotto an excess of information, of connotation, is produced through various oppositions:

The *linear* versus the *curvilinear* (the straight lines of Christ's nose and forehead, as against the convexity of Judas's nose and the concavity of Judas's forehead; the emphasis on the line between the lips in the case of Christ, and on the everted outer curves of the mouth in the case of Judas; the straightness and *rectitude* of Christ's eyebrow, as against the sinuous and deviant eyebrow of Judas; the taut severity of the hair of Christ, the lax, highlighted curls of Judas). We find *vertical* against *non-vertical* alignment (the bridge of the nose, the forehead, and the first tangent of the halo establishes a clear upward or *ascensional* axis for Christ; with Judas, the first tangent of the protuberant bone above the eye tends towards a horizontal, *mundane* axis, matched by the asymptotic tendency of the concave nose, the line below the chin, and the lines in the cloak below the neck and along the arm). We find *expansion* versus *contraction* (with Christ, the distance between eyebrow and hairline is extended and unbroken...with Judas, the distance between eyebrow and eyelid is correspondingly reduced and interrupted...). (pp. 62–3)

And so the argument concludes that "the 'effect of the real' consists in a specialised relationship between denotation and connotation, where *connotation so confirms and substantiates denotation that the latter appears to rise to a level of truth*" (p. 62, italics original).

In the tradition of Chinese graphic art, traces of the body and the motor act whose labour produces the visual sign is always on display inviting pursuit by the ever-mobile Glance of the viewer:

Chinese painting has always selected forms that permit a maximum of integrity and visibility to the constitutive strokes of the brush: foliage, bamboo, the ridges of boulder and mountain formations, the patterns of fur, feathers, reeds, branches, in the 'boned' styles of the image; and forms whose lack of outline (mist, aerial distance, the themes of still and moving water, of the pool and the waterfall) allows the brush to express to the full the liquidity and immediate flow of the ink, in the 'boneless' styles. (p. 89)

In stark contrast, the Western tradition is defined by its attempt to disavow the material process through which graphic representation becomes a site of production, an attempt characterised by a necessarily double strategy in which: (1) the two-dimensional surface of the image is to be integrated and harmonised as far as possible with the three-dimensional world represented within it; (2) the process of looking (of the painter, of the viewer) is to be reduced to a single point, the instant of the Gaze, so that "spatially and temporally, the act of viewing is constructed as the removal of the dimensions of space and time, as the disappearance of the body: the construction of an *acies mentis*, the punctual viewing subject" (p. 96). For the signified (as already discussed in the case of Giotto) this means a layering of connotations to foreground the presence of represented reality. But for the signifier there are other strategies which produce a position for the viewer by denying that production. These work in the field of vision.

In *The four fundamental concepts of psycho-analysis* Lacan recalls the story of a small boy on a fishing trip who pointed to a floating sardine tin and told him, "*You see that can? Do you see it? Well, it doesn't see you*" (1977b, p. 95, italics original). The tin doesn't see you but *someone* there might, since whatever you can see is a point from which you could be seen. The optic field allows me as a subject to see an object within it but only on condition that I could equally be seen from that point, become an object for another subject: "I see only from one point, but in my existence I am looked at from all sides" (p. 72).

To maintain itself in its relation to sight the ego misrecognises itself, presuming only that it sees the Other when in fact it always appears at a point within the Other, for the Other. Historically the effect becomes even more extreme after the development of the system of monocular perspective and the emergence in the seventeenth century of the Cartesian subject. For this subject aims to be "itself a sort of geometral point, a point of perspective" (p. 86). Such perspective, as Lacan argues at length (pp. 65–119), functions through the intersection in the surface of the picture of two imagined cones, one converging on the vanishing point, the other on the implied viewpoint. In Byzantine images of God, God's eye as the gaze of the Other fixes his look on me; in the perspective tradition that place is taken by the vanishing point of the perspective, a void, which thus appears to me not as somewhere I can be seen from but rather as an *object* for which I am a *subject*.

But further, in a yet more subtle turn, since I am *both* situated by the viewpoint of the perspective (one cone converges on my eye) *and* appear to master the vanishing point (on which the other cone converges) it seems to me as viewer that I both see myself and "*I see myself seeing myself*" (p. 80, italics original), a full subject indeed. This is "the gaze of the painter, which claims to impose itself as being the only gaze" (p. 113), the Other of which I am an effect misrecognised and internalised as though it were an effect of me, mastered by my look. *Vision and painting* mobilises the Lacanian analysis directly in its account of the developing history of the Western tradition (see Bryson 1983, p. 181, fn. 14).

In the Byzantine tradition the image is presented in a minimal schema and "the viewing subject is addressed liturgically, as a member of the faith, and communally" (p. 96). *Vision and painting* plots the rise of the Quattrocento tradition in two stages. In the first epoch of perspective, discussed explicitly in Alberti's *De pictura* of 1435 and exemplified by Bryson in Raphael's "Marriage of the Virgin",

> the eye of the viewer is to take up a position in relation to the
> scene that is identical to the position originally occupied by

the painter, as though both painter and viewer looked through the same viewfinder on to a world unified spatially around the centric ray, the line running from viewpoint to vanishing point. (p. 104)

The viewer is thus positioned as a physical presence but with a particular effect, pulling off its greatest feat at the juncture of greatest risk. The centric ray, the theoretical axis extending between vanishing point and viewpoint raises the possibility of a radical alterity, precisely that I could be seen as an object from that vanishing point I observe.

But the Albertian regime only does this, so Bryson argues, in order to contain signifier in relation to signified, hold representation on to represented. Thus: (1) my body is situated by the image since I am addressed in a specific position (at the viewpoint); (2) as viewer I am interpellated by the system of perspective representation as mastering the field of vision, including the proffered viewpoint *and* the vanishing point. There is thus "an impersonal arrangement, a *logic* of representation which changes the viewer himself or herself into a representation, an object or spectacle before their own vision" (p. 106). In the flattering misrecognition so provided by such visual texts it is as though I see myself seeing myself.

In a second, culminatory epoch, the production of a position for the viewing subject is not simply contained — the attempt is rather to efface it completely. This is illustrated in relation to Vermeer. A vanishing point is dispensed with, and in, for example, "The Artist in his Studio", the scene is not arranged around an act of inspection (the artist, for instance, has his back to the viewer). Perception is recorded with unprecedented accuracy but is not presented to a viewer addressed directly in a bodily situation. Rather "the viewing subject is now proposed and assumed as a notional point, a non-empirical Gaze" (p. 112).

(Analogies are always dangerous, especially analogies between different modes of representation, each of which must persist in its own specific effectivity, its own peculiar time. Nevertheless, there is a tempting analogy between the system of perspective so analysed and the metrical system of iambic pentameter of English poetry since the Renaissance, deriving as it does from the effect of counterpoint between the metrical pattern and the intonation of the individual utterance. The speaking subject seems to discover a position as master of the signifier (whose materiality insists in the repetitions of the metric) when actually he or she is positioned as an effect of the metrical signifier. Again, in an even more risky analogy, Bryson's first epoch can be read as corresponding to the Augustan period in poetry whose strategy is to contain the signifier and the second to the rhetoric of Romanticism which aims to efface altogether the process of enunciation.)

Traversing and underwriting both stylistic epochs there is the Western regime of visual representation. The Glance, active in the process of tracking the materiality of the visual signifier, is repressed by the would-be temporal and spatial fix of the mastering Gaze and so "constructed as the hidden term on whose disavowal the whole system depends" (p. 121). The difference and differentiation of the Glance is to be denied by the repetition and identity of the Gaze. And so "against the Gaze, the Glance proposes desire, proposes the body, in the *durée* of its practical activity...exactly the terms which the tradition seeks to suppress" (p. 122). Yet after opening this horizon, deep within the recesses of the subject, *Vision and painting* makes its way back to the open plains of the social formation. Having analysed both comprehensively and in scrupulous detail the specific formal possibilities of the visual signifier, it returns to affirm the inevitable polysemy of any act of reading.

The viewing subject and the act of viewing

Painting, as the most material of the signifying practices, imposes its set of signifiers in closest proximity to the viewing subject — who takes up what they impose only with a difference. Not for the first time *Vision and painting* draws on Bakhtin when asserting that "the sign exists only in its recognition, 'dialogically', as interaction between the signifiers presented by the surface of the image or of the text, and the discourses already in circulation" (p. 151).

Of this the book delivers a finely judged instance, when it discusses the connotations and excess of information which give the effect of the real from Giotto onwards. After its carefully detailed discussion of the kiss between Judas and Christ it points out a significant distinction. Whereas the denotation of a schema is formally coded and may be looked up in an iconological dictionary, "no equivalent lexicon exists" for "the codes of the face and body in movement (pathognomics), the codes of the face at rest (physiognomics), and the codes of fashion or dress", the very foundation of codes of connotation (p. 68). If denotation belongs to an internal order of the image, these codes operate within the general social formation and so are available to realise and transform the signifiers of the image.

Realise *and* transform: at this point the analysis is prised away from a purely 'internal' account of meanings generated within the four sides of the frame and towards discourses flowing across both text and reader. Because the signifier takes on meaning only when immersed in the process of the social formation, every meaning offered is altered in its realisation:

> If the image is inherently polysemic, this is not *by excess* of a meaning already possessed by the image, as hagiography would have it, but *by default*, as a consequence of the image's dependence on interaction with discourse for its production of meaning, for its *recognition*. (p. 85)

From this it follows that whatever position a painting may furnish for the viewing subject, that position is always exceeded in any act of viewing. So although *Vision and painting* has the closest possible engagement with a traditional formalism — aims in fact to occupy exactly that territory, generally the least hospitable to radical intervention, by means of its detailed analysis of the regime of the Gaze and the Glance in terms of subject position — the book does not find its centre in such formalist, textual analysis. That account is offset by a commitment to historical materialism and insistence on signification as active process.

A conclusion may then be brief. *Vision and painting* takes its place firmly within the tradition of British post-structuralism, drawing as it does on the work of *Screen*, to describe textual effectivity in terms of subject position. In fact, the book is exemplary in this respect, as this account has sought to document. But it is exemplary of British post-structuralism in another way, for the work on subjectivity and positioning is taken up within a firmly Marxist perspective. In this Bryson's text is intertextual, an intervention in a collective endeavour.

And considered like this the book yields only one surprise, which is the question why it did not pick up decisively Laura Mulvey's work on scopophilia and the *masculinisation* of the Gaze. Mulvey's cinematic examples of 'woman as image' calls out for development in relation to representation of the female nude from Giorgione's "Venus" of 1510 to Manet's "Olympia", a trajectory which would clearly touch on the feminisation of landscape in that tradition. In a work so rigorously and convincingly comprehensive as *Vision and painting* the omission points to a need for further work, though one that trenches on the problematic issue of the 'female look' and how it is inscribed — if it is at all — in the masculine scopophilic regime of Western art.

9
Musicology

Consonance and dissonance are not essentially different —
the entire realm of possible sounds is contained within the notes
that nature provides.

Anton Webern

The Western harmonic idiom is "a more or less common piece of theoretical knowledge nowadays" (Chanan 1981, p. 233). It is surprising therefore that more work in a post-structuralist perspective has not been directed at the area of musicology (for a thoroughly Marxist account, see Shepherd 1977). *If* the analogy with language holds for it, music seems so invitingly to be a mode of the signifier without a signified. And it remains a deeply entrenched fortress of naturalism and essentialism in which conventional musicology confidently derives the Renaissance tradition of Western tonal harmony from nature, from the physics of acoustic sound such that a vibrating string produces fainter overtones along a half and a third of its length (and so on) which are respectively an octave and a fifth above the note of the whole string (and so on in hierarchic ordering): "This phenomenon provides us with the first evidence of harmony in nature, and in fact it has instinctively served as the basis of our harmonic system" (Karolyi 1965, p. 61). Relations between two or more notes can arise from the selection and combination of sounds both as this occurs 'horizontally' (paradigmatically) in scales and harmonies and 'vertically' (syntagmatically) in melodic and thematic construction and in chord progressions. According to the dominant conventional theory consonance defines an interval or chord which gives a satisfying effect because the notes producing it share one or

124

more overtones, dissonance an effect of tension because they do not.

However, the problems of translating the physics of acoustics into musical effects to be contrasted as consonance and dissonance are well indicated by Charles Rosen when he points out that thirds and sixths were considered unequivocally dissonant until the fourteeenth century when they came to be accepted as consonant while fourths were classified as consonances until the Renaissance when they were re-classified as dissonances:

> It is not, therefore, the human ear or nervous system that decides what is a dissonance, unless we are to assume a physiological change between the thirteenth and fifteen century. A dissonance is defined by its role in the musical 'language', as it makes possible the movement from tension to resolution. (Rosen 1976, p. 33)

The way would seem opened here to an analysis of the Western post-Renaissance system of tonality as a form of 'musical space' providing an historically determined position for the subject.

The conditions of music

Alan Durant's *The conditions of music* (1984) often promises to be just such an analysis, a historical account of music comparable to Heath's account of the history of narrative space and Bryson's of the gaze. Sensitive, scrupulous, reticent, allusive as well as elusive, *The conditions of music* sketches such an account in a way which corresponds more to historical materialism than post-structuralism, and this reading will run somewhat against the grain of that text, both in the degree to which the argument is made explicit and in its co-option to a post-structuralist project.

In a first chapter on "Music and its language" Durant cites Deryk Cooke's widely influential work, *The language of music* (1959), to deny that music can adequately submit to a semiological analysis in terms of codes, 'vocabulary' and 'syntax', because "assigning meaning depends on positions of perceiving and interpreting" (1984, p. 12). In support of this view Durant evidences the historical variability of the key terms in musicology, 'instrumental', 'technique', 'concert' and 'orchestra'. A structuralist account of music on the analogy of language rests on a notion of "founding psychological and acoustic resources" (p. 13) and so ignores the construction of the musical text as an effect in address to positions made available within institutions of performance and social relationships historically determined. *The conditions of music* then concerns itself with what its title anticipates, musical effect determined by the material conditions of performance (church, concert-hall, nightspot, disc in the living room) in relation to musical technology, spectacle and audience.

Yet this attempt to foreground act over structure, reading over text, encounters a welcome return of what it intends to bypass, especially when a chapter on "Tuning and dissonance" re-examines judgements of whether music sounds 'in tune' or 'out of tune' as justifying kinds of audience response. Denying the 'naturalistic fallacy' in musicology from Helmholtz onwards (that intervals as self-sufficient acoustic realities correlate to effects of consonance or dissonance) Durant emphasises that "dissonances have varying functions in music" (p. 62) and in the Western post-Renaissance harmonic tradition, according to the conventional assumption of musicology, have a certain meaning: "Tonal music is created in exactly an alternation between what is agreeable, tolerable and stable (the resolutions), and the tensions, suspensions and displacements of dissonance" (p. 72). The exchange between dissonance and its subsequent resolution in consonance seeks to produce "dramas of feeling and perception which are conducted through dissonant suspensions, leading finally into a coherence of resolution and identity" (p. 72).

Modulation may be defined as the exchange of one key centre for another, a procedure which enlarges the possibilities of suspension and resolution:

> In the traditions of Greek music and to a lesser extent in medieval religious music, modes and scales had specific characteristics and associations. But the new tonal music required instead as far as possible an equivalence between scales, to accentuate a compatibility which alone, particularly on keyboard instruments, might achieve repeated modulation, and make a continuity of thematic material in different keys a compositional possibility. (p. 74)

Such rationalising standardisation in the musical system affected both composition and musical technology. Symbolic qualities previously attached to individual scales and the physical properties of instruments become transferred to textures and orchestration instead: "Increasingly it is individual resources of compositional technique, rather than socially ordained character, which are taken to generate music's emotional, ethical or religious effect" (pp. 74–5).

In contrast to medieval music, the post-Renaissance tonal tradition works to inscribe a different position for its reader:

> Incorporation of expressive dissonance, and delineation of a developmental experience of listening, define in terms of musical form an accentuated individualism of tonal music...In tonal music, dissonances had a function both formally, projecting the music harmonically forward towards cadence, and subjectively, establishing a dialectic of desires and expectations which are subsequently gratified in pleasures of resolution. (p. 75)

But in the new, atonal concert music of the twentieth century from Schoenberg onwards the meaning of dissonance is entirely revalued. After reviewing contemporary accounts of dissonance as negation of humanistic rationality and control (Hindemith), as emancipation (Webern) and as reflection of alienation under capitalism (Adorno, Hanns Eisler), *The conditions of music* ends its discussion of tonality by affirming that the signifying effect of dissonance depends "on surrounding conditions both of musical forms, and of the institutions through which these forms are represented" (p. 84), thus restoring its argument to its previous ground, the interpretative act and conditions of performance.

Consonance, dissonance and the subject

Each history of representation has its own time, its own specificity within an uneven development. Yet what *The conditions of music* outlines in epitome could easily be extrapolated into an account comparable with Heath's analysis of narrative space and Bryson's of the post-Renaissance tradition of graphic art. For it defines the tonal system in terms of its specificity, its history, and, by implication, as a regime of representation providing a particular position for the subject.

Just as *Vision and painting* begins by breaking with the naturalist fallacy in art history, so *The conditions of music* emerges from a critique of the conventional assumption that tonal harmony is founded in the physics of acoustic sound and psychology. Tonality is constructed as a relation between dissonance and consonance, modulation and resolution, with ensuing consequences for specific forms of musical composition, technology and performance. Through equivalence between scales it constitutes a would-be universal, rational and reified system, one directly analogous to the universal and seemingly unproduced system of linear perspective. In Durant's account tonality is an historical system demarcated by its innovation at the Renaissance against the medieval modes with their socially distinct associations and at the other end by its modernist dissolution in the twentieth century.

As a regime of representation tonality aims to position the subject by incorporating dissonance, which is "expressive", within the rational systematicity of consonance. In the linear process of the musical text, through the selection and combination of sounds, both effects become possible, establishing "a dialectic of desires and expectations which are subsequently gratified in pleasures of resolution". Dissonance/consonance, expectation/resolution, mobility/clarity, difference/repetition, desire/pleasure: the overriding system of tonality operates to fix the process of the subject and secure for it a position which is unified and unifying.

Since its attention is elsewhere, however, *The conditions of music* refuses to flesh out its analysis in close historical detail. In terms of the early Renaissance period it would surely be possible to contrast the socially ordained and connotative medieval modes and the new tonality along the lines proposed by Bryson's distinction between the schema or stereotype image inherited from the feudal tradition and the "singularity" introduced to give the effect of pictorial realism. Again, there is nothing equivalent in Durant's account to Bryson's analysis of the historical differences between high Renaissance painting producing the viewer as body, as an empirical point of view (Raphael's "Marriage of the Virgin"), and the later development of a position for the viewing subject as non-empirical Gaze (Vermeer's "The Artist in his Studio"). Despite its deliberate abbreviation, however, *The conditions of music* demonstrates that, as do represented spaces, musical systems "live and die like societies". The tonal system of harmony has been surpassed, at least in high cultural forms; meanwhile popular music in the West continues in the main to recycle the old harmonies in a form influenced by Afro-American sources but otherwise only marginally different from that of the Church of England's *Hymns Ancient and Modern*.

But in contemporary Western culture music may carry a quite different kind of meaning, as is proposed by Carol Flinn in a recent account. Reviewing a number of different kinds of texts — from musicology, composer's manifestoes, the journalism of film music composers — Flinn is able to demonstrate that music has accrued a signifying connotation identifying its position and meaning as "static, meaningless, enigmatic and feminine" (1986, p. 57). These suggest that music is predominantly read as an articulation of "the maternal body and voice" (p. 58). Her conclusion cuts across but does not contradict Durant's analysis: "It is one thing to suggest that music offers woman a discursive place in which her desire is provisionally articulated; it is entirely another to argue that music is essentially, irrevocably 'feminine'" (p. 72). This simultaneously avoids the dangers of essentialism and opens the possibility that music may represent an expression otherwise denied.

10

Philosophy

Fog in Channel: Continent Isolated

Times headline, 1911

Post-structuralism in philosophy must mean above all the writings of Jacques Derrida. There is almost nothing to say about British philosophy and Derrida's deconstruction because no mainstream major philosopher in England has engaged with what is generally regarded as an alien tradition, 'metaphysics'. Those interventions there have been are effectively marginal. David Wood, who has written a number of essays on Derrida, edited a collection of essays about his work, *Derrida and différance* (1985); and John Llewelyn's *Derrida on the threshold of sense* (1986) is rightly regarded as one of the most acute and sympathetic expositions of Derrida's work. The workshops on philosophy, sponsored by the University of Warwick, have given serious attention to Derrida, and a conference specifically on his work was held at the University of Essex in 1986. Richard Kearney, whose interest is phenomenology, has recorded an instructive interview with Derrida (1984), and Alan Montefiore has edited a collection, *Philosophy in France today* (1983), which includes an essay by Derrida.

More typical of the British reaction — or lack of it — is Quentin Skinner's edition of essays well named as *The return of grand theory in the human sciences* which includes a short expository chapter on Derrida. A facetious paragraph in the editor's introduction regards Derrida merely as a figure in literary criticism where he is "the leading iconoclast" (1985, p. 8). Even though Alan Montefiore invited Derrida to speak in Oxford (where he purchased the now famous postcard of Plato and Socrates from MS Ashmole

304, fol. 31 verso which is still selling well in the kiosk at the Bodleian), this centre of British analytic philosophy has, like Socrates in the design, stared straight ahead, ignoring the Plato behind his back.

As much serious work on Derrida has been done in Britain by literary critics as philosophers. Eagleton, for example, has fully taken on board the Derridean challenge, defending deconstruction against the *New Left Review* (1986a, pp. 89–98). And Ann Wordsworth, a teacher of literature who has so far published only sparingly, exercises a deep knowledge and understanding of Derrida's texts.

Besides the general stagnation that increasingly affects the dominant surfaces of British culture, two things in particular may account for the failure of British philosophy to face up to the challenges of the 1980s. One is that analytic philosophy has traditionally maintained a much higher official status in Britain because it has enjoyed a privileged association with logic and with 'hard' science. This has allowed it to follow a trajectory beyond the currents of contemporary Marxism, which was precisely where post-structuralism was taken up in other disciplines and areas of study.

A second reason, related to this first, results from the form taken by what opposition there has been to conventional philosophy. A Marxist intervention in philosophy has so far failed to establish itself in Britain, as it should have done, for example via the journal *Radical Philosophy*. Founded in 1972 with the task of making just such an intervention, *RP* has not fulfilled its mission and shows little signs of doing so. It should have entered thoroughly into a critique of the prevailing tradition, fighting the battle of ideas on that ground. Instead, after a few skirmishes, it has tended to leave the orthodox tradition largely in place and gone for the making of an alternative tradition, putting its energies into versions of Marxist philosophy, writings about and in the Marxist tradition, along with an interest in various figures and issues from outside the mainstream. Except for David Wood's essay of 1979, serious debate in it about Derrida has been slight.

In contrast, philosophy in America, especially in the work of Richard Rorty, has opened itself to confrontation with Derrida and deconstruction. In 1985 *Post-analytic philosophy*, edited by John Rajchman and Cornel West, was published in the United States and included essays by Rorty, Hilary Putnam and Donald Davidson. Quite apart from the assumption of the title, the force of its claimed intervention is summarised in John Rajchman's introduction as follows:

> The very idea of logical analysis has been challenged. There may be no such thing as the method or logic of science, nothing 'philosophical' to study. There may be no such thing as analytic sentences, and nothing for analytic philosophers to analyse. Rorty puts it bluntly: "The notion of 'logical analysis' turned upon itself and committed slow suicide."

And the two comments printed on the cover of the book are well worth repeating, the first by Jean-François Lyotard:

> The essays it brings together attest to the vitality of American thought...in its encounter with foreign traditions and endeavours in thought, in particular, European ones. I see in this one of a number of signs of a reopening of the borders which have segmented Western intelligence for two centuries.

The second is from Derrida:

> Through the differences and internal divisions which also make for its richness, I am convinced that something essential is brought together and is fully revealed in this collection: what, in point of fact, is new within North American thought today. This event is important in itself in the United States; but I think it is also suited to transform the space of philosophical exchange with Continental Europe, and, in a singular way, with French thought.

Instead of seeking encounter with the Derridean oppositions, which can be named over as "speech/writing, life/death, father/son, master/servant, first/second, legitimate son/orphan-bastard, soul/body, inside/outside, good/evil, seriousness/play" (Derrida 1981a, p. 85), British philosophy has pursued its obsession with the real and continued to privilege the familiar binary, "truth/falsehood", as the only one worth serious attention. At present this is the only note on which one may close this sad chapter.

11
Literary Theory

Critics, as 'barking dogs', are of two sorts: those who merely relieve themselves against the flower of beauty, and those, less continent, who afterwards scratch it up.

William Empson, *Seven types of ambiguity*

For a few weeks in 1980, post-structuralism was front-page news in Britain. When Colin MacCabe, a young assistant lecturer in the Faculty of English at Cambridge, was not confirmed as a full lecturer, the so-called serious newspapers picked up his dismissal and tried to explain what caused it. Apparently he lost his job because he taught "structuralism", an error denounced by his professor, Christopher Ricks, when he claimed it was the job of a literature teacher to "uphold the canon" (MacCabe's side of the story is told in the Foreword to his *Theoretical essays* (1985), and grim reading it makes too about what, in the generation after 1945, was the best English Faculty in the world).

Re-reading English, a book of essays edited by Peter Widdowson, was published in 1982 with an Introduction subtitled "The crisis in English studies". For the crisis the solutions proposed were mainly Marxist and post-structuralist. In the *London Review of Books* (which is a Social Democratic/Liberal journal) the book was given a hysterical denunciation (17 June 1982) naming it as "Stalinist" and, in what was regarded as an even worse term of abuse, "unEnglish". The *Times Literary Supplement* (a Tory publication now owned by the right-wing media millionaire, Rupert Murdoch) commissioned a review of *Re-reading English*, which was generally favourable towards the book. However, this review was not published, and when a second appeared instead (10 December 1982) it consisted of a long, pompous attack ("billowings of sheer untalented modishness") which actually criticised the publisher for letting the book come out (it has since sold 6,000 copies (see Davies 1987)). This initial moral panic at the entry of post-structuralist ideas into the sacred garden of Englit (not only *ideas* but *French* ideas at that) has since given way to more rational debate, so much so that in November 1985 an issue of *PN Review* (no. 48) was given over to discussion of post-structuralism as what it called — with wild exaggeration — "the new orthodoxy".

Englit at the centre, *Screen* at the margins

Because of the particular inheritance of the national culture, Englit has come to hold a place very close to the ideological heartlands of Britain, a place of privilege and intimacy markedly different from that occupied by study of the national literatures in North America. Told several times (see Doyle 1982, Goulden and Hartley 1982, Baldick 1983) the story of the rise of Englit comes down to one thing: a study of the national literature was promoted by educationalists especially in the years after the First World War because it promised to bring conflicting class interests together by transcending them in a unified national domain.

The immense power of the position occupied by Englit at the centre means that it was very well worth attacking but also that the polemic flies off in all directions (Leavis against the world, for instance, back in the 1950s). Consequently, a number of different strands of post-structuralist theory run through recent work and debate in literary studies but are contrasted here as two, one concerned with literature as discourse providing a position for the subject, the other being what will be called 'left deconstruction'. Both are Marxisms but in the first the prevailing influence is Althusser while in the second it is Foucault.

In following through the Althusserian problematic post-structuralist work on literature relies heavily on the precedent of *Screen*, as its practitioners acknowledge. Colin MacCabe cites *Screen* in the Preface to *James Joyce and the revolution of the word* (1978) and gives ten pages to it in his *Theoretical essays*, affirming that "Throughout the 1970s in Britain, the most important consistent attempts to discuss and analyse the relations between culture and signification took place in the pages of the film magazine, *Screen*" (1985, p. 4). Again, Catherine Belsey in *Critical practice* (1980): "In what follows I have drawn very freely on recent work on film in *Screen* magazine, probably one of the most important sources of critical theory in Britain at the moment" (p. 69). Or again, with a reference to the regional reading groups established by *Screen*'s parent organisation, SEFT (Society for Education in Film and Television): "As the main contribution to this book I should like to acknowledge the help I have had from working with the Manchester Reading Group of the Society for Education in Film and Television" (Easthope 1983a, p. ix). Theoretical concepts, domesticated in relation to cinema (and described in Chapter 3), are worked through in specific application to literature and will be exemplified here by writing on the three main genres, novel, drama and poetry, as well as feminist literary criticism.

Conventional literary study in Britain takes place within "a perfect and virtually unbreakable circle" (Williams 1977, p. 45). *Screen* made the progress it did because, in taking cinema as its object, it was able at a stroke to step outside the ideological enclosure. But having done so, and moved forward, it was inevitable that the terms of analysis would be brought to bear on literature. In the first appearance of British post-structuralism in literary analysis, MacCabe's book on Joyce, the transposition leads to loss as well as gain. The clear benefit lies in the clarity and confidence of the theoretical exposition but its application to literature brings with it a concomitant limitation. Partly there is the struggle to establish the terms on the grounds of the encircling discourse of literary criticism but there is also the problem that the object of study is a single author generally relegated to the periphery of the canon in virtue of being Irish and therefore a 'sport'.

The novel: MacCabe's *Joyce*

Joyce's writing produces a change in the relations between reader and text, a change which has profound revolutionary implications...It is only given the essential homogeneity of experience and a position from which the elements within it can be judged that it is possible to talk of a representational theory of language...Joyce's texts, however, refuse the subject any dominant position from which language could be tallied with experience. *Ulysses* and *Finnegans Wake* are concerned not with representing experience through language but with experiencing language through a destruction of representation. (MacCabe 1978, pp. 1, 4)

Thus *James Joyce and the revolution of the word* places at the theoretical centre of its analysis a conception of the dialectic between text and the reader's position as its subject. In detailing this theoretical programme it contrasts the classic realist text with Joyce's modernism, developing its account with reference to object language and metalanguage, the distinction between enunciation and enounced, and to narrative. These are illustrated from Joyce's writing so that the book in this respect covers the same terrain as conventional Joyce criticism, from the short stories to the *Wake*.

MacCabe's discussion of realism in the cinema had already anticipated the advance into literary studies by exemplifying classic realism from George Eliot. In *James Joyce* Eliot is again the instance of classic realism defined as a rhetorical strategy by which the manifest local particularities of an object language are meant to submit to a full general understanding revealed in the metalanguage, that metalanguage thus being able to claim "direct access to a final reality" (p. 17) and provide the reader with a position of dominant specularity. The modernist texts of Joyce deny any such stability to their subject.

The production of a specular position for the reader can also be analysed in terms of the difference between subject of enunciation and subject of the enounced. Although this conceptualisation was introduced in *Screen* (by Stephen Heath 1975, pp. 49–50) as a linguistic distinction (or rather a linguistic distinction mobilised within psychoanalysis by Lacan) it acquires much greater purchase when applied to written texts and novels, as it is by MacCabe in contrasting the realism of Balzac's *Illusions perdues* with its subversion in Joyce's *Stephen hero*.

In 1957 Roman Jakobson introduced the distinction between "the speech act" (*énonciation*) and "the narrated event" (*énoncé*), together with subjects of the speech act and, in contrast, the narrated event (1971, pp. 133–4). Lacan took up the distinction and commented on the absurdity of the opinion of philosophy that a statement such as "I am lying" constituted a paradox: "*I am lying*, despite its paradox, is perfectly valid...the *I* of the enunciation is not the same as the *I* of the statement (*énoncé*)" (1977b, p. 139; cf. MacCabe 1978, fn. pp. 34–5). Lacan distinguishes between the real, the imaginary and the symbolic. Corresponding to these terms there is the speaking subject, the subject of the enounced, the subject of enunciation. An individual can only become a speaking subject by entering discourse but can only enter discourse as a split *(Spaltung)* between two positions (strictly, between a position of fixity and a process of which that fixity is an effect) as these are constructed in relation to the signifier and to the signified, to enunciation and enounced, to narration and narrated.

Thus, as speaking subject I am dependent on the temporal process of enunciation, the effectivity of the chain of the signifier (which operates both syntactically and paradigmatically), the differentiation of phonemes, the rules of syntax, and only from this basis can I talk about myself. So even when I do talk about myself ("I am 26 and have long, fair hair", etc., etc.), I can only do so by figuring as a character *represented* in and by the coherence of my own discourse. This is a misrecognised identity because I can only identify myself there by speaking from *somewhere else* in the process of discourse, as subject of enunciation.

A novel, in so far as it constructs a coherent represented — character, narrative and 'what happens' — provides a position for the speaking subject (now the reader) as subject of the enounced; in so far as it acts in a process of construction — through language, stylistic effects to create a sense of character, etc., a narration — it produces the reader as subject of enunciation. Crucially, in the classic realist novel, when the enounced is foregrounded over enunciation the reader is offered a position as subject of the enounced while that as subject of enunciation is denied. A modernist text, aiming to display the process of its own enunciation, disrupts the fixity of its reader as subject of the enounced.

Drawing on the distinction between enunciation and enounced MacCabe is able to show how Joyce's texts, chronologically in increasing degrees, undermine the reader's identification with the hero as position privileged within the represented. But the distinction yields further mileage. The essentially static relation between enunciation and enounced can be extended into an account of the process of novelistic narrative. This *James Joyce* does in outline by developing antecedents in the work of *Screen*, in particular that of Heath on narrative space (1976) (though see also MacCabe 1976).

Desire is a process without closure. Once opened up by the necessary non-satisfaction of lack, the condition of speech is that "something is always missing" (MacCabe 1978, p. 6) and so pleasure is offered to us by the misrecognition that desire can be satisfied. Hence precisely the pleasures of the coherent narrative in a realist text, for "classic realism disrupts the position of pleasure only to reassure us of its return, it is this gap which produces the heightened tension we experience as narrative" (p. 46). A stitching together of the concatenated narrative of realism provides the pleasure of closure but constantly undoes that stitching for fresh closure, a new position of fixity and plenitude. In this respect realism seeks a "neurotic negation of desire" (pp. 35, 104), while Joyce's modernism enacts an affirmation of desire. What counts for the political question of art is not what a text says but what it does; not whether it has a correct political line but whether it confirms its reader's identity/identities or transforms these into "a network of relations which thus become available for knowledge and action" (p. 156).

What knowledge and (political) action is not specified. What is specified is the effect of modernism in terms of gender. Thus, Lacan proposes that the difference insisting in language through the system of differentiation materialised in the signifier becomes analogous for the subject with difference as it is constituted by sexual difference. *James Joyce* mobilises the imbrication of linguistic and sexual difference theorised by Lacan to argue that "the condition of existence of narrative is a simultaneous recognition and denial of the problem of difference; a problem which materialises as one of women and language" (p. 53). "Women and language": at this juncture MacCabe's text is prepared to argue that Joyce's modernism, specifically that of *Finnegans Wake*, leads to a revolutionary politics because in denying the reader's pleasure it opens the reader's desire.

Joyce and écriture féminine

It becomes clear that *James Joyce and the revolution of the word* is committed far more to a politics of gender than a politics of narrowly social revolution. At the level of theory this outcome has been prepared from the beginning. Thus it is argued in the first chapter that psychoanalysis is especially appropriate for the understanding of literature since "the theory of psychoanalysis has been as dependent on literature as on the analytic situation" (p. 11), as with Freud and Sophocles' *Oedipus*. On this basis MacCabe argues that Joyce's denial of realism in *Finnegans Wake* constitutes an expression of feminine writing (there being no necessary correspondence between the gender of an author and the gendering of a text). It is important to follow this through because the question of the gendering of a text will return in the work of Toril Moi.

Realism is masculinist, MacCabe contends, because it is a form of fetishism, that being an especially male prerogative (pp. 109–10), a masculine desire to disavow the lack of the Mother's phallus by erecting an apparently self-sufficient (textual) reality in its place. Thus the substantiality of realism — its metalinguistic plenitude, the effacement of enunciation by the enounced, the narrative coherence — all these textual features correspond to "the fetishist's world" which is

> the world of communication where because desire is under control (the imaginary possession of the phallus confers an imaginary control), the differential nature of demand can be ignored. Language is reduced to a pure meeting of minds.

After encountering lack of the phallus in the Mother's desire the male child aims for a narcissistic (or imaginary) reaffirmation of his possession of the phallus in identification with the Father, to disavow lack by experiencing absence in a way which promises "unification in the articulation of the phallus" (p. 148).

The effect of the *Wake* is to make this impossible. A reading of it encourages the view that "language is a constant struggle between a 'feminine libido' which threatens to break all boundaries and a 'male fist' which threatens to fix everything in place" (p. 146). Through its puns, lapses, jokes, lacunae, polyvalent terms and coined words with no place in the English dictionary the *Wake* constantly demonstrates for its reader "the differences and absences with which language is constituted" and exemplifies a writing which "allows a constant openness to the feminine" (p. 147), a feature noted by the *Wake* itself when it refers to "gramma's grammar" (cited pp. 148–9). This, in the main emphasis of MacCabe's account, is what makes for the revolutionary consequences of Joyce's textual intervention. That the radical potential of these texts is diminished by what the book admits as the lack of "any definite notion of an audience" (p. 156) or indeed any audience outside the academic was fastened on by reviewers in 1978 and is only partly disarmed when it is said that in *Finnegans Wake* Joyce "is still writing in our future" (p. 148).

Textual analysis and theoretical perspective come together to give this argument, though both can be contested. The textual analysis proceeds by identifying the materiality of language — what is experienced as language rather than representation — with language at the level of the phonetic, paradigmatically exemplified in the puns of the *Wake*. It is enough to indicate here that, the possibility of feminine writing itself once granted, another account of it would develop if attention is given not to the *phonetic* but the *syntactic* level of language. So it is in the now famous passage where Virginia Woolf praises "the psychological sentence of the feminine gender" because it is "of a more elastic fibre than the old, capable of stretching to the extreme" and "enveloping the vaguest shapes" (1979, p. 191). This identifies feminine writing not with phonetic play but rather with sentence organisation, one which is paratactic rather than syntactic, more like what we read in the novels of Woolf than those of Joyce.

In any case MacCabe's defence of the *Wake* as feminine cannot but rest on an essentialism, an essentialism inscribed within its psychoanalytic theory. For *James Joyce* a little girl's first identification must be "fundamentally different from the male" (p. 150), that foundation being sexual difference, not political contradiction. Psychoanalysis rather than an Althusserian account of the subject in ideology is the more consistent framework in MacCabe's text.

This is one reason why the book is such a hard read. Although the conceptual basis from Lacan is thoroughly and originally worked through into English it remains thoroughly and unrelievedly abstract. And the problem of the book's theoretical exposition is compounded rather than helped by its illustrative topic. Thus, the book aims to cover and indeed capture the territory conventionally held by the Joyce of literary criticism. Accordingly it moves forward across the texts of a single author considering each in chronological order. But this consecutive order of exposition is set the task of integrating *at the same time* with a theoretical order of exposition, so that Joyce's early texts are required to be the appropriate examples for the elementaries of critical theory and his later texts for its full complexity.

Neither of these difficulties is faced by Catherine Belsey's *Critical practice*. It avows itself as a rehearsal of theory and so is able to go there first and suit examples to that admitted priority. At the same time as a volume in the 'New Accents' series it had to be readable by students in higher education, a process achieved by the benign censorship of the series editor, Terry Hawkes, who lets its writers say whatever they want so long as they say it clearly. For both these reasons, though *James Joyce* may be, within English, the more original work, *Critical practice* (which draws many of its examples from drama) has been a far more significant intervention and has been taken by those who attack post-structuralism in literary theory as its exemplary text.

Belsey's *Critical practice* (1980)

Each version of British post-structuralism begins by breaking with the naturalist fallacy dominating its particular area of concern (in art history, the doctrine of the 'Essential Copy', in musicology the derivation of musical effect directly from acoustics). In literary studies that place is occupied by what Belsey names as "expressive realism". Based in the humanist assumption that "'man' is the origin and source of meaning, of action, and of history" and that language is by nature transparent to meaning, expressive realism is the theory "that literature reflects the reality of experience as it is perceived by one (especially gifted) individual, who *expresses* it in a discourse which enables other individuals to recognize it as true" (1980, p. 7). After illustrating how such views permeate the critical writings of Ruskin and Leavis, *Critical practice* turns to alternatives — New Criticism, Frye's account of archetypes in *Anatomy of criticism*, the reader-response theories of Fish, Jauss and Iser — to show that they too fail to break with the common-sense view of language, that underlying Frye's formalism "is a concept of human nature" (p. 23), that Iser's theory "suppresses the relationship between language and experience" and repeats the familiar concept of (more or less) transparent "communication between individual subjects" (p. 36). This humanist conception cannot be sustained in the face of post-Saussurean critical theory.

On the grounds (1) that the relation between signifier and signified is by nature arbitrary though they are brought together in the 'social fact' of language and (2) that the signifieds of a given language produce meaning only through their relations to each other Belsey re-affirms the Saussurean principle that "language is not a nomenclature, a way of naming things that already exist, but a system of differences with no positive terms" (p. 38). Language constructs meanings and this construction is ideological not only in that language is always a social fact but, crucially, because the process of construction itself may be overlooked so that "the differences it constructs may seem to be natural, universal and unalterable when in reality they are produced by a specific form of social organisation" (p. 42). That meaning production can become naturalised is then suavely exemplified by analysis of six photographic advertisements for perfume, *Chique, Rive Gauche, Estivalia, Blasé, Charivari* and *Charlie,* an analysis that slides without tremor into an account of the first paragraph of George Eliot's *Middlemarch* (just how disconcerting this elision feels for conventional literary criticism is registered in Barry 1981).

As the development of British post-structuralism envisages, linguistics opens the way to ideology and to a conception of subjectivity. Althusser's account of how ideology works to constitute subjects as apparently constitutive together with Lacan's account of how a seemingly transparent discourse enables the subject to misrecognise its identity as self-present are taken to justify the assertion that "ideology suppresses the role of language in the construction of the subject" (p. 61). On this basis *Critical practice* analyses the realist text as constructed to present itself to the reader as natural and spontaneous expression, supporting MacCabe's discussion of George Eliot by arguing that a metalinguistic hierarchy of discourse produces the realist effect in *The Mill on the floss* (pp. 70–2), along with other central texts in the nineteenth-century realist tradition: *Jane Eyre, Oliver Twist, Emma, Bleak House.*

Analysis of *Bleak House* (pp. 79–80) begins by noting the two contrasted narratives that open the text, Esther Summerson's and the anonymous third-person narrator. Gradually however a "literary unwritten discourse begins to emerge, the discourse of the reader" (p. 80), in possession of a metalinguistic understanding of the text from a point beyond the other two narratives. At the end the three discourses "converge to confirm the reader's apparently extra-discursive interpretation and judgment" (p 81). By this means the text constructs a reality which appears complex and many-sided but which is aligned with a single, non-contradictory discourse in which Esther, the ironic narrator and the reader come to share "a 'recognition' of the true complexity of things" (p. 81). By thus smoothing over contradictions in the interests of a single, unified and coherent 'truth' the text of *Bleak House* "offers the reader a position, an attitude which is given as non-contradictory, fixed in 'knowing' subjectivity" (p. 81).

Expressive realism is a discursive operation aiming to deny its own operation by particular technical strategies (hierarchy of discourse, stylistic illusionism, centring of point of view, narrative closure) whose aim is consistent:

> in this way heterogeneity — variety of points of view and temporal locations — is contained in homogeneity. The text interpellates the reader as a transcendent and non-contradictory subject by positioning him or her as "the unified and unifying subject of its vision". (p. 78)

This last phrase, cited from Heath (1981, p. 38) explicitly rejoins Belsey's account of novelistic realism with *Screen*'s account of mainstream cinema.

Realist text/interrogative text

Realism, however, can be opposed to modernism and, in Belsey's terms, the classic realist text can be contrasted with the *interrogative* text. If expressive realism in the form of the classic realist text functions ideologically by seeking to pass itself off as natural, in the interrogative text the world represented may be perceived at what Althusser calls "an internal distance" from the ideology in which it is held (1977b, p. 204), enabling the reader to perform a critique of this ideology. While the realist text aims to install its reader 'outside and looking on' from a transcendental position,

> the *interrogative* text, on the other hand disrupts the unity of the reader by discouraging identification with a unified subject of enunciation. The position of the 'author' inscribed in the text, if it can be located at all, is seen as questioning or as literally contradictory. (Belsey 1980, p. 91)

The interrogative text works to unfix the position of the reader.

Not surprisingly, Brecht's own modernist enterprise of epic theatre serves as preliminary illustration of the interrogative text, *Galileo*. But as Brecht noted himself in *The Messingkauf dialogues*, Shakespeare's is "a theatre full of A–effects" (1965, p. 58), and *Critical practice* goes on to illustrate the interrogative text with *Julius Caesar, Coriolanus* and *Winter's tale*, as well as Marlowe's

143

Tamburlaine. If this means reading historically specific Elizabethan texts as though they were examples of contemporary modernism, then, so it is argued, "we have no choice" but to do so (Belsey 1980, p. 144). The instances demonstrate well how the interrogative text positions its subject as a site of contradiction but the issue of historical versus contemporary reading brings with it a deeper difficulty in *Critical practice*, one to which attention will return.

For the classic realist text itself can be *read* as a form of interrogative text. Following Barthes in *S/Z*, *Critical practice* argues that since the realist text always was a construct, an effect of the signifier, it is available for *deconstruction*, "that is, the analysis of the process and conditions of its construction out of the available discourses" (p. 104). It is significant that this text of 1980 mentions Derridean notions of deconstruction in a footnote to this sentence (pp. 150–1), yet confidently co-opts the term for its own purposes. Thus, since the text is in fact composed of contradictions it becomes "*plural*, open to re-reading" (p. 104) and this, in the spirit of Barthes's programme, will transform the reader from passive to active, "make the reader no longer a consumer, but a producer of the text" (Barthes 1975, p. 4, cited Belsey, p. 125). Literary criticism is unequivocally politicised:

> It is this contradiction in the subject — between the conscious self, which is conscious in so far as it is able to feature in discourse, and the self which is only partially represented there — which constitutes the source of possible change. (p. 85)

Intervening to demonstrate the text as always a construct and the reader's position as always its effect, literary criticism becomes politically progressive if it acts to interpellate readers as "pepetually in construction, perpetually contradictory, perpetually open to change" (p. 132).

Reflections on Critical practice

Critical practice has now itself achieved the status of a classic text in British post-structuralism (and as such, for example, is singled out for a badly argued and depressingly facetious denigration in Patrick Parrinder's *The failure of theory*, 1987 pp. 18–30). Yet

Critical practice has won its position even despite a certain vacillation or instability in its structure of concepts, as can be appreciated if certain terms and oppositions are reconsidered, specifically: text/reader, implied reader/actual reader; historical meaning/present reading; knowledge/effectivity.

As noted already with reference to the *Screen* problematic itself, there is a play or difference between the implied position of the reader as structurally determined by the text and any actual position taken up. *Critical practice* accordingly stresses that "meaning is never a fixed essence inherent in the text but is always constructed by the reader, the result of a 'circulation' between social formation, reader and text" so that "to argue that classic realism interpellates subjects in certain ways is not to propose that this process is ineluctable" (p. 69). Opening a gap between text and reader, between a position inscribed and one actually assumed, is necessary to sustain the argument regarding deconstruction, that the text can be read against the grain so that a classic realist text can be understood as actively constructing a position for its reader. But a difficulty is posed for the coherence of the argument when this distinction becomes superimposed on one between positions historically inscribed by the historical text and positions imposed on the reader in the present.

In this *Critical practice* can be seen to hover in the space it opens between two possibilities. One is an Althusserian problematic in which texts and the positions they inscribe are real, historically determined (albeit in the autonomy of their own specificity as literature), and can be known in their effects. The other is a more radically post-structuralist problematic within which there are no texts, real or otherwise, but only readings actively produced in an unceasing present. At many points *Critical practice* founds itself on the Althusserian real. Ideology is defined as "both a real and an imaginary relation to the world" (p. 57), beyond which, it is asserted, people may grasp "their relation to the real relations in which they live" (p. 66). This is the real of class struggle and mode of production invoked when Macherey's position is summarised as seeing it as the task of criticism to establish the unspoken in the text so as "to produce a real knowledge of history" (p. 136).

Elsewhere, however, the real is less reliable — and less relied on. As remarked, the position for the reader inscribed by classic realism can be re-worked by a present reading. And the readings offered of Shakespeare's texts as interrogative texts are not just readings in the present but readings which take no account at all of any actual Jacobean reader situated historically after feudal allegory but before the seventeenth-century institution of realism in poetry and prose. At such points *Critical practice* is not trying to construct a knowledge of the real and, indeed, it is part of the strength of the text that it aims to reflect on itself by facing the arguments of Hindess and Hirst set out in *Mode of production and social formation*.

Accepting that epistemology is impossible (for the reasons given by Hindess and Hirst), *Critical practice* confronts the danger that "the total rejection of epistemology may present us with a world...in which one discourse (and therefore mode of action) is as good as any other" (p. 63) (a position very close to that of classic North American deconstruction) but does so only to reject it on the grounds that a way out of the circle "lies in the concept of knowledge as *discursively produced*, the product of the recognition and resolution of contradictions within and between the existing discourses of ideology" (p. 63). This is attractively consistent with the pervading arguments about contradiction (even if it may work the founding notion of contradiction very hard indeed). Undeniably it steps outside the ideology/science opposition but only by committing itself to a concept of knowledge which may not be enough to count as knowledge at all ("the product of the recognition and resolution of contradictions").

Critical practice on its own account presents itself less as a text giving a knowledge of history (or anything else) than as an intervention to produce politically progressive readings. Again, it is part of the rigour of the text that it aims to confront this issue in a final section ("The problems") that begins by asking: "Is literature most usefully seen as a means of access to history (Macherey), or as a way of grasping the present (Lacan and Barthes)?" (p. 143). The answer given is that "there is more work to be done" (p. 145). If the problem is that posed by the fact that the literary text is on the one hand a structure and on the other the result of an act of interpretation, then from a vantage point some years later it can be said that the work has been done but that the problem has not been resolved. Meanwhile, after MacCabe and Belsey, post-structuralism in Britain was ready to advance from the novel and drama into the sacred groves of poetry.

Poetry as discourse

In *Etudes Anglaises, Poetry as discourse* (Easthope 1983a) was reviewed as follows (Cusin 1985):

> The theory of discourse which the author proposes to apply to English poetry is presented in a clear and explicit manner: "what defines a discourse is the *role accorded* to enunciation in it" (1983, pp. 102–3); or again "Ideology can no longer be ghettoized as belonging only or mainly to the signified" (p. 23). Jacques Lacan is the major reference here, but as re-read by Althusser, who is himself corrected by Paul Hirst *(Law and Ideology)*. If the approach is Marxist, it is a long way from the analyses of a Christopher Caudwell (for whom the tight closure of the heroic couple in eighteenth-century England was to be explained by the stringency of import controls). The argument is simple and attractive especially for those aware that recent literary criticism is no longer stuck in a narrow structuralism. Poetic discourse in England, from the Renaissance to Romanticism is characterised by the position it provides for the reader — that of the full subject, of a "transcendental ego", and this through a double strategy: by closing the poem's syntagmatic chain and either denying or effacing the process of enunciation.
>
> The argument is supported first by a study of iambic pentameter, which is charged with all the crimes of bourgeois ideology: its hegemony favours abstraction, disguises its own production and (Whiggishly?) reconciles order and liberty for the benefit of an *imaginary* imperialism (in the Lacanian sense of the term) and thus to the disadvantage of the subject of the signifier.
>
> An analysis contrasting a medieval ballad ("The Three Ravens") and Shakespeare's "Sonnet 73" leads to the first conclusion: "The two forms exemplify opposed kinds of discourse: one collective, popular, intersubjective, accepting the text as a poem to be performed; the other individualist, elitist, privatised, offering the text as representation of a voice speaking" (p. 77). It is not surprising that the reader is next led, through analysis of a section of *The Rape of the Lock*, to consider the pseudo-transparency of poetic discourse in Pope; on the other hand, some thought is needed perhaps before adopting the view that the Romantics, supposing they could

147

challenge the traditional poetic discourse, in fact only perpetuated its forms. For William Wordsworth, isn't the new poetry that which seeks to be entirely without rhetoric, enunciation removed altogether: "All good poetry *is* the spontaneous overflow of powerful feelings" ("Preface" to the Lyrical Ballads, cited p. 124, italics added)? From which Easthope can conclude that "Tintern Abbey", the opening of which is analysed in detail, "gives the effect of the presence of the speaker by denying its presence as a poem" (p. 132).

In contrast, and with a firm logic, modernist poetry — Pound's "Canto 82" serves as the example — because it privileges paratactic juxtaposition to the disadvantage of imaginary coherence, admits a space for the reading subject. Antony Easthope ends this chronological survey by praising what, following certain phoneticians, he prefers to call "intonational metre" rather than *vers libre*, and whose practice sustains the new poetic discourse of Modernism. The work's conclusion, "A Future for Poetry", returns the reader from the dimension of the imagination to that of ideology.

Post-structuralism in feminist literary criticism

Toril Moi's *Sexual/textual politics* intends "to develop a critical presentation of the current debates within feminist literary criticism and theory" (1985, p. 93). As such the book divides its subject matter roughly into three categories:

(1) theories concerned with gender in terms of authorship;
(2) theories concerned with gender in terms of the characters represented, or, in the title of Chapter 2, "'Images of women' criticism";
(3) gender as a possible category for style of discourse itself, particularly the idea proposed of an *écriture féminine*.

In the first two areas the text stays largely within the confines of literary criticism, but with the third, as is consistent with the promise of feminism, it moves beyond literary criticism and the academic itself to pose larger questions about gender, identity and feminist theory. Followed through with rigour and great consistency, the argument of *Sexual/textual politics* weaves together three strands of post-structuralist thinking, from Althusser, from Derrida and from the fact of the book's intervention in the context of British post-structuralism.

In its own equivalent to the usual founding gesture by which a post-structuralism breaks with the version of naturalist thinking dominant in its area of concern, *Sexual/textual politics* recalls the established practice among feminists of using 'feminine' and 'masculine' "to represent social constructs" while reserving 'female' and 'male' for the biological aspects of sexual difference (p. 65) and argues that "patriarchal oppression consists of imposing certain social standards of femininity on all biological women" in the name of *nature*. But there is no more nature, in this sense, for "though women are undoubtedly *female*, this in no way guarantees that they will be *feminine*" (p. 65). From this basis the argument means to go on much further, to subvert any definition of masculine and feminine.

When Derrida's *Dissemination* lists the inherited categories of conceptual oppositions cited above (p. 132) it does not include masculine/feminine. *Sexual/textual politics* deploys its argument around the opposition masculine/feminine following closely the procedures of Derridean deconstruction — it takes a binary polarity in which 'masculine' is privileged in dependent relation to the denigrated 'feminine', demonstrates that the terms, far from being "stable, unchanging essences" (p. 154), are in fact reciprocally interdependent, and does so with the aim, not of reversing the polarity (by privileging 'the feminine'), but of undoing the polarity altogether. Moi's strategy differs from North American deconstruction, however, for in aiming "to deconstruct the opposition between traditionally 'masculine' and traditionally 'feminine' values" it means to go beyond the terms "to confront the full political force and reality of such categories" (p. 160).

To deconstruct "the opposition between masculinity and femininity" it is necessary challenge "the very notion of identity" (p. 12) because masculinity within patriarchy claims to have the universality of an essence and an identity as source of itself rather than as effect. It is part of the strategy of *Sexual/textual politics* to attack this "traditional bourgeois humanism of a liberal-individualist kind" (p. 6) in whatever argument relies upon it:

> What feminists such as (Elaine) Showalter and (Marcia) Holly fail to grasp is that the traditional humanism they represent is in effect part of patriarchal ideology. At its centre

is the seamlessly unified self — either individual or collective — which is commonly called 'Man'. As Luce Irigaray or Hélène Cixous would argue, this integrated self is in fact a phallic self, constructed on the model of the self-contained, powerful phallus. Gloriously autonomous, it banishes from itself all conflict, contradiction and ambiguity. In this humanist ideology the self is the *sole author* of history and of the literary text: the humanist creator is potent, phallic and male — God in relation to his world, the author in relation to his text. (p. 8)

In this crucial paragraph (which is supported in detail in the rest of the book) two different conceptual structures are brought into coherence. One is Derrida's analysis of the Western metaphysical tradition as simultaneously logocentric and phallogocentric: metaphysics, founded in ideas of being, presence and self-origin, is at the same time phallocentric in that presence and origin coincide with the attributes of a God the Father ("It is one and the same system: the erection of a paternal logos...and of the phallus as 'privileged signifier'", Derrida 1973, p. 311). And the second is Althusser's critique of humanism. Both are drawn on in the examples, of which three main ones will be mentioned here.

Gilbert and Gubar's widely influential *The madwoman in the attic* (1979) proposes that even within patriarchal literary standards women novelists managed to express "a distinctive female power" (cited Moi, p. 59), one which postulates "a *real* woman hidden behind the patriarchal textual façade" (p. 61), a humanist and implicitly phallocentric assumption therefore. While the work of Hélène Cixous on feminine writing displaces the problem of women and writing from author to textual style, "away from an empiricist emphasis on the sex of the author towards an analysis of the articulations of sexuality and desire within the literary text itself" (p. 110), yet, as Moi's account clearly exhibits, this admirably anti-essentialist and anti-biologistic project is contradicted by Cixous's argument that femininity in writing finds its source in voice and presence, especially as the Voice of the Mother, and that in this respect "a deconstructive view of textuality" is undercut by a "an equally passionate presentation of writing as a female essence" (p. 126). And the same structure of analysis and critique discovers again a humanist and thus phallocentric core in the writing of Irigaray, whose dilemma is that "having shown that so far femininity has been produced exclusively in relation to the logic of the Same" (rather than difference), nevertheless "falls for the temptation to produce her own positive theory of femininity" and thus into the difficulty that "to define 'woman' is necessarily to essentialise her" (p. 139). (Though not discussed, MacCabe's account of "gramma's grammar" in Joyce is liable to the same charge of essentialising.)

What can resolve this dilemma? Within patriarchy *either* woman is defined as a Woman, a negative and passive essence complementary to Man; *or* she attempts to produce a positive theory of femininity — which ultimately becomes recuperated and restored within the phallocratic empire of metaphysics, nature and essences. Turning from Cixous and Irigaray to the work of Kristeva, Moi's argument finds a resolution in the concept of positionality.

Kristeva writes that "*Woman as such* does not exist" (cited Moi, p. 165), refuses to define 'woman' and denies the concept of feminine writing yet discusses sexuality and writing via concepts of language, ideology and the unconscious. Thus in terms of language as process the subject is decentred, the speaking subject posited as the "place, not only of structure and its repeated transformation, but especially, of its loss, its outlay" (Kristeva, cited Moi, p. 152). Kristeva does not have a theory of 'femininity' but she does have "a theory of marginality, subversion and dissidence", and, "in so far as women are defined as marginal by patriarchy, their struggle can be theorized in the same way as any other struggle against a centralised power structure" (p. 164). To complete this "uncompromising anti-essentialism" (p. 164), Kristeva's analysis of the subject is thoroughly (and originally) psychoanalytic, a process in which 'masculine' and 'feminine' are constructed effects.

If femininity has a definition, then, Moi concludes, it is a relational definition as "that which is marginalised by the patriarchal symbolic order" (p. 166), and this entails a means of viewing "the repression of the feminine in terms of *positionality* rather than of essences" (p. 166). Identity, in sum, is a position contradictorily lived out by the speaking subject as it is unevenly assigned in signifying practice, ideological practice, the process of the unconscious.

This conceptualistion of subjectivity as position is not newly introduced by *Sexual/textual politics*. It derives from Althusser's stress on the subject as support for a position as well as from Lacan's account of the ego as misrecognition and the subject as

151

effect of discourse. The work of Kristeva gives currency to the notion of subjectivity as positionality (as discussed above with reference to *Screen*, pp. 42–3). And certainly the clear logic of Moi's thinking, leaning as it does on Derridean deconstruction, pushes the argument to the conclusion it achieves. However, it is fair to point out that these texts and concepts were available to other writers addressing the issue of women's writing but are not so directed elsewhere — in fact as the comprehensiveness of Moi's critique of other feminist writing evidences, the line taken has considerable originality, though less so if it is seen as it must be in the context of post-structuralist work in England (the influence of Catherine Belsey is acknowledged in Moi's Preface, p. xv). *Sexual/textual politics* develops the analysis it does because as a text it also intervenes within the problematic of British post-structuralism which, departing from Althusser's anti-humanism, has always taken the subject and its positioning as central to a political analysis.

Sexual/textual politics ends with a paragraph citing a passage from Derrida which writes of a possible relationship to the other which would not be asexual but would be constituted "beyond the binary difference that governs the decorum of all codes, beyond the opposition feminine/masculine, beyond homosexuality and heterosexuality" (p. 173). This conclusion has been dismissed by Lisa Jardine as simply Utopian, "a meticulous analysis of feminist critical theory...validated, in the end, by Derrida in a frock" (1986, p. 217, fn. 16), a criticism which indicates a more serious problem, following from the mapping together of Derrida's critique of *conceptual* oppositions and categories with oppositions whose force and specific effectivity lies in a different domain entirely, that of the unconscious as understood by psychoanalysis. And between these two there may be no easy homology or indeed any homology at all. As *Sexual/textual politics* is fully aware, "the opposition between feminine and masculine does not exist in pre-Oedipality" (p. 165): if the wish for an end of such binaries cannot find a place in the Utopia of history, it certainly does in the Paradise of infancy. But in that case escape from sexual difference in mere undifferentiated difference is not where we're going to but where we've come from.

Left deconstruction

There is a politics concerned with the struggle for the meaning of words — 'democracy', 'freedom', 'justice' are examples, 'deconstruction' is another. Following *Screen*, Belsey's *Critical practice* appropriates the term by saying "the object of deconstructing the text is to examine the *process of its production*" (p. 104) and foresees that process being applied to the concept of literature itself by asking "whether we should continue to speak of *literature* at all" since there is no particular authority for "the assumption that there is a body of texts, with their own specific practices, which can usefully be isolated as 'literature'" (p. 144). Belsey practises what she preaches, for throughout the book aesthetic texts are deconstructed to evidence the operation of the signifier by which they achieve their effects *and* literature itself is deconstructed when officially literary texts *(Bleak House, The Winter's Tale)* are analysed alongside and in exactly the same theoretical framework as non-literary texts (perfume advertisements, the Sherlock Holmes stories).

One main direction of British post-structuralist thinking, exemplified in the work of MacCabe and Belsey, pursues an analysis of texts in terms of the position they offer to their reader. But another powerful version takes the form of putting in question the discursive practice and institutional mode of academic Englit, deconstructing its self-assumed privilege (over the study of popular culture, for example) by exhibiting the process of its production. Deserving to be named as left deconstruction, the strategy shares with much American deconstruction a tendency to deny the text any material identity or potential effectivity and assert that it *only* exists as an act of interpretation. In this respect left deconstruction is post-structuralist in the bracketing of the material reality of the text. Such an approach is anticipated when Raymond Williams at the end of "Base and superstructure in Marxist cultural theory" (1973, reprinted in Williams 1980) posits the study of literature on the basis of an either/or: since literary texts are "not objects but *notations*", we should "look not for the components of a product but for the conditions of a practice" (see Chapter 2, above). The road is opened for an analysis of literature not as texts but as a practice of reading in which they are institutionally constructed. One of the first texts to explore this path is Tony Bennett's *Formalism and Marxism* (1979).

Either/or

Bennett begins by following through the trajectory of Russian Formalism. That project tried to define the literariness *(literaturnost)* of the literary text in terms of its artifice or device *(priem)* which leads to the effect of *defamiliarisation (ostranenie)*, the feature in which its literariness resides. But this can be seen as a problematic concept if it is remarked that the text which defamiliarises in 1912 does not defamiliarise in the same way in 1922. Accordingly, the Russian Formalist project develops from the attempt to define the literariness of literature 'in itself' into the recognition, signalled vividly by the 1928 essay of Jakobson and Tynanov, "Problems in the study of literature and language" (1971), that literariness is a function of the text in relation to the historically situated reader.

Bennett praises Formalism for speaking of literature "not as a *thing* with an *essence*...but a *relationship* and a *function*" (p. 130) and uses this as a basis from which to criticise others in the Marxist tradition who treat literariness as an essence inherent in the literary text — an essence always and everywhere the same (for example Althusser's "A letter on art" (1977b, pp. 203–8), which asserts that literature enables ideology to be perceived, or Eagleton in *Criticism and ideology* which similarly assumes the aesthetic as a special category introducing "a certain curvature in the ideological space in which the text plays" (1976, p. 180)).

In arguing that literature is not an essence but a practice of reading *Formalism and Marxism* partakes of the same view as Harold Bloom when he observes "that there are *no* texts, but only interpretations" (1979, p. 7). Such versions of American deconstruction presume the immateriality of the text in order to open it to a libertarian plurality of readings: Bennett's is a left deconstruction because it stresses that readings are not free for the individual but collectively determined, that "the political effects of literary texts" depend on "the historically concrete and varying modes in which they are appropriated" (1979, p. 136). A final chapter describes how literary texts in Britain, from Arnold to Leavis, have been constructed in a literary practice which "attempts to heal or placate class and ideological contradictions" (Bennett 1979, p. 161).

Difficulties are encountered when the argument denies the view that the text exists as an essence by denying it any material reality at all. In a series of formulations *Formalism and Marxism* follows

Williams in posing a 'not...but': "The question is not what literature's political effects *are* but what they might be *made to be*" (p. 137); a political reading "does not restore to the text contradictions which were 'always there' but hidden from view; *it reads contradictions into the text*" (p. 146); again: "The text is not the issuing source of meaning. It is a site on which the production of meaning — of variable meanings — takes place" (p. 174). There must be questions here. Surely what something might be made into is determined in some measure by what it is? Can any contradictions — any at all — be read into the text? And what *is* this "site" on which the production of variable meanings takes place? It looks as though this either/or problematic reproduces the essentialist binaries it means to oppose. The claim of conventional literary criticism that meaning resides in the text itself, not at all in the reading, becomes reversed into the assertion that meaning is produced only in the reading and not at all from the text.

In a review of *Formalism and Marxism* Terry Eagleton asked:

Does it follow from arguing that the 'text in itself' is an illusion that we can never actually know that *Macbeth* isn't about Manchester United? Doesn't the text in some sense constrain the possible range of its interpretations? (1979, p. 20)

In arguing that literature is a practice of reading as much as it is a text read he might well have invoked the Marxist principle that production "not only creates an object for a subject, but also a subject for the object" (Marx 1973, p. 92). When Eagleton himself subsequently deconstructs literariness it is with a qualification which avoids denying the reality of texts while bracketing out the reality of literature in an analysis of Englit as a discursive practice on a model drawn from Foucault.

Eagleton: *Literary theory* (1983)

In 1976 Eagleton published *Criticism and ideology*, a theoretical text whose basis was thoroughly Althusserian in approaching literature as a relatively autonomous practice ultimately determined by economic practice. In the years after 1976 even the Althusserian modification of traditional Marxist categories regarding base and superstructure came under critique, as has already been discussed

155

with reference to Hindess and Hirst. Eagleton's *Walter Benjamin: towards a revolutionary criticism* (1981) is a work of transition which at one point offers an auto-critique of *Criticism and ideology*, accusing it of being "theoretically limited" by its Althusserian problematic, this leading to a "residual idealism and academicism" which is now to be rejected in favour of Raymond Williams's "bold efforts to shift attention from the analysis of an object named 'literature' to the social relations of cultural practice" (1981, p. 97).

Self-criticism can be less vaguely phrased. Between *Criticism and ideology* (1976) and *Literary theory* (1983) there has been a complete change of position (Macherey, central to the first, is not even mentioned in the second). *Criticism and ideology* rests on a distinction between literature as ideology and its own status as a science of literature (hence Chapter 3, "Towards a science of the text"). It also underwrites the existing literary canon. Denying that there is any such a thing as literature, *Literary theory* works only by attacking other theories and refusing to outline one of its own. It acknowledges that the Conclusion would have been impossible without the work of Foucault, and "its influence there is pervasive" (1983, p. 134). Here the text will be read with attention to its post-structuralism.

Thus it begins by undermining the currently dominant naturalism, and that, in Englit, consists of the presumption that a canon of texts of 'imaginative' literature is self-evidently of supreme value. Eagleton's opening page shows just how fluid the canon is, able to encompass Bacon's essays, possibly Hobbes's *Leviathan* as well as Shakespeare and Milton — more like what Shelley defines as 'poetry' in his *Defence* than is ever admitted on a list of set texts. *Literary theory* then takes on two accounts of literariness, both of which are seen off for the same reason. Whether literature is defined as what 'defamiliarises' ordinary language or as 'non-pragmatic' discourse, both depend on "how somebody decides to *read*" (p. 8). Literariness as fact cannot exist apart from literary criticism as an evaluative activity, a form of knowledge which, as the work of Foucault demonstrates, contributes to "the maintenance and reproduction of social power" (p. 15).

At this point what *Literary theory* does not do is as important as what it does. For it does not argue that there are no texts but only readings. It does not therefore collapse everything into discourse, and, scrupulously avoiding an unnecessary either/or, writes of literature being "as much a question of what people do to writing as

156

of what writing does to them" (p. 7) and again of literature as "less" some inherent quality "than" as ways people relate themselves to it (p. 9). The persisting materiality of writing and the text is maintained though it is argued that "any belief that the study of literature is the study of a stable, well-definable entity, as entomology is the study of insects, can be abandoned as a chimera" (p. 11).

This is a post-structuralism which does not mean to surrender the capacity of a discourse of knowledge to refer more or less accurately to reality. As far as entomology is concerned, the reality of insects is not doubted but the reality of insects does not in itself guarantee the protocols and criteria by which the science of entomology constructs knowledge of its object (insects indeed can get into a scientific discourse in many different ways, and a mosquito will figure very differently in pathology on the one hand and aerodynamics on the other). Nor is entomology beyond the effects Foucault analyses as power/knowledge. At issue rather is the relative stability of entomology dependent on both its method and its object of study contrasted with literary study and its 'object'. *Literary theory* is unequivocal that "any attempt to define literary theory in terms of a distinctive method is doomed to failure" because as an object literature has insufficient stability, and so, "the unity of the object is as illusory as the unity of the method" (p. 197).

Again, what's not denied is as notable as what is. The cinema certainly exists, as do popular music, television programmes, advertisements, drama, written novels and poems; but

> it is most useful to see 'literature' as a name which people give from time to time for different reasons to certain kinds of writing within a whole field of what Michel Foucault has called 'discursive practices', and that if anything is to be an object of study it is this whole field of practices...whether one calls it 'culture', 'signifying practices' or whatever. (p. 205)

This view would transform 'literary texts' by constructing them within a different discourse. On the basis of this argument it becomes possible to analyse how and with what effects conventional literary critical discourse produces texts as 'really' great, etc., for it is of course in this respect that all such criticism is political.

"Departments of literature in higher education, then, are part of the ideological apparatus of the modern capitalist state" (p. 200).

Within such institutions, "critical discourse is power" and exercises authority by policing the classification of writing into high cultural and popular, selecting candidates for admission to the discourse and certificating "those who have been judged to speak the discourse better or worse" (p. 203). It is not the signified content but the discursive mode of literary criticism that matters: "Nobody is especially concerned about what you say, with what extreme, moderate, radical or conservative positions you adopt, provided that they are compatible with, and can be articulated within, a specific form of discourse" (p. 201). This, so *Literary theory* suggests, is above all a means of individualising, for it assumes "that at the centre of the world is the contemplative individual self, bowed over its book, striving to gain touch with experience, truth, reality, history or tradition" (p. 196).

Althusser and Foucault in English literary theory

Between the two wings of post-structuralist theory discussed here there are divergences as well as compatibilities. That deriving from Althusser as interpreted by *Screen* argues from the materiality of the text towards the position assigned to its implied reader while the later inflection departing from the work of Foucault would seem to deny any effectivity to the text except that accorded to it within the institutional discourse of Englit. Yet there are important distinctions here.

That tendency promoted by Williams and later by Bennett earns its title as left deconstruction by dematerialising the text into 'notations' or a 'site', a procedure conforming to that advocated by Harold Bloom ("there are *no* texts, but only interpretations"). Denying *any* effectivity to the text, reducing it into an equivalent with the act of reading, this view is entirely incompatible with an analysis such as that proposed by MacCabe or Belsey of textual difference in terms of the position of subjects. From this either/or it would follow that there are no implied readers, only actual ones.

This however is not the view adopted by Eagleton and *Literary theory*. Although the legitimacy of literature — or rather Literature — as a self-sustaining canon of great works is denied, no risk of idealism is taken in the careful insistence on the reality of texts and writing, that a text constrains the possible range of its interpretations, that writing does something to people. Among the possible effects of texts would be that of providing a position to its reader.

Yet *Literary theory* is completely silent about work influenced by *Screen*, about Heath, MacCabe or Belsey. As mentioned earlier, hostilities here stretch back to the notorious *Screen* review of *Criticism and ideology*, if not further. *Literary theory* makes no reference to any of the writings discussed here as British post-structuralism and in fact this present work in part hopes to balance a certain one-sidedness in Eagleton's otherwise extraordinarily comprehensive account.

Whatever its reason the omission is regrettable. Negatively, the ascription of a materiality to the text renders *Literary theory* not incompatible with the analysis of texts and the positioning of the reader; positively, Eagleton's project stands to gain in two different ways. One is that *Screen*'s work on cinema or Belsey's deliberately shocking negotiation between advertising media and *Middlemarch* perfectly enacts the called-for stepping aside from literature into confrontation with discursive practices. But secondly, the theoretical material concerned with the subject and position would only help to strengthen and support analysis of Englit as a discursive practice. It would follow through the Foucauldian project by sketching in the way literary criticism provides an object for its discursive practice and a subject positioned in relation to that object through modes of identification.

Thus: as an object Englit offers an identity to its subject as academic (as against everyday), masculine (canonical authors are almost all male), national (neither international nor regional) and ruling class (the high cultural tradition). And it provides this identity through a specific mode of *identification*. The paradigm of conventional criticism elides four instances at each of which the material process of discourse interposes:

(1) the author and his experience;
(2) the text and the author's experience;
(3) literary criticism as discourse constructing the text;
(4) the reader positioned by the superimposing of (1), (2) and (3).

Within and across each of these four, discourse is assumed to operate with unmediated transparency so that the reader is meant simply to re-experience directly the author's experience. Literary criticism in this respect has compared itself to a child listening to a

159

story at its mother's knee (see Gardner 1982, p. 32). The subject of literary criticism, therefore, is positioned as a subject of experience (not knowledge), within pleasure (not work) and as centred in an imaginary plenitude (exactly comparable to that of mother/infant dyad).

Literary theory explicitly takes up a very hostile position towards post-structuralism, which it does not clearly discriminate from deconstruction. In the relevant chapter, despite certain strengths (mainly identified with the work of Foucault), post-structuralist ideas are discussed as the product of the retreat from politics into subjectivism and "erotic play" (p. 142) following the defeat of the 1968 initiatives in France. This would be a more accurate characterisation of American deconstruction (as will be suggested in the next chapter). And it would certainly not be an accurate account of what has been discussed here in relation to film theory, art history and literary theory as British post-structuralism.

12

Deconstruction

...in truth the loss of what has never taken place,
of a self-presence which has never been given
but only dreamed of...

Derrida, cited *Oxford Literary Review*

This present chapter concerns deconstruction proper, that is, the American development from sources in Derrida of a particular set of protocols for reading texts. Since those texts are most often literary texts, this is really a second chapter on literary studies. The line of march is less clear, for reasons that will become apparent.

Althusser and de Man on literature

We may begin by setting alongside each other two contrasting passages on literature and literary theory. The first, written in 1966, is from Althusser's "A letter on art":

> What art makes us *see*, and therefore gives to us in the form of *'seeing'*, *'perceiving'* and *'feeling'* (which is not the form of *knowing*), is the *ideology* from which it is born, in which it bathes, from which it detaches itself as art, and to which it *alludes*. Macherey has shown this very clearly in the case of Tolstoy, by extending Lenin's analyses. Balzac and Solzhenitsyn give us a 'view' of the ideology to which their work alludes and with which it is constantly fed, a view which presupposes a *retreat*, an *internal distantiation* from the very ideology from which their novels emerged. They make us

'perceive' (but not know) in some sense *from the inside*, by an *internal distance*, the very ideology in which they are held. (1977b, p. 204)

The second is longer and occurs in Paul de Man's *Blindness and insight*, published in 1971. Referring back to the work of critics (Lukács, Poulet, Blanchot) it has discussed, it claims that their critical stance is defeated by their own critical results, and from this continues:

A penetrating but difficult insight into the nature of literary language ensues. It seems, however, that this insight could only be gained because the critics were in the grip of this peculiar blindness; their language could grope toward a certain degree of insight only because their method remained oblivious to the perception of this insight. The insight exists only for a reader in the privileged position of being able to observe the blindness as a phenomenon in its own right — the question of his *[sic]* own blindness being one which he is by definition incompetent to ask — and so being able to distinguish between statement and meaning. He has to undo the explicit results of a vision that is able to move toward the light only because, being already blind, it does not have to fear the power of this light. But the vision is unable to report correctly what it has perceived in the course of its journey. To write critically about critics thus becomes a way to reflect on the paradoxical effectiveness of a blinded vision that has to be rectified by means of insights that it unwittingly provides. (1983, p. 106)

If there were a paragraph which founded deconstruction, it would be that from de Man, followed almost at once by this:

The critics here assembled all have in common a certain degree of immanence in their approach. For all of them, the encounter with the language of literature involves a mental activity which, however problematical, is at least to a point governed by this language only. All strive for a considerable degree of generality, going so far that they can be said to be writing, not about particular works or authors, but about literature as such. Nevertheless, their generality remains grounded in the initial act of reading. Prior to any

162

generalisation about literature, literary texts have to be read, and the possibility of reading can never be taken for granted. It is an act of understanding that can never be observed, nor in any way prescribed or verified. A literary text is not a phenomenal event that can be granted any form of positive existence, whether as a fact of nature or as an act of the mind. It leads to no transcendental perception, intuition, or knowledge but merely solicits an understanding that has to remain immanent because it poses the problem of intelligibility in its own terms. This area of immanence is necessarily part of all critical discourse. Criticism is a metaphor for the act of reading, and this act is itself inexhaustible. (pp. 106–7)

"Art makes us *see...ideology*"; a literary text "leads to no transcendental perception": besides the fact that the main arguments here are in flat contradiction, these extracts from Althusser and de Man are also opposed in many other ways.

In style Althusser is abstract and literal, while de Man seeks out the metaphors of a Christian "journey" towards the light, a journey, however, which misses transcendence since you can only see God when you are blind. Althusser calls on the shared discourse of a political tradition, de Man pursues images of blindness and insight in his own way. Althusser pronounces truth in a style which aims to ratchet up certitude by italicising words specially weighted as technical terms, de Man enjoys paradoxes such as that according to which blindness is able to move towards the light because it need not fear its power. In this respect, Althusser is wholly serious while de Man is at play.

For Althusser literary study is an act of reading leading to knowledge, for de Man it leads back towards an act of reading. For Althusser the process of literary study assumes a degree of closure while for de Man it remains potentially infinite ("itself inexhaustible"), guaranteed by the infinite reversibility and incommensurability of blindness and insight in any reading or series of readings (and this becomes grounds for arguing that interpretation is 'undecidable'). However, though Althusser's argument invokes the closure of knowledge on to a truth, it opens the way to shared political action, while de Man's closes on the inexhaustibility of subjective experience, said to be beyond observation, prescription, verification. The effect of Althusser is to instate the reading of literature in a political context, an extra-literary domain, by reading it in relation to ideology; that of de Man is to restore literature to its traditional place by rendering it in terms of the antinomies of merely individual experience, both literal and metaphorical — to be blind/to have vision, blindness/ insight. De Man re-reads and replaces the social and discursive binaries of Derrida with binaries which are in and for *the subject*, and the subject of literary reading at that.

Perhaps more than the others this last difference may provide a preliminary explanation for the extraordinary charisma de Man and deconstruction seemed able to exercise in North America, a charisma which remains largely a mystery in Britain. Separate pieces of literary criticism have gained currency but the simple fact is that deconstruction as such has made almost no impression on British post-structuralism. And even when it has been introduced it has appeared in ways significantly different from the American precedents.

Deconstruction over Britain

No full-length literary study within the protocols of deconstruction has yet been produced in Britain though it is promised (see Ellman 1987 and Young, forthcoming). Two texts by Christopher Norris, *The deconstructive turn* (1983) and *The contest of faculties* (1985), consist of essays rather than a single, developed argument, and are in any case texts which work in a most interesting way at and on the margin between literature and philosophy rather than specifically literary studies. Norris's *Deconstruction: theory and practice* (1982) is a text about, not of deconstruction. As far as literature is concerned British deconstruction is represented by a handful of essays, most of which have appeared in the *Oxford Literary Review*, two of whose editors teach at the University of Southampton. Though also a port, Southampton is not Newhaven.

Deconstruction in Britain is therefore hard to define. In 1981 Robert Young, founding editor of the *Oxford Literary Review*, published *Untying the text: a post-structuralist reader*. This comprised essays by Barthes and Foucault, as well as "On Literature as an ideological form" by Etienne Balibar and Pierre Macherey, a Marxist text that had also appeared in the *Oxford Literary Review* in 1978, translated by three editors of the *OLR*, Ian Mcleod, John Whitehead and Ann Wordsworth. Yet *Untying the text* exhibits a firm commitment to deconstruction, reprinting, for example, essays by Barbara Johnson, J. Hillis Miller, Paul de Man and Richard Rand. The native element is represented in essays by Maud Ellman and Ann Wordsworth, though this latter, a brilliant and innovative account of Tennyson's *In Memoriam*, owes less to deconstruction than to psychoanalysis. The editor's contribution, "Post-structuralism: an introduction", after a patient exposition of Saussurean linguistics and differences between structuralism and post-structuralism, proceeds via Macherey and Althusser to a lucid and uncontroversial account of work by Foucault, Lacan and Derrida (1981, pp. 1–28), its main gesture in the direction of Yale being no more than the remark that "it is Derrida who is often associated most closely with post-structuralism because it is he who has most carefully investigated and exposed the contradictions and paradoxes upon which structuralism is formed" (p. 15). We have to look elsewhere to find something of the edge deconstruction has acquired in North America.

Founded in 1976, the *Oxford Literary Review* for two years included a range of modernist and post-structuralist writings about the arts until it narrowed in 1978 to a particular concern with deconstruction and literature (Number 2 of that year appears in a new format and is devoted entirely to readings of Derrida). In 1981 the University of Southampton sponsored a conference on literary theory in association with the *OLR* and followed this with further conferences in 1983 and 1985. Except for occasional references and a paper by Catherine Belsey, the 1981 conference made no formal engagement with feminism, though this absence was more than made good at the 1985 conference on "Sexual Difference" (reprinted as the *Oxford Literary Review* for 1986). However, very little in this collection owes much to American deconstruction, and the main discourse invoked is that of psychoanalysis.

Certain papers from the first Southampton conference for 1981 were selected for later publication in the journal, and in default of other contexts it is to these that a reader in quest of deconstruction is forced to turn. More explicitly polemical than other *OLR* texts and accompanied by some of the verbal response they excited on delivery, they illustrate well the intervention of deconstruction and the attempt to graft it on to the British post-structuralist tradition.

Young's post-structuralism

Robert Young's conference lecture, "Post-structuralism, theory, text", was printed in *OLR* as "Post-structuralism: the end of theory" (1982, pp. 3–20). Once again names are a site for contestation, and Young's intervention has the effect of co-opting the word post-structuralism for a definition mainly in terms of deconstruction, though one subtly re-tinctured through its immersion in the British tradition.

Young's analysis is structured across essentially three points, centred on the seemingly modest assertion that: "Post-structuralism is criticism that attends to the movement, the lability, and the instability of meaning and representation in the play of the signifier" (p. 5). This seems tame but is in fact decisive for, thus essentialised, the signifier (the trace, *écriture*, writing) can be set up in opposition to an equally essentialised notion of metalanguage.

Since Lacanian psychoanalysis has shown that the subject is always positioned in relation to the object through "the workings of the unconscious and the structure of desire", and since Derrida has shown how language entails a "process upon which cognitive processes depend", then the effect of their work is to "dissolve the status of metalanguage" (p. 6). A metalanguage would seek to stand apart from an object language, transcending it in the form of theory or of science and presenting it as secondary to itself. This is impossible since in discourse the signifier is everywhere, and thus "it became clear that language could never produce an objective discourse upon itself" (p. 6). The condition for such an (impossibly) objective discourse is covertly assumed to be the *absolute* transparency of discourse, as becomes evident when Young's paper (with implicit allusion to MacCabe's account of realism) remarks it as ironical "that some contemporary criticism, while criticising what it considers to be the the realist novel for assuming this transparency of language, nevertheless itself assumes a transparency in its own use of metalanguage" (p. 7). Crucially, the impossibility of metalanguage will affect literary criticism because it will mean the end of theory — "textual analysis is no longer an *application* of theory" (p. 8) and literary criticism "can no longer be theoretical as such" (p. 9).

The third point in Young's structure, not at all explicit in his account, concerns the subject. The Lacanian account of subjectivity is invoked to confirm that "the subject while reading a text is also read by it" (p. 12), and thus, so it seems to be assumed, textuality, the inherent instability of meaning in the play of the signifier, will dissolve metalanguage and with it a metalinguistic position of mastery. Finally, the paper seeks a *rapprochement* with politics. Since "the power play of the mastery of meaning, the narrative of successive interpretations that attempt to master each other, is the very substance of literary criticism" (p. 11), then to act out the impossibility of literary theory is to undermine mastery, and this — as the paper implies through a final, brief appropriation of Foucault — conforms to "a struggle against power, a struggle aimed at revealing and undermining power where it is most invisible and insidious" (Foucault 1977b, p. 208, cited Young 1982, p. 14). Each of Young's three topics has to be assessed in relation to the prevailing tradition of post-structuralism within which his argument seeks to intervene.

Writing

The work of Derrida signals a recognition that language as typically instanced in writing is inherently polysemous, that there is always an unstoppable flow of meaning beyond any fixity in a dissemination which is potentially infinite. Thus, against J. L. Austin's *How to do things with words* (1962) Derrida's argument is that no meaning can be finalised in a 'speech act' since it is in the nature of a text as writing that it can be cited:

> Every sign, linguistic or nonlinguistic, spoken or written (in the usual sense of this opposition), as a small or large unity, can be *cited*, put between quotation marks; thereby it can break with every given context, and engender infinitely new contexts in an absolutely nonsaturable fashion. (1982, p. 320)

A 'single' intended meaning cannot saturate a text, since the text can always be reiterated beyond its 'original' context, as for example when this sentence of Derrida's is cited here. However, Derrida's assertion of the potential infinity of contexts for the sign is immediately qualified when the next sentence explains that "this does not suppose that the mark is valid outside its context, but on the contrary that there are only contexts without any center of absolute anchoring" (p. 320). The potentially absolute infinity of meaning is carefully distinguished from acknowledgment of its actual limitation in a given context of reading.

However, the influence of Derrida on Barthes, especially evident in *The pleasure of the text* (French 1973, English 1976), appeared to legitimate the view that writing *(écriture)* could be hypostasised as though it were autonomously effective. So Barthes writes in *S/Z* that it is "in fact the function of writing...to dissolve metalanguage as soon as it is constituted" (1975, p. 98), as though writing actually performed this operation 'in itself' and not in conjunction with an act of reading. It is very much this Barthesian reading of Derrida that is co-opted in Young's paper.

In Robert Young's argument the idea of the play of the signifier is privileged into an abstraction denuded of specific discursive force or specific institutional effectivity. It thus becomes liable to the criticism that a conception of *écriture* has transposed the traditionally absolutist notion of an author on to "a transcendental anonymity" raised by Foucault in his paper "What is an author?" when he asks, "In granting a primordial status to writing, do we not, in effect, simply reinscribe in transcendental terms the theological affirmation of its sacred origin or a critical belief in its creative nature?" (1977a, p. 119). Young (1982, p. 10) alludes to the paper which makes this criticism, one which had been reprinted in *Screen* in 1979. Young's intervention is set the task, therefore, of making its way upstream, establishing itself in a cultural context in which this critique would already be to hand.

That context would also have taken note of an interview with Derrida recorded in Scotland in 1980 during which Derrida unequivocally rejected a reading of his work as legitimating a dehistoricised abstraction of writing, affirming, rather, against the view that for deconstruction "any interpretation is as good as any other" the position that "some interpretations are more powerful than others" since

> Meaning is determined by a system of forces which is not personal. It does not depend on the subjective identity but on the field of different forces, the conflict of forces, which produce interpretations. (1980, p. 21; see Appendix III below for full transcript).

Metalanguage

Young's inflection of post-structuralism towards deconstruction has to struggle even harder to establish itself if writing is opposed to a generalised and undefined notion of "metalanguage" and its presumed precondition, "transparency". In the first place his own paper's untroubled adoption of a metalanguage situated beyond the ideas of the writing it treated as an object for exposition was picked up in questioning and he was forced into the conventional defence that "one cannot help but use metalanguage, a discourse on a discourse" (1982, p. 17), a version of that deconstructive heroism wittily characterised by Terry Eagleton when he notes that "at this point, the standard deconstructionist move is to mutter something about the inescapability of metaphysics, which gives your radicalism a toughly stoical edge, a no-flies-on-Charlie 'realism'" (1984b, p. 135).

Secondly, it would cut no ice with British readers of Althusser to be told there could be no theory and no metalanguage because all discourse took place on the grounds of signifier, that "belief in the possibility of a transcendent model and metalanguage was crumbling" because "language could never produce an objective discourse upon itself" (1982, p. 6). The Althusserian account of science had from the first insisted — against empiricism — that knowledge was the effect of a theoretical discourse and precisely of a process of construction. Althusser had specifically denied that the discourses of science, of theoretical practice, were transparent and had worked hard to elude just the either/or Young perpetuates — *either* wholly transparent metalanguage standing wholly outside its object *or* no science, no knowledge, no metalanguage at all. In this respect Young's position has to be identified as that of a 'wild' deconstructionist, who, like the traditional metaphysician, suspects "that unless you have the 'whole truth' you have no truth at all" (Eagleton 1986a, p. 85). He thus steps around the arguments of Hirst about knowledge though readily cites his comments on ideology (1982, p. 11).

Once again with reference to knowledge, the argument proceeds by ignoring the specificities of discourse, their social situation and ensuing effectivity, in favour of some kind of universal. It becomes possible to equate the fictional effect of metalanguage (George Eliot) with the metalanguage of a theoretical discourse (Colin MacCabe on *Middlemarch*). At this level all differences disappear: as a questioner objected at the time, "If you take an article from *Nature* about enzymes, and all you've got to say about it is that it assumes the transparency of discourse, and a position of mastery for the subject, you've said nothing" (p. 17).

The subject

Young saves his time on the question of the subject because at the same conference Ann Wordsworth gave a paper on deconstruction and the subject from a stance whose implications came out most clearly in answer to questions. In response to the presentation, printed as "Household words: alterity, the unconscious and the text" (1982, pp. 80–95), it was immediately asked, "What about ideology? What about the political?" (p. 93). This was followed by an intervention from a questioner asserting the historicity of the subject: "Lacan says explicitly that the transcendental ego emerges historically as the Renaissance. That is why it is referred to by Lacan as the Cartesian ego" (p. 94). The same intervention invoked an argument made by Stephen Heath in *Screen* (see Heath 1976, p. 62).

> You cannot privilege the subject as constructed in the dynamic of the unconscious *over* the subject of ideology, that is, the subject as constructed historically within ideology. You cannot pose one over against the other. You have to see the subject as historical and then tie in the unconscious subject; failure to do that is to confirm, for example, patriarchy as eternal. (Wordsworth 1982, p. 94)

The reply given was: "It's difficult to answer this, because there isn't a subject in deconstruction at all; there's no pure state that makes the classical notion of consciousness possible" (p. 94). The exchange is exemplary: on the one hand a claim for a historicisation of subjectivity and an affirmation of politics, on the other the familiar deconstructive manœuvre around an either/or: either the full subject in a "pure state" of consciousness or no subject at all. If there is no subject, there can be no critique of ideologically based conceptions of the subject, and no analysis of the text as providing a position for the subject.

The 1981 Southampton conference proceedings as published in the *Oxford Literary Review* and Robert Young's paper in so far as it can be treated as representative together are symptomatic of resistances to the establishment of deconstruction in Britain. The engagement with politics is well outside Marxism as when Young cites as apparently a conclusive end of the affair Foucault's comment that "Marxism exists in nineteenth century thought like a fish in water" (1982, p. 10) and refers casually in passing to "the end of the Althusserian experiment" (p. 10) in a tone which earned him a rebuke at question time for "complacency and self-satisfaction" (p. 17). But what most relegates it to the margins of the mainstream British tradition is its general effacement of politics and a sense of the historical in favour of a generalised conception of writing.

British and American deconstruction

Cut off on one side from an underpinning in Marxism, the kind of position taken in Young's paper does not on the other side find a home in the trans-Atlantic tradition. It is remarkable how far it sets itself apart from American deconstruction *au pied de la lettre* and how much it is pulled into the gravitational field of British post-structuralism. With the American model in mind Jonathan Culler in *On deconstruction* confidently defines deconstruction as follows:

> deconstruction does not elucidate texts in the traditional sense of attempting to grasp a unifying content or theme; it investigates the work of metaphysical oppositions in their arguments and the ways in which textual figures and relations, such as the play of the supplement in Rousseau, produce a double, aporetic logic. (1983, p. 109)

Culler bravely proceeds to catalogue the strategies through which deconstruction carries out its chosen task of reaching the desired cul-de-sac by producing a reading in which the meaning of a text becomes undecidable by: (a) inverting hierarchies; (b) looking "for points of condensation"; (c) being alert to forms in which the text exhibits "difference from itself"; (d) seeking out the text's self-referentiality; (e) interesting itself "in the way conflicts or dramas within the text are reproduced as conflicts in and between readings of the text" (pp. 213–14).

Culler's exposition follows de Man in the passage cited at the start of this chapter in foregrounding deconstruction as leading to an impasse in which blindness and insight interminably reverse each other. Young's introduction makes no mention of classic Derridean deconstruction, analysis of and the possible breaching of binaries, nor does it list any such strategies for exhibiting the text's division from itself. Far closer in fact to Barthes in *The pleasure of the text* than to de Man in *Allegories of reading*, "Post-structuralism: the end of theory" steps carefully aside from any notion of committed deconstructive undecidability, though it appeared elsewhere at the conference and in the papers published by the *Oxford Literary Review*, notably in the presentation by an American, Richard Rand. And Young's essay retains a commitment to politics, at least in the Parthian shaft citing Foucault at the end.

A sense of the differences between the effectivities of the two traditions of national culture emerged vividly in some British responses to Richard Rand's paper, "o'er-brimm'd" (*sic*, 1982, pp. 37–58), which took as its point of departure Keats's 'To Autumn' but did not aim to read it as a text. It provoked the following exchange:

> *Question*. I'm trying to find a question you can't make a joke of...I found your analysis interesting and entertaining, but suspected that it wasn't actually serious.
>
> *RR*. It is not serious, I promise you it is not serious.
>
> *Q*. You were concerned with language, somewhat concerned with subjectivity and the place of the unconscious, not at all concerned with ideology. On what grounds would you say that your reading was preferable to any other?
>
> *RR*. I don't regard it as preferable, but I found it very pleasurable to elaborate. I've no concern for the matter of being serious. The idea of being serious is a highly repressive one. (1982, p. 56)

Marginal and incidental as this little piece of dialogue seems, it may well discover more about the failures of deconstruction to implant itself in Britain than any of the preceding account of the content of arguments. Rand's determinedly American playfulness contrasts dramatically with the questioner's politicised British seriousness. The authority that seriousness commands descends into literary debate via Leavis from the particular British national tradition of moral seriousness and obsession with 'the real'.

Up Aporia Creek: British readings of deconstruction

Besides the weight of inherited forces, there are at least three other, more immediately conjunctural responses for the American failure to export their version of deconstruction successfully. One is — as has been the theme of this book — the fact that what brevity will phrase here as 'French ideas' had already begun to arrive in Britain with Althusser, and their radicalism had been subsumed into a re-working of Marxism. Symptomatic of this is the relatively insouciant manner that writers in *Screen* believed they could accommodate the proposals of Derrida without unsettling their general project.

A second is that Hindess and Hirst had already thrown into question a number of topics that in North America were broached by deconstruction. They had argued against any view that the social formation might be conceived as centred structure with a point of origin in the mode of production. More to the point, in the field of the theory of knowledge, their work had initiated a thorough critique of the possibility of: (1) theoretical practice as a form of absolute truth to be opposed once and for all to ideology; (2) any notion of a discourse of knowledge as a metalanguage able to escape the logic of the signifier whereby "the represented exists as an effect of a process of signification" (Hirst 1979, p.68). It was, then, one thing to introduce new questions, quite another to ask ones that seemed very like those already exhausted in debate.

These two factors help to explain why none of the writers associated with the *Screen* project responded to the challenge of Derrida's writing in anything like the same way that challenge was taken up in the American context (the final chapter will suggests how that response itself may be understood as a moment in the tradition of the national culture in the United States). But there is a third reason. The advance of deconstruction was blocked by the intervention of one writer who, partly because of a visiting Fellowship at Cornell in 1981, had fully engaged with American deconstruction: Terry Eagleton. In three separate books Eagleton savaged deconstruction, and although the books were aimed in part at an American audience, they were widely read in Britain (one in fact, *Literary theory*, has so far sold over 70,000 copies world-wide, extraordinary for a work of literary theory). Thus, ironically, British readers were throughly warned off deconstruction, often before seriously encountering its texts. An account of responses to deconstruction in England cannot ignore this negative presentation.

173

Written in a tone of baffled rage which would offer succour to his opponents, Eagleton's critique of deconstruction opens in *Walter Benjamin* (1981) with a furious denunciation culminating in a political–moral judgement perfectly in accord with the seriousness of the inherited discourse: "It is not certain that Marxists should be tolerant of this stance: in a world groaning in agony, where the very future of humankind hangs by a hair, there is something objectionably luxurious about it" (p. 140). Avoiding this tone, the mode of address in a corresponding section of *Literary theory* (1983) is more measured, stressing the internal contradictions of deconstruction. *The function of criticism* (1984a) provides the most sustainedly fluent yet coldly analytic attack, one which engages more than the others with the writings of Paul de Man and which develops an account of the subject of deconstruction that renders it the most devastating of the three.

Following on from *Blindness and insight*, notably in *Allegories of reading* (1979) de Man expanded the deconstructive rejection of 'truth' and 'metalanguage' by arguing that because of the irremediable dependence of language upon *écriture* a literary text could always be shown to undermine its own meaning, through a difference from itself analysable in terms of such binaries as logic vs. rhetoric, literal vs. metaphoric. That point at which reading grounded its insight most confidently in the text was precisely the juncture at which it was most blind to the effects and assumptions of the text making that first insight possible and so indicating the necessity for another, opposed reading. The only possible interpretation, therefore, was that which through self-conscious irony acknowledged its own aporia poised between opposed interpretations that were 'undecidable'.

Viewed synoptically, Eagleton's criticisms of this kind of theoretical position can be grouped under five headings, three pertaining to the logic of deconstruction (truth, ideology, undecidability) and two to its institutional practice as this provides a position for the subject.

1. Truth and metalanguage

For Eagleton, as mentioned already, the deconstructive version of the impossibility of knowledge rests on a false alternative, a noose you don't have to put your head into:

The model of science frequently derived by post-structuralism is usually a positivist one — some version of the nineteenth-century rationalist claim to a transcendental, value-free knowledge of 'the facts'. This model is actually a straw target. It does not exhaust the term 'science', and nothing is to be gained by this caricature of scientific self-reflection. To say that there are no absolute grounds for the use of such words as truth, certainty, reality and so on is not to say that these words lack meaning or are ineffectual. Whoever thought such absolute grounds existed, and what would they look like if they did? (1983, p. 144)

This is the apposite moment to cite Derrida's remark during question time for his paper at the Baltimore conference: "I believe in the necessity of scientific work in the classical sense" (Macksey and Donato 1970, p. 271).

2. Ideology

Eagleton points out that "ideology for the Yale school would seem in the first place to signify fascism and Stalinism" and that to treat these as "prototypes of the ideological is drastically reductive and essentialist" (1984a, p. 101). Though given little prominence in deconstruction, the concept of ideology is mentioned by de Man when he writes that "what we call ideology is precisely the confusion of linguistic with natural reality, of reference with phenomenalism" (1986, p. 11). Mirror image of the essentialist definition of *écriture* noted earlier in Robert Young, this conceptualisation reproduces a simple binary opposition "between 'ideology' — conceived as relentlessly closed and seamlessly self-identicial — and *écriture*" (Eagleton 1984a, p. 102), an opposition deconstruction has failed to dismantle.

3. Undecidability

It is only by seeking to excise the literary text from the discursive practices and social institutions within which, and only within which, its potential meanings are realised, that deconstruction can claim undecidability as the defining characteristic of the text. Here Eagleton recalls Saussure's foundational arguments that the relation between signifier and signified, by nature arbitrary, make up a completed sign in the social fact of language:

Meaning may well be ultimately undecidable if we view language contemplatively, as a chain of signifiers on a page; it becomes 'decidable', and words like 'truth', 'reality', 'knowledge' and 'certainty' have something of their force restored to them, when we think of language rather as something we *do*, as indissociably interwoven with our practical forms of life. (1983, p. 147)

On this Eagleton is closer to Derrida than is deconstruction. In the *Literary Review* interview Derrida answers the question, "How does one decide that certain terms are 'undecidable'?" by denying it is a matter of individual decision but rather one of the "historical and theoretical situations" in which some terms "can appear to have this indeterminacy" and then only for a reader similarly inscribed in the situation (see Appendix III).

"There cannot be a universal object named literature", Eagleton argues following Lentricchia on de Man, yet for American deconstruction "rhetorical 'undecidability' is the essence of all literature" (1986a, 54). Attention must therefore be refocused on the practices and institutions as these act to determine meaning. And the path is opened to a political deconstruction of the academic and institutional site of deconstruction.

4. Institution

For Eagleton history defines deconstruction as a contradictory moment in which its "disownment of authority is plainly in line with the politics of the '60s" (1984a, p. 102), serving a generation who lived through the counter-culture, while at the same time it is recuperated within the prevailing discursive and institutional matrix. Deconstruction is thus kept "alive by what contaminates it" (1981, p. 137), a movement of ceaseless disavowal of the given on which it depends, one which unwittingly and so the more effectively provides space for the reproduction of existing structures: practical criticism; literature; the academy. The "deconstructive gesture" must be performed again and again, interminably, so promising the literary critic that it will "keep you in a job indefinitely" (1984a, p. 105); since the apparent self-reflexiveness of literature gives it a privilege over lesser discourses (film, television, etc.), deconstruction rejoins conventional literary studies in affirming "the centrality of literature", this becoming in fact "the centre from which all centring is denounced" (p. 104); and these combined ensure "the interminable reproduction of the academy" (p. 105). In sum, it is this discursive and institutional practice which, in Eagleton's most recent and incisive critique, offers an identity and position of security to the subject of deconstruction.

5. *The subject of deconstruction*

As recuperation works in the practices of deconstruction, so denegation inscribes its subject, for deconstruction constitutes "a liberalism without a subject" (1981, p. 138 and again 1984a, pp. 98–9). It would be a mistake to suppose that classical liberalism ascribed only to the subject as unified and apparently self-sufficient — it always confronted the subject in its divisions, was "racked by a conflict between the autonomy of the self and its plurality" (p. 99), between supposedly transcendent selfhood and the social constitution of the self in and through ideology (Eagleton might well have instanced the fourteen books of Wordsworth's *Prelude* though he doesn't.) Recognising that "the humanist doctrine of autonomy is increasingly implausible", deconstruction sought to retain a space for the liberal subject by foregrounding its plurality, its evanescence, its *loss*:

> Ideological closure can no longer be opposed by the free, positive self-fulfilments of the individual; but it might be countered instead by the more negative free play of the signifier, which can escape the deathly embrace of some terroristic meaning exactly as the liberal self once hopelessly believed it might do. (1984a, p. 99)

The discursive mechanisms guaranteeing this manœuvre are the effect of pathos, the tone of stoicism and the dramatisation of self-consciousness.

Here the British inflection of deconstruction comes closest to its trans-Atlantic precedents. The subject is "always a fading thing that runs under the chain of signifiers" (Lacan cited Young 1982, p. 12); "there isn't a subject in deconstruction at all" (Wordsworth 1982, p. 94). Constitutive lack in the subject can pass itself off as pathos for the loss of the full subject, a pathos in turn covered by a fully traditional stoicism — which is why Eagleton's quip about radicalism with "a toughly stoical edge, a no-flies-on-Charlie 'realism'" (1984b, p. 135) is much more than a quip. For this reason deconstruction "reproduces a blending of bleakness and euphoria, affirmation and resignation, characteristic of the liberal humanist tradition" (1984a, p. 99) and hence "deconstruction's dual sensibility, at once stoically conformed to the ineluctability of metaphysics and enraptured by a *jouissance* or *mise-en-abyme* which promises to shatter that whole enclosure" (pp. 99–100).

The process of disavowal by which the self's self-conscious self-reference seeks to make good its actual constitutedness is explicit in de Man: traditional liberalism is torn between "an empirical self that exists in a state of inauthenticity and a self that exists only in the form of a language that asserts the knowledge of this inauthenticity" (1983, p. 214, cited Eagleton 1984a, p. 100). De Man correctly perceives that "the only authentic bourgeois subject is the one who recognises that transcendence is a myth" but fails to see that the subject of deconstruction, "wryly conscious of its own inescapable complicity with what it views", reinstates in a plausibly contemporary form the "familiar image of the bourgeois liberal...crippled, marginalised, self-ironising" (p. 100).

(Eagleton mentions T. S. Eliot, Henry James, E. M. Forster but his remarks envisage an extended critique of the liberal subject. Such a critique would pick up Catherine Belsey's discussion of the subject in Locke citing the elegiac tone in which Locke writes of the certainty that "we have in us something that thinks" but takes the "very doubts about what it is" to "confirm the certainty of its being" (1985, p. 84). From the first, nothing can dispel "the solitude and uncertainty that haunt the humanist subject" (p. 92), nothing that is but the rhetorical strategy of seeking to recuperate the impossibility of the full subject as *pathos*.)

What gives such force to Eagleton's third critique is that, in addition to evidencing the social practice of deconstruction through a not untraditional Marxist sociology of knowledge, it is now able to get inside the deconstructive process and define the subject of deconstruction inscribed by the denegations of its discursive practice. His analysis is prepared to do so by the readiness with which it can draw on the British strand of post-structuralism which, as has been argued throughout, takes as its point of departure Althusser's essay on ideology. It is then no accident, as they say, that it is precisely Althusser's theoretical intervention to the effect that the subject is constituted to misrecognise itself as constitutive which is most scrupulously omitted from the otherwise admirably comprehensive and pluralist reading list of American deconstruction.

The return of the repressed?

American deconstruction, as urged for example by J. Hillis Miller in his essay, "The critic as host" (1977), likes to see itself as a parasite which invades a body and takes it over from within. A violent desire to expel certainly looks like a symptom of the disease in the case of Eagleton's first polemic against deconstruction or the Southampton questioner's McEnroe-like cry to Richard Rand, "You cannot be serious." But after this initial reaction British Marxists and post-structuralists have tended to graft deconstruction to the parent stock, incorporating it in the way Eagleton foresaw when he wrote that "deconstruction, as a particular set of textual procedures, can operate as a radical force is surely undeniable" (1981, p. 140). However, it has been the deconstruction of Derrida, particularly his analysis of binary oppositions and of the significance of difference, which has been brought in, not the American revisions.

It was fairly predictable that in the struggle to refound literary studies Shakespeare and Renaissance literature should become a main arena for contestation since it represents the hegemonic centre of conventional literary criticism. Criticism of Elizabethan literature has been occupied by a body of work which may best be named as that of the British Renaissance Foucauldians, this including Barker (1984), Dollimore (1984), Drakakis (1985), Dollimore and Sinfield (1985), as well as Stallybrass and White (1986). Strongly influenced by the work of Stephen Greenblatt, this critical writing can be characterised as Marxist except that it brackets mode of production as real centre of the social and discursive formation, yet as post-structuralist on the British model in its concern with the subject as a subject of discourse constituted in a subjectivity that is ineradicably historical. To represent this area and to measure any change of position since *Critical practice*, one text has been selected, Catherine Belsey's *The subject of tragedy* (1985). Renaissance criticism was also chosen as the point of intervention for Eagleton's book on Shakespeare (1986b), which will be reviewed first to assess how and in what ways a writer so expressively opposed to deconstruction has in fact come to live with it.

Starting with an analysis of *Macbeth* (pp. 2–4) Eagleton's *William Shakespeare* (1986b) opens with one of the most polemic affirmations in literary criticism: "The witches are the heroines of the piece, however little the play recognises the fact, and however

179

much the critics may have set out to defame them." That's clear enough. In comparison with "a society based on routine oppression and incessant warfare" (Macbeth's Scotland? bourgeois society since the Renaissance? twentieth-century Western society under the nuclear threat?) the witches' chosen place on the outside and at the margin, for all its seeming obscenity, is a better one.

But this "sisterly community" is not just separatist, a space or enclave hollowed out at a distance from the butchery of a "hierarchical social order". Their difference comes to infiltrate and undermine Macbeth from within:

> The witches signify a realm of non-meaning and poetic play which hovers at the work's margins, one which has its own kind of truth; and their words to Macbeth catalyse this region of otherness and desire within himself, so that by the end of the play it has flooded up from within him to shatter and engulf his previously assured identity. In this sense the witches figure as the 'unconscious' of the drama, that which must be exiled and repressed as dangerous but which is always likely to return with a vengeance. That unconscious is a discourse in which meaning falters and slides, in which firm definitions are dissolved and binary oppositions eroded: fair is foul and foul is fair, nothing is but what is not. (p. 2)

Three distinct but overlapping theoretical frameworks are superimposed here. One is Macherey's Marxist theory according to which the assured, 'official' meaning of a text, what *Macbeth* recognises about itself, depends on the ideological contradictions from which it is produced being effaced into a sense of unity. A second is Lacan's psychoanalytic account of how the signifier and linguistic difference operate in a way analogous to gender and sexual difference, the witches opening up desire in Macbeth's previously enclosed selfhood and manhood. And a third is Derrida's constant demonstration that the materiality or 'graphematic' feature of the signifier always leads to a play of meaning which exceeds any fixity imposed upon it.

The society of the play tries to maintain itself by privileging the left-hand term of three sets of oppositions that can be set out as follows:

    hierarchical social order/the witches
    military/sisterly
    centre/margins

These are the political and ideological binaries. Then:

    conscious/unconscious
    being/lack
    self/other

These psychoanalytic oppositions pertain to the subject and especially the figure of Macbeth. Thirdly:

    signified/signifier
    meaning/non-meaning, play
    fixity/dissemination

The analysis via binaries is thoroughly Derridean. But for the witches "'Fair is foul'": in the world of the play "foulness — a political order which thrives on bloodshed — believes itself fair, whereas the witches do not so much invert this opposition as deconstruct it". The witches may (or may not) subvert these binaries, but, crucially, does this *reading* of the play in affirming the denigrated right-hand term, deconstruct or invert the binaries it analyses?

Does Eagleton's reading of *Macbeth* show that, as Macbeth is undermined by the witches, the former castigator of deconstruction has now been infiltrated by it? No, it does not, for it is grounded in a Marxist problematic rather than one of Derridean deconstruction. With regard to the processing of hierarchised binaries Derrida firmly discriminates between inversion and deconstruction: inversion reverses the two terms from the outside (and so retains the hierarchic structure though changes its content), deconstruction aims to inhabit them and undo them from within, relativising each in relation to the other (see 1976, p. 24, and 1981a, p. 42). Although it is argued that the witches operate within the world of the play to deconstruct the oppositions on which it is founded, Eagleton's *Macbeth* is not a deconstructive reading because it does not hesitate to privilege the previously subordinated term: the witches ("radical separatists who scorn male power") are resoundingly endorsed.

Far from being surreptitiously won over by it, Eagleton's Marxist–feminist reading deliberately engages with deconstruction in order to turn it (as a spy is turned) for radical political purposes, as is quite clear by the end of the book. Seeking to integrate linguistic and psychoanalytic accounts, along with a Foucauldian recognition of the body as always exceeding its representations, into a thoroughly historical perspective, the conclusion is that Shakespeare's dramatic allegory hopes to imagine how the energies of discourse and the body released in the new bourgeois order may yet be synthesised with the inherited structures of social order into "a fruitful reconciliation between capitalism and feudalism" (p. 99). *Shakespeare* is excitingly suggestive and a major threat to the conservative sentimentality of conventional Shakespearianism; but arguably it is a reading limited by what might be called its 'contentism', its brusque effacement of textuality in favour of signified meaning, a limitation which it would elude if it gave more attention to the specificity of the plays as forms of signifying practice (drama) and what particular position they might offer to the reader — and their audience. It also has the effect of leaving Shakespeare in his place in the literary canon. Such reservations could not be entered against Belsey's new text; nor, in working with deconstruction, does it lose its political effect.

Critical practice six years on

Catherine Belsey's *The subject of tragedy* (1985) (subtitled "Identity and difference in Renaissance drama"), like Eagleton's *Shakespeare*, represents a second wave in British post-structuralist writing on literature. While the first was concerned with theory in general, this second aims for theory realised, to intervene by working out new theoretical understanding in a practice of 're-reading' literature (the title of the 'New Accents' text edited by Peter Widdowson in 1982 and adopted by the series of literary criticism Terry Eagleton now edits for Blackwell). In this spirit *The subject of tragedy* promises to move on into cultural studies, cultural history. That is immediately signalled in its own discourse, no longer so abstractly Althusserian but now more concretely engaged, always wittily lucid, always most sweetly reasonable when its assertions are most radical. Since concern here is with the theoretical underpinnings and the qualities of their difference from those of *Critical practice* (1980) details of the analysis of Renaissance drama will be outlined schematically.

When Lacan, in a typically uncitable dependent phrase, refers to "the beginning of the seventeenth century, in that inaugural moment of the subject..." (1977b, p. 223), he must mean that it was the (bourgeois) humanist would-be transcendental subject, and especially the Cartesian subject, which emerged at the beginning of the seventeenth century (see Venn's account of the birth of the bourgeois subject discussed in Chapter 7). After illustrating from Renaissance drama the dramatic and rhetorical strategies by which the supposedly self-originating subject seeks to establish itself, *The subject of tragedy* contrasts the feudal and bourgeois subjects. Or rather, the subjects of "discursive" and "empirical" knowledge. Both define themselves in a subject/object relation.

Thus while the discursive (or late feudal) subject seeks to be at one with its object — God, Logos, truth, being, the transcendental signified — "absorbed in total presence" (p. 56) in a relation for which knowledge is not instrumental but constitutive, "a condition of being" (p. 58), the new (bourgeois) empirical subject in contrast emerges in

> a difference between the knowing subject and the objects of its knowledge, and this difference becomes definitive for the subject. The subject is now defined as that which knows, in contradistinction to that which is known...The subject consequently takes the place of God and becomes the author and guarantee of its own (subjective) truth. (p. 65)

On this basis Belsey's text argues the impossibility of either construction of the subject: the discursive subject since "absolute presence, eliminating difference, is precisely the dissolution of the subject" (p. 59); and the empirical subject since (the subject/object relation itself being reconstituted as subjectivity) *either* the objects of its knowledge, its experience, *or* the knowing subject itself must be construed as constitutive, in which case "the problem presents itself of what precisely it is that does the reflecting and contemplating" (p. 85).

From this point *The subject of tragedy* goes on to show how the empirical subject endeavoured, in the seventeenth century, to resolve the dilemma posed for its own self-validating authority as bearer of knowledge by relying on an institutional establishment of knowledges in the social order — only to find its sovereignty in that wished-for relation undercut by contradictions within the social order itself: absolutism, supposed to guarantee the sovereign subject, in fact came rapidly to deny it. And so also did the attempt to impose sovereignty in the domain of gender and of sexuality.

In this arena, so it is proposed, the project of the empirical subject, working with different strategies in different historical periods, necessarily produces two insurmountable kinds of resistance. At first the absolutist version of marriage sought to instate women as "objects of exchange and the guarantee of dynastic continuity" (p. 192) but managed thus only to assign them subject-positions (in the oppositions father/mother, husband/wife, parent/child) which "cannot be held simultaneously without contradiction" (p. 155), so denying women a single position in which they too might identify themselves as empirical subjects. Subsequently, the development of the affective family and the liberal version of marriage as a free exercise of choice between autonomous subjects came up against the contradiction so tersely exposed by Mary Astell in *Some reflections upon marriage* (1700): "If *all men are born free*, how is it that all women are born slaves?" (cited Belsey 1986, p. 218).

It was argued (above, pp. 145–6) that *Critical practice* hovered between two possibilities, one an Althusserian problematic in which texts are determined by their place in the real, 'in the last instance' by economic practice, another radically post-structuralist, in which they are read in an unceasing present. *The subject of tragedy* lands firmly on the side of Foucault. The real is bracketed, and the concept of mode of production as the (ultimately) real centre of the social formation is surrendered in favour of the Foucauldian conception of power as omnipresent, dispersed unevenly across the discursive and social practices within which the subject is constituted, especially in discursive modes which deploy power by exercising knowledge. Accordingly, in *The subject of tragedy* mode of production is seen to do no more than exert pressure as when the Tudor and Stuart monarchy acts "under pressure from an emergent mode of production" (p. 93). In the book's account of the social and discursive formation as a decentred structure in dominance, 'in dominance' now appears only under erasure (this manœuvre itself is symptomatic of a deeper theoretical revision of the base/superstructure model affecting much more than this particular example of British post-structuralism and will be taken up explicitly in the concluding argument).

Whereas *Critical practice* trusted in the Althusserian account of how ideological practice interpellated the subject as means to analyse texts in terms of the position they offered to the subject, in *The subject of tragedy* subjectivity itself, as defined both in discursive and social practices, becomes the central term for analysis:

> The destination of meaning is the subject. To be a subject is to have access to signifying practice...held in place in a specific discourse, a specific knowledge, by the meanings available there...Subjectivity is discursively produced and is constrained by the range of subject-positions defined by the discourses in which the concrete individual participates. (p. 5)

Notably, the impress of the writings of Foucault catches up and reinforces modes of analysis of texts developed by the work of *Screen*. Such is evident in the mobilisation of the concepts of signifying practice and indeed of subject-position itself (there are issues here regarding the relation between the Althusserian problematic and the work of Foucault which will be returned to). And the *Screen* problematic also resurfaces in the way Belsey's work blocks the question of the interminable dissemination of meaning by distinguishing between actual and implied positions and claiming only that "A specific text *proffers* [my italics] a specific subject-position from which it is most readily intelligible" (p. 6).

Undeniable gains ensuing from this re-worked theoretical framework can be summarised as follows:

(1) The Foucauldian account of subjectivity allows any discontinuities between textuality and social formation, discursive and social practices, to be crossed with ease (hence the powerfully developed historical contrast between the 'discursive' and 'empirical' subjects).

(2) And this enables *The subject of tragedy* to move between an account of the social formation (under absolutism) and analysis of relations of gender (otherwise notoriously resistant to theorisation in terms of 'social roles' derived from 'mode of production').

(3) While constantly indicating their points of interaction, *The subject of tragedy* conspicuously refuses to prioritise among the diversity of discursive and social practices it discusses, between seventeenth-century family structures and the work of John Locke,

between *Hamlet* and *Arden of Faversham*, between soliloquy, theatre design and the tradition of family portrait painting.

(4) So the conventionally instituted boundary between high cultural 'Literature' and the texts of popular culture is deliberately breached, and this situates the book within left deconstruction, the struggle for the death of literature.

(5) Nevertheless, through the concept of the positioning of the subject, a real sense of the specificity of (literary) textuality is retained throughout.

(6) Finally, Belsey's revised theorisation gives a better reflection on its own epistemological status.

In the earlier text, knowledge is able "to produce a real knowledge of history" (Belsey 1980, p. 136), though, it was argued here, the text presents itself less as giving a knowledge of history than as an intervention to produce politically progressive readings. In *The subject of tragedy* knowledge, specifically as the self-ascribed knowledge of the empirical subject, is construed only as a form of power, in terms of its discursive effectivity. From "written texts we produce a knowledge of a world which is no longer present. And yet it is always from the present that we produce this knowledge" (p. 1). And Belsey's own text does not advance itself as a form of knowledge of history but unequivocally as an intervention in which empirical accuracy is claimed only as a discursive effect. History is what we make it.

Foucault but even more so, and at a deeper level, Derrida. It is significant that the index of a text which claims an alignment with Marxism should have twenty entries for "difference" and for "dialectic" zero. Difference grounds historical change, for to imagine the conditions of a past century as the same as ours would be "to eliminate difference" (p. 2). Difference is of course also language for "the space between signifier and signified" is "the place of difference" (p. 64). In *The subject of tragedy* the subject is understood not in psychoanalytic terms (these are fiercely ejected on pp. 53–4, "a chimera") but in terms of difference. The subject is "always other than itself" (p. 52) because it is a speaking subject and "meaning is perpetually deferred by its existence as difference within a specific discourse; it is perpetually displaced by the trace of alterity within the identity which is no more than an effect of difference" (p. 6).

Difference has also (and this is a markedly original turn in literary criticism) an application in logic since British Renaissance rationalism sought "to fix difference as antithesis" (p. 94), to restrict imaginable possibilities to oppositions, so helping to institute an ideological formation operating "a series of oppositions between the individual and society, private and public, family and state, in which the first is always understood to be threatened by the encroachment of the second" (p. 199). And difference as sexual difference presents itself comprehensively as the patriarchal project of eliding difference into the binary opposition by which "women are defined by their difference from men" (p. 148), a project which guarantees resistance, and has produced it historically, as Belsey shows from a wide range of women's writing. *The subject of tragedy*, then, aims to undo the eternally repeated sameness of liberal humanism in the name of difference.

British post-structuralism and deconstruction

Introduced as far back as 1964 by Lacan (see 1977b, p. 161) the term 'deconstruction' has come to carry several different meanings. In this and the previous chapter on "Literary theory" it has been used in five ways:

(1) A criticism designed to challenge the realist mode in which a text aims to naturalise itself by demonstrating its actual constructedness, to exhibit the means of representation by which the represented is brought about ("The object of deconstructing the text is to examine the *process of its production*", Belsey 1980, p. 104; "in deconstructing the tenets of perceptualism what analysis begins to see...is a shadowy activity *behind* the image, manipulation of the sign as plastic substance", Bryson 1983, p. 130).

(2) Deconstruction in a Foucauldian context, a procedure for revealing the inter-discursive dependencies of a discourse (see Chapter 7).

(3) Deconstruction in the sense of 'left deconstruction': the project of annihilating the category of 'Literature' by uncovering the discursive and institutional practices which uphold it.

(4) American deconstruction: the set of procedures and critical practices deriving mainly from the Paul de Man's reading of Derrida which aims to discover how a text always differs from itself in a critical reading whose own text, through self-reflexive irony, aims towards a similar undecidability and aporia.

(5) Derridean deconstruction: a critical analysis of inherited binary oppositions in which a left-hand term claims privilege through its denigration of the right-hand term on which it depends, the analysis aiming not to reverse the values of the opposition but rather to breach or undo them by relativising their relation.

British post-structuralism, for reasons discussed in relation to the *Oxford Literary Review* and its Southampton conference of 1981, has remained largely uninterested in deconstruction in definition (4), American deconstruction. An existing theoretical situation already grounded in a critique of the subject, a recognition of the insistence of the signifier and an awareness of the 'debate over epistemology' was unlikely territory for any such colonisation. Nevertheless, in different ways in different writings the post-structuralist enterprise in Britain has sought to mobilise, for the purposes of its avowedly political and frequently Marxist project, deconstruction in definitions (1), (3) and especially (5). Of this Eagleton's *Shakespeare* and Belsey's book on Renaissance literature are sufficient evidence.

Having reached close to the concerns of contemporary debates — what natural scientists call 'the state of the art' — it is appropriate to open some consequent questions. The first, once again, must be the issue of base and superstructure, the problem of social and economic determination. Under the banner of Foucault *The subject of tragedy* confidently reaches across between social practices (the legal institution of marriage in the seventeenth century, the political power of monarchic absolutism) and specifically textual or signifying practices (Shakespeare's *Hamlet*, family portraiture). The question here must be an old Althusserian one. For the risk is that, claiming to bracket the real with a new sanction from that undeniably abstracted concept, "power", everything can go on as before, as it did in the historical writing of Edward Thompson and indeed in the social history of Trevelyan. The content of Belsey's history is certainly different but is it a different kind of history?

If the decentred structure in dominance is now to be understood as a decentred structure in which the source of power is everywhere, there must be a new danger of historicism. Historicism is best defined as a conception of time as linear, homogeneous and thus susceptible to essential section in the sense that the whole of a given social formation is present at any moment. In this case the notion of power may function as an absent centre for a revived view of the social formation as an expressive totality: the 'specific effectivity' of different levels of discourse and practice, each acting in their *peculiar time*, may be overlooked. Can the time of patriarchy be so easily assimilated to the time of political sovereignty? Can the time of the Foucauldian subject as relay and resistance in the circulation of power be held comfortably in place with the time of the psychoanalytic subject, the time, that is, of the unconscious and desire? It may be more than an aberration in *The subject of tragedy* that the subject of psychoanalysis is so expressly hustled out of the theatre of history.

This question of totalising leads inevitably to another: how far can the meaning of a text be understood as an historical meaning without reduction? It is a topic very much at issue between, on the one hand, American deconstruction with its readiness to approach the text ahistorically and atemporally in a (disavowed) relation to the reader as its subject correspondingly posed as beyond history and time, and on the other hand the constantly presumed necessity within British post-structuralism to give priority to historical meaning. It may be enough here to allude to that extraordinarily entangled Parisian debate (charged too with the endless negotiation of fathers and sons) between Derrida and Foucault recorded as "Cogito and the history of madness" (Derrida 1978, pp. 31–63) and partly translated into English as "My body, this paper, this fire" (Foucault 1979, pp. 9–28). Foucault argues that the meaning of a passage in Descartes has an historical meaning to be understood in relation to the seventeenth century; Derrida replies that it must mean more than this. If we accept that they are both right, what follows?

A response cannot adequately be made on theoretical grounds alone. It must also take into account the context of the debate, the field of forces within which it comes to issue. In this respect the differences between American deconstruction and the attempted incorporation of Derridean deconstruction into British post-structuralism must be grasped in relation to different national cultures, or rather international ones, since here the British tradition finds its place as European.

Within the British left inheritance, whether represented by the Marxism of Eagleton or the post-structuralism of the writers of *Changing the subject*, Bryson, Durant, Belsey (but *not* Hindess and Hirst for whom history exists only "in the modality of its current existence, its representations", 1975, p. 309), it is an almost automatic and uninterrogated assumption that a sense of the historicity of meaning, however defined, must come first. And, appropriately qualified, this is the position of Derrida when he says:

> Meaning is determined by a system of forces which is not personal. It does not depend on the subjective identity but on the field of different forces, the conflict of forces, which produce interpretations...one cannot read without trying to reconstruct the historical context but history is not the last word, the final key, or reading. (See Appendix III, p. 238 below)

Work in England following the post-structuralist trajectory generally proceeds on the basis that history is a text but not just a text, for it is both what hurts and helps. But that assumption itself is no exception to the rule it specifies if what makes it is itself a history, as it were, behind our backs, the field of forces within which a set of concepts (a critique, a problematic) has been appropriated into different national cultures. These must now be interrogated in an attempt to understand the Englishness of 'British post-structuralism'.

13
Post-structuralism and the English Tradition

My Englishness is my very vision.

D.H. Lawrence

The tradition of all the dead generations weighs
like a nightmare on the brain of the living.

Karl Marx

The concluding chapter in Freud's *New introductory lectures* reveals him as a reader of Marx's *Critique of political economy* (1859) but not of *The Eighteenth Brumaire of Louis Bonaparte* (1852), from which the epigraph to this concluding section is chosen. It is ironic therefore that Freud should announce as a main limitation of the Marxist theory of base and superstructure its failure to recognise that "the past, the tradition of the race and of the people, lives on in the ideologies of the super-ego, and yields only slowly to the influences of the present and to new changes" (1975, p. 99).

Nairn's nationalism

Since the development of the modern nation state at the beginning of the capitalist epoch a conscious and unconscious reproduction of the national culture has been one of the most powerful, insidious and damaging ways dead generations have lived on in the present. Yet the bibliography on nationalism amounts to no more than a shelf of books, and most of them no more than a few theoretical gestures rapidly sliding into descriptive histories of particular nation-states. One remarkable exception to this, Tom Nairn's *The break-up of Britain* (1977), a committedly Marxist analysis, starts its concluding chapter by admitting that "the theory of nationalism represents Marxism's great historical failure" (p. 329), though it does so with some confidence it can repair that failure.

On national cultures there is still less, despite the essay by Anderson discussed earlier (Chapter 2). Yet this remains a crucial area for future work: once the logocentrist fantasy that rational consciousness is universally present to its objects without mediation is rejected (and post-structuralism is not alone in rejecting it) attention must be directed at the field of forces in which 'ideas' are appropriated and take on effectivity. Although the present study is committed necessarily to commenting on the specific tradition in which 'post-structuralism' becomes 'British', what follows here can expect only to open up some possible lines of thought.

Nairn discusses nationalism with reference to the nation state defined in terms of a national market and national law. What needs to be explained in nationalism is the co-presence of 'white' and 'black' nationalism, that on the one hand it appears as "a good thing" (1977, p. 331) as in the Vietnamese struggle for independence, on the other, as in the case of Nazism, as soaked in the worst excesses of barbarism and irrationalism. Nairn argues that nationalism must be understood in terms of the contradictions of capitalism's 'uneven development', development that is uneven between capital and labour, imperial power and colony, nation and competing nation, centre and periphery.

Nationalism therefore is constituted in a double movement, simultaneously compelled to look back to some irrationally conceived national identity or tradition which it can use as sanction and legitimation for reaching forward to take over for itself the most modern, 'socially necessary' forms of production:

> nationalism can in this sense be pictured as like the old Roman god, Janus, who stood above gateways with one face looking forward and one backwards. Thus does nationalism stand over the passage to modernity, for human society. As human kind is forced through its strait doorway, it must look desperately back into the past, to gather strength wherever it can be found for the ordeal of 'development'. (pp. 348–9)

Beginning at the margins, in the colonies, this mode of nationalism is then reproduced back at the imperial centre which thus becomes no less engaged in the same two-edged structure.

A national culture consists of many layers between 'concrete' and 'abstract', between the wide range of social practices in which it is reproduced (annual national days, flag-flying, phallic totems such as presidents and monarchs) and the discursive and ideological forms in which it is constantly reshaped and reactivated, between, that is, practices in which signification is not dominant and those in which it is. These latter will be the main object of attention here. And it would follow from Nairn's analysis that a national culture will be correspondingly two-faced, with one side turned outwards to conscious appropriation of the new but appropriation only on the unconscious condition that the new can be silently stitched into the old. Tradition in this respect will operate most strongly because it works behind the backs of its participants.

England/France

Because, as a central instance of nationalism, the tradition of a national culture is similarly two-faced, always harking back to a naturalised account of its origin in order to confront and integrate the new, the defining characteristics of a national culture are determined — though not fixed — in its founding moment, that is, by the particular conditions in which the economy of a nation state and its political structure break with feudalism and an *ancien régime* (or in the case of developing countries, a particular imperialism). For Marx and Engels in *The German ideology* this becomes a basis on which to approach differences between the two otherwise similar national cultures divided by the Channel, the well-known contrast between the English empiricist and the French rationalist traditions.

It is theorised that those differences derived from their contrasted experiences of 'the bourgeois revolution', England in the English Revolution of 1642–60, France in 1789 and after. Hobbes and Locke, founders of the English tradition, "had before their eyes both the earlier development of the Dutch bourgeoisies...and the first political actions by which the English bourgeoisie emerged from local and provincial limitations" (Marx and Engels, 1970, p. 111); Helvétius and Holbach (singled out to represent French Enlightenment philosophy) were confronted not only by English theory — and earlier practice — but by a French bourgeoisie "which was still struggling for its free development" (p. 111). Hence, it is proposed, "the theory which for the English still was simply the registration of a fact becomes for the French a philosophical system" (p. 112), and this difference between historical achievement and aspiration, between fact and system, goes some way to explain the operation of an empiricist as against a rationalist tradition.

Lacan sets out to attack the French inheritance of Cartesian rationalism in rewriting "I think therefore I am" as "I think where I am not, therefore I am where I do not think" (1977a, p. 166), and post-structuralism has had a particular effectivity against that inheritance, as Terry Eagleton has pointed out: France is a society "whose ruling ideologies drew freely upon a metaphysical rationalism incarnate in the rigidly hierarchical, authoritarian nature of its academic institutions" and so in this context "the Derridean project of dismantling binary oppositions and subverting the transcendental signifier had a radical potential relevance" (1984a, p. 98). But it would take the argument well beyond its limits here to go any further down this road on which appears the question of how far post-structuralism in France challenges that national culture. Instead the concern will be rather with the English tradition as this begins to become visible through a contrast with American national culture (the tradition, that is, of the country, since the United States has been able to co-opt the name of a continent for itself).

"We are the World"

For Marx and Engels, writing in 1846, "the most perfect example of the modern State is North America" (1970, p. 80) because it had most completely escaped feudalism and any *ancien régime* with the foundation of the most thoroughly and homogeneously bourgeois society in the world. And this is just the point of analysis picked up by Louis Hartz in *The liberal tradition in America* (1955), which begins a very suggestive account by noting that it is precisely because the United States lacked a feudal tradition to rebel against, an *ancien régime* able to inspire both Rousseau and Marx, that the United States "lacks a genuine revolutionary tradition" (p. 5). Hence the difference for Hartz between Locke in the British tradition and Locke in America: whereas in the former Locke's foundational liberal arguments define themselves in opposition to the aristocratic, residually feudal position of the royalist, Robert Filmer, in the latter Locke rules alone, a consequence Hartz indicates by saying:

> There has never been a 'liberal movement' or a real 'liberal party'in America: we have only had the American Way of Life, a nationalist articulation of Locke which usually does not know that Locke himself is involved. (p. 11)

Accordingly for Hartz, who is writing under the conditions of McCarthyism and what he terms "redscare" (p. 13), there is in the American liberal tradition a "danger of unanimity" (p. 11), for it functions without "that sense of relativity, that spark of philosophy which European liberalism can acquire through an internal experience of social diversity and social conflict" (p. 14).

There could hardly be a better example of national culture as a field of forces in which the 'same' ideas take on different weight and value than Hartz's contrast between the American and British Lockes, that is, bodies of writing identical at the level of content but, if Hartz is correct, very different in meaning and effect. However, this is not the reason why Hartz is introduced here but rather because his text has been re-launched through a re-reading by Samuel Weber (1983), one which is valuable in the degree to which it goes well beyond the letter of what Hartz wrote in 1955.

Hartz through Weber directs attention at three main effects through which American national culture structurally reproduces itself. Firstly, it universalises. Because of its separation from the struggle between conservative and radical interests perpetuated in the European tradition, the United States tradition "came to hypostasise itself as an absolute, a tendency that was reinforced both by the universalist and naturalist character of liberalist categories and values...and by the real absence of a strong, prebourgeois ('feudal') social tradition in the New World" (Weber 1983, p. 248). Hence, the peculiar difficulty American national culture experiences in responding to any form of cultural or regional difference except by transmuting it into a version of what Hartz calls simply 'the American Way of Life'.

Secondly, and correlative to this static universalisation, the American (liberal) tradition acts to define and delimit conflict, ethical, epistemological, political, under a certain mode. It is not so much that it excludes conflict as that "it delegitimates conflict, in the name of pluralism" (p. 249). Thus

> pluralism allows for a multiplicity of coexisting, even competing interpretations, opinions or approaches; what it does not allow is for the space in which the interpretations are held to take place to be itself considered conflictual. (p. 249)

That space Weber names as "the institution", by which he does not mean only social institutions but rather the discursive practices and discursive formations they promote.

On this showing, then, American national culture functions to transform discursive conflict (conflict between as well as conflict within) by re-presenting it in the mode of a merely *personal* interpretation, another competing expression of autonomous subjectivity rather than of social contradiction — in sum, to reduce social being to the form of consciousness. The Hartz/Weber thesis can immediately be put to work — and evidenced — if it is applied to the American re-working of post-structuralist theory into deconstruction.

The Americanness of deconstruction

The writings of Derrida, Lacan, Foucault and others (but *not* Althusser) were transformed when they were imported into the United States. Their work, suggests Weber, has been subject to universalisation, become "purged of its conflictual and strategic elements and presented instead as a self-standing methodology" (1983, p. 249).

To institutionalise the manœuvre of denying the possibility of absolute metalanguage and knowledge of truth (even while it is repeated in the abstracted and generalised terms of 'truth' and 'metalanguage'), however threatening in local instances, can be seen to be correspond to a deep strand in American national culture, appropriated by it rather than challenging it. "Every natural fact is a symbol of some spiritual fact" (Emerson 1950, p. 15): in so far as the transcendentalism of the famous essay on 'Nature' typifies American tradition, deconstruction took to the post-structuralist bracketing of the real like a duck to water. On this basis and with aid from the inherited tendency to iron out discursive conflict it became possible to hypostasise the specific effectivities of different discourses into an entropic uniformity — the universe of discourse (and only discourse). And on this basis conflict could reappear but in a similarly abstracted and transhistorical mode, as the essentialised binary, *écriture* versus 'ideology' (= "the confusion of linguistic with natural reality", de Man). And this binary, corresponding to an empirical subject and "a self that exists only in the form of a language" (de Man), realised in the interminability of textual interpretation, provides a space for 'a liberalism without a subject', a universalised, abstracted, dehistoricised, non-conflictual space in which the subject finds itself only in its own lack of plenitude, in irony, undecidability, aporia.

Put these together — a bracketing of the real, a dehistoricising and dematerialisation of discursive conflict, a covert domain scooped out for the liberal subject in the very denegation of the possibility of that subject — and the American national culture insists once more by disavowing the reproduction of the literary institution deconstruction makes possible. In this respect deconstruction's re-working of a foreign intervention exhibits the structural double movement Nairn defines in nationalism. In reaching forward to the new, the old is reinstated — deconstruction as a form of personal expression in the foreground continues in a traditional manner to make invisible conflict in the discursive practice enabling it.

Two short examples, one particular, one more generally speculative. A later argument will concur with and cite approvingly the main tenor of William Ray's admirably deconstructive text, *Literary meaning*, but meanwhile a reservation against its concluding assertion can be noted here. For in an unguarded moment, though one consistent with its avowed position, it voices the fear (somewhat unnecessarily) that the masses will get off on deconstruction and so spoil it:

> as ironic reading gains popularity and epigones proliferate, then what commenced as revolutionary gesture becomes institutional norm. When deconstruction becomes the unexamined truth for a significant number of students, it will, true to its own paradigm, mean something entirely different — something predictable and shared. (1984, p. 209)

Quite. As actuality of the discursive practice of deconstruction emerges for a moment from its usual invisibility, it compels admission that the "gesture" of American deconstruction must remain a purely personal one, defined precisely *against* any chance of shared, institutional change.

Secondly, perhaps, the American reading of Foucault. In Britain the work of Foucault is regarded on all sides as dangerously subversive because it takes as its point of departure a bracketing of the real. In contrast, in the United States, Foucault is already finding a comfortable place in and around the academy. Why? Arguably because certain features of the project assimilate without too much resistance into American national culture: a pragmatic concern with microstructures; a generalised interest in power; a tone of underlying fatalism ("You can't beat City Hall"). And all of this in a perspective which does not clearly distinguish between a "natural fact" and "a spiritual fact".

So far, this attempt to connect deconstruction to American national culture has suggested an exclusively negative assessment of it. But, as Weber says, the emigration of post-structuralism to the United States has a negative and a positive feature, that, in "reinforcing the liberal delegitimisation of conflict", it "is also undermining it" (1983, p. 251). There are horses for courses, specific engagements within specific fields. A radical discourse can only intervene effectively on the terrain it means to contest even with the concomitant certainty that to some degree it will be appropriated by it.

A positive face of deconstruction in America could be indicated in terms of the subject and position. While in the European tradition, with its institutionalisation of discursive conflict (as Hartz argues), there have always been a variety of ways to encounter and if so desired oppose Marxism, in America there has been one in chief, inscribed at the heart of the liberal tradition, namely to affirm the sovereignty of the autonomous subject (in this sense, as Weber hints, Marxism is the *necessarily* excluded other of American national culture). This may now be proving a weakness rather than a strength. Deconstruction may deserve all the criticisms showered on it by a Marxist such as Eagleton but, in the decade between 1970 and 1980, it certainly achieved one thing: however much it secretly recuperated a position for the liberal subject as 'a fading thing', it made it impossible to oppose Marxism from a basis in the claims of the full or absolute self. The demise of deconstruction (now a dead horse?) left scorched earth which could only be occupied by one thing, Marxism. Into this vacuum Jameson's *The Political unconscious* was launched in 1981.

Notes towards a definition of English national culture

At this moment the shelf of books on Englishness, previously and symptomatically so empty, is beginning to fill rapidly (see for example *Formations* 1984, Colls and Dodd 1986 and forthcoming). There is no mystery here. At a conjunctural level the Falklands escapade put Englishness firmly on the agenda. At an epochal level there is a more depressing reason for this new interest. For there is now a growing perception that the great British imperialist bourgeois endeavour, which began around 1660, is coming to an end. The crisis of the British economy appears not chronic but terminal because the decline of manufacturing production seems to be irreversible. The North Sea oil bubble has masked a continuing loss of Britain's share of world trade just as hysterical re-affirmation of Royalty and greatness conceals weakening of real power. Nairn points out that the English, because their national identity has been subsumed into and made invisibly equivalent with imperialism, have actually been deprived of a substantial sense of national identity. As the imperialist heritage slides away a sense of Englishness becomes more perceptible.

It will be enough here to sketch an account of English national culture sufficient to enable assessment of how British post-structuralism both challenges and is appropriated to it. Setting aside the range of social and cultural practices through which English national identity is produced and reproduced, the national culture will be defined as an organising structure within the *discursive* ensemble through which a central tradition is expressed, shaped and renewed.

Clearly enough that tradition originates in the seventeenth century when the gentry, the English bourgeois class, having won the battle for economic and political supremacy, set out to work through its victory by diffusing its hegemony into the cultural domain. After the (so-called) Restoration of the Monarchy in 1660 the founding of the national culture is undertaken, all but consciously, by any number of writers, among whom one would especially commend John Dryden and Alexander Pope for their efforts in working through discursive themes into the less perceptible and therefore more easily reproduced mode of stylistic forms. This public sphere of so-called "Augustan" culture established in the period 1660–1720 after the revolutionary triumph of the new class has maintained a continuity to the present day. Relative to the French rationalist tradition, constantly troubled since 1789 by radical interruptions (1830, 1848, 1870, the Vichy regime of 1940–5) the British tradition has marched along a single continuum in parallel to the continuing rule of the English gentry whose comparatively untroubled inheritance was easily able to contain the threats of 1832 (the First Reform Bill) as well as 1867 (the Second), of 1926 (the General Strike), and who emerged in 1945 intact at the price of nothing more than a state socialist Labour government (1945–51).

In the first place we must accept that the effect of the disavowal Weber discerns in the American tradition — competing individual expressions foregrounded so that actual conflict can be excluded from the institution itself — may be a defining feature of all kinds of *bourgeois* national culture. In *The Eighteen Brumaire* Marx writes brilliantly and sardonically of such bourgeois national cultures. In order to substantiate its own hegemony the new class in each new nation state looks back, past the feudalism which it has "knocked...to pieces" (Marx and Engels 1950, vol. 1, p. 226), to "the ante-diluvian Colossi" of the 'classical' empires, Greece and Rome, so it may dress itself in the new ideological forms of neo-Classicism (superimposing, for instance, the design of the Parthenon, the Bank of England building and the radiator grill of a Rolls Royce). In doing this it looks forward to its own rule for it is thus able to present its interests as eternal and universal though they are in fact local and sectarian, to speak in the accents of all 'civilised men' even though its claims are narrowly class-based.

But in the England of 1642–60, as distinct from the France of 1789, the same process happened with a difference. In England the bourgeois revolution was made in the seventeenth century, within the terms of a *religious* culture, not those of the French Enlightenment: "Cromwell and the English people had borrowed speech, passions and illusions from the Old Testament for their bourgeois revolution", though, as Marx adds in a finely laconic conclusion to the famous paragraph, after the real aim of the gentry had been achieved in 1660, "Locke supplanted Habbakuk" (p. 226). This judgement may be over-optimistic.

Marx's analysis has been applied to the founding of the national culture in the Augustan period. Describing the innovation of a public sphere after 1660 Terry Eagleton in *The function of criticism* points to the distinction between "interested" and "disinterested" discourse. In so far as the individual subject addressed itself according to real material interest, it was discredited from participating in the discourse of the public sphere, since "one's title as a speaker is derived from the formal character of one's discourse, rather than the authority of that discourse derived from one's social title" (1984a, p. 15). In the same structure of disavowal Weber uncovers, English common discourse makes interest its concealed problematic, "the very enabling structure of its disinterested inquiry" (p. 16).

Nevertheless, even through both may operate on this basis of disavowal, two differences in English national culture are indicated if Weber's account is drawn on for comparison. While American national culture seeks to deny real competing interests in the institution, English national culture in contrast admits such conflict within discourse in order to *recuperate* it into a renewed unity. Settlement, compromise, *negotiation* are the crucial strategies, as they are so clearly in the aim of the English Locke to come to terms with Filmer, while that competing tradition is simply omitted in the American reading of Locke, as Hartz says. The English cultural tradition is consistently *adversarial*, a discursive operation deeply influenced by the corresponding adversarial practices of English law (prosecution, defence, judgement) and the British parliamentary system (government, loyal opposition, the monarch) (television discussion programmes today similarly adopt without hesitation the format of two opponents and a point of balance represented by the chair).

Instead of the transformation of conflict into competing individualities inside the discursive institution — whose invisible coherence is thus secretly maintained — socially conflicting views are as far as possible admitted to the sphere of the national culture where the strategy is to resolve and synthesise them into a form of unity, a recuperation in which the re-presentation of social contraries as merely individual is only *one* of many discursive manœuvres. To grasp this tactic of making good means first taking measure of the unity into which difference is recuperated.

The unity of English national culture functions through the deployment and management of weighted oppositions. Of these the foundational opposition is that between the apparent and the real, what seems to be the case and what really is. There is little need to labour again the empiricist preconceptions on which this opposition is based (in France, in contrast, the real/apparent distinction opens on to a rationalist conception of the real). It develops in a scenario which requires an object, a subject and a means of representation able to pose these two in a reciprocally constituted relation.

The Johnsonian stone on which rests the English obsession with the real is well known as "common sense". Noting how "sense" replaces "wit" in usages from the Renaissance, the *Oxford English Dictionary* very usefully exhibits how this epistemology is dramatised by giving three main meanings for the term, meanings which correspond to perception of the object, the faculties of the subject, and the discursive formation itself in which these two are represented and sustained in a relation. Thus, "(1) An 'internal' sense...centre of the five senses, in which the various impressions received were reduced to the unity of a common consciousness; (2) The endowment of rational intelligence possessed by rational beings; (3) The general sense, feeling, or judgement of mankind, or of a community".

Sense is common in that it is immediately available, objectively and impartially, to any 'reasonable gentleman' ("the general maxims we are discoursing of are not known to children, idiots and a greater part of mankind", Locke 1947, p. 13) and thus to a collective, not private, reason. But this version of rationalism differs profoundly from the rationalism of the French tradition because of its claim to base itself in an empiricist real. What is common is *sense*. So, for example, Edward Thompson, in the very process of arguing against the New Left critique of the English tradition as constituted by *empiricism*, convincingly confirms that it is profoundly *empiricist* when he notes wittily with reference to the English reception of Darwinism that the *Origin of species* excited comparatively little in the way of intellectual controversy via "signed manifestoes" etc. because "Darwin addressed a protestant and post-Baconian public, which had long assumed that if God was at issue with a respectable Fact (or if a dogma was at odds with a man's conscience) it was the former which must give way" (1978, p. 62) (this implicit identification of "fact" with "conscience" will be returned to).

Since the real is set up as already given 'in itself', its corresponding subject is posed as similarly self-originating and autonomous. What was earlier discussed symptomatically may be retrieved here substantially, for English national culture presupposes what Catherine Belsey describes as 'the empirical subject'. Since the self-evident nature of reality presumes that the only problem posed "is to go and look and see what *Things* there are" (MacCabe 1985, p. 39), this subject is constituted in a position of dominant specularity. But in addition it possesses on the inside attributes and qualities co-relative to the discursively constructed real on the outside: givenness, solidity, substantiality, a significance ultimately *transcendental*.

The condition of existence for this object and this subject is the assumed transparency of discourse. Brought about largely through continuous pamphleteering and prose during the Revolutionary period, after 1660, as Stanley Fish asserts, "the plain style wins the day" (1974, p. 379). Despite variations and renovations it persists as an enabling discursive form to the present day (for analysis of a contemporary instance from a 1977 issue of the *Times Literary Supplement*, see Easthope 1979). The means of production of knowledge and experience of the real must be effaced for the real to stand in itself. A plain or natural or common, in short a would-be styleless style through which the real shall be as fully evident as it seems to be for sight is the necessary condition for this effect — it is not just an "idiom" but an "ideology" (see Thompson, 1978, p. 63). Hence metaphors of clarity and vision saturate English national culture to a degree which makes any attempted avoidance of them sound merely idiosyncratic (for this reason in this present text they have not been avoided).

Managing the oppositions

This English real is maintained by means of an opposition between real and apparent in which the first term is privileged by a denigration of the second. From this central opposition fields of force radiate and reproduce it in a structure which really calls for a multidimensional representation impossible for writing. A preliminary catalogue would show how power operates in and across this discursive formation through strategies of inclusion and exclusion.

Inclusion first. There is the re-presentation of *contradiction as synthesis*. This is done through a kind of synecdoche, when parts are made to stand for the wholes of two opposed positions and the joining of these parts is claimed as a resolution of the wholes. A classic instance here, from the nineteenth century, is Mill on Bentham and Coleridge.

In the increasingly conflictual conditions of English culture from 1790 onwards, the public sphere is preserved within the mode not of rationalism but rather of liberalism. Thus the Augustan denial of interest in favour of a disinterested public space is re-worked as a split in the subject of that communal terrain. In his essays on Bentham (1838) and on Coleridge (1840) Mill asserts that "whoever could master the premises and combine the methods of both would possess the entire English philosophy of his age" (Mill 1965, p. 293) and his account proceeds to try to add together Bentham's comprehension of "the merely *business* part of the social arrangements" (p. 268) and "material interests" with Coleridge's understanding of society's "spiritual interests" (p. 267). Another example would be the way Arnold in *Culture and anarchy* construes class difference between Barbarians (the landed gentry), Philistines (the commercial bourgeoisie) and Populace (the working class) in terms which point towards their transcendence into a higher unity: one's "ordinary self...differs according to the class to which one belongs" (1960, p. 107) so that we are "at war" (p. 95) but "by our *best self* we are united, impersonal, at harmony" (p. 95). Thus, 'apparent' oppositions are brought together into a 'real' unity, or their underlying unity is 'revealed'.

A second inclusion works through the tactic of *always already*. An oppositional intervention is incorporated when it is shown that its apparent radicalism is 'really' only already part of the tradition (in which its attraction can be explained away as 'fashionable', a key term whose covert opposite is the supposedly unchanging nature of the tradition). Example: when the work of Derrida is said to be that of an 'heretical Rabbi', thus as another expression of religion (albeit not Christian). A third tactic for incorporation consists of *point of view*. This far-reaching metaphoric trope asserts that the real is one and indivisible but that it is perceptible from different individual points of view. So a licence to criticise is extended by the notion of point of view, a licence which since Dryden has been granted to otherwise disinterested participants in the public sphere of the national culture to indulge in satire and attack on condition that such criticism is limited to personal expression (and what could be more personal than criticism of an individual's look in the English tradition of political caricature and cartoon?). Against the reality of the public sphere, personal criticism counts only as apparent, to be assimilated ultimately with caprice and whimsy (see below).

Then there is exclusion. Hypostasisation of the real supports the opposition *objective/subjective*, which, overdetermined by equivalence with real/apparent, becomes a means for expelling a point of view which is so threatening as to be ruled outside altogether. In the foundational Augustan period this opposition acquired content in specifically religious terms as that between

Protestant and Roman Catholic, founding a continuing trope by which 'dogma' is opposed to 'common sense' and feeding into contemporary oppositions between 'ideology' and 'common sense'. Objective/subjective extends into *concrete/abstract* (cf. 'facts'/'ideas' and 'experience'/'theory' and otherwise 'fact'/'value') and becomes mapped on to yet others from social practice (yielding for example 'gentleman'/'not a gentleman', 'amateur'/'professional', 'common sense language/jargon', and 'practical'/'intellectual').

Presumed primacy of the real, the socially constructed real of English empiricism which denies its own construction, encourages superimposition of the 'philosophic' oppositions objective/subjective and concrete/abstract on to the social and political opposition, *centre/extremes*. Admitting opposed points of view only in order to exclude them stretches back at least to Dryden's *Religio laici* of 1682 which defends the centre, in this case the Church of England, against the equated extremes of Catholicism and Dissent. The tone of the poem's conclusion is as significant as its theme:

> What then remains, but, waving each Extreme,
> The Tides of Ignorance, and Pride to stem? ...
> Faith is not built on disquisitions vain;
> The things we *must* believe, are *few*, and *plain*: ...
> For points obscure are of small use to learn:
> But *Common quiet* is *Mankind's concern*.

Centre/extremes, clarity/obscurity, things/ideas, common/private — it's all there, as surely as three centuries later in the trope by which British television news habitually discriminates political right from left as "moderates" and "extremists".

Dryden becomes a classic instance of what may be called the figure of *terminal settlement*, "What then remains..." That same trope constantly recurs in the national culture via such phrasings as "In the end...", "After all...", etc. In a tone of weary finality it points decisively away from appearance towards the self-evidently real, regarded equally a matter of truth and shared judgement.

Two further workings of the real/apparent opposition deserve attention. One takes the form *serious/play* or serious/silly. "Silly", meaning argument rationally pursued beyond the bounds of common sense, is able to connote false and subjective and abstract and extreme. And it is distinguished as a term for exclusion from

205

something like whimsy or the fanciful which is included by partaking of licensed self-indulgence. Another crucial operation of real/apparent takes the form of classic irony, an utterance which apparently or literally means one thing while actually meaning another. Enormously versatile, this discursive effect depends on transparency of discourse to recuperate an oppositional view or position by avoiding any explicit statement which would lead to the clear staking out of its own position. Classic irony cites a radical statement as object language from an unstated position of metalinguistic certainty. It therefore implicitly invokes the real as traditionally conceived and a shared subject position in a way which never risks exposing the interdependence of that object and that subject.

In sum, then, English national culture is predicated on the real, persistently in the guise of Nature (whether, as Basil Willey argues, (1962) in its eighteenth-century form as *natura naturata*, or, with Romanticism, as *natura naturans*). This real has immensely strong but entirely covert transcendental connotations and associations, for two reasons: it comes into existence in the seventeenth century as the bourgeois real able to overthrown feudal definitions and therefore, invisibly nestling within it, from the period of its origin it carries forward a powerfully religious meaning (the Lockeian real is *always* contaminated with Habbakuk); it guarantees but refuses to acknowledge its dependence on the empirical subject and therefore, as Thompson so acutely remarks, there is always a trade off between "Fact" and "a man's conscience". Thus the most real quality of my inward self-consciousness derives from my determined hold on the externally real (whether as God or Nature's God or God in Nature). So the opposition *fact/fiction* can be drawn on to characterise moral consciousness: self-deception (obedient to the Pleasure Principle) leads to fantasy and fiction, self-awareness (corresponding to the Reality Principle) grips on tightly to fact. In English national culture the real is from first to last a moral category.

At this point the backward look of English nationalism becomes visible. While looking forward and capable of flexibly incorporating innovation, even opposition and radicalism, into itself, the national culture does so by recuperating novelty to its own concealed tradition. In this respect it can manage the contradiction Pope at the end of the first epistle of *An essay on Man* names as the one, clear truth in which fact and value, real and apparent, finally coincide: "'Whatever IS, is RIGHT'".

The Englishness of British post-structuralism

It's a pleasure to quote once again Nairn's finely disabused account of the English tradition: "English separateness and provincialism; English backwardness and traditionalism; English religiosity and moralistic vapouring, paltry English 'empiricism', or instinctive distrust of reason..." (Nairn 1964, p. 48). In the first place British post-structuralism intervenes critically against the imperialist provincialism of this tradition by virtue of its internationalist, albeit Europocentric, commitment. It would be hard to recall a period when contemporary French thought has exercised such fascination for the radical intelligentsia of Britain as it has in the past decade.

At three points British post-structuralism engages critically with English national culture: over the real, over the subject, over the transparency of discourse. In each instance criticism is not made from a standpoint outside; rather British post-structuralism is valuable in so far as it *inhabits* the discourse it wishes to oppose, engages with it on its own terms, and, so, inevitably risks reiterating it, as will noted.

Against the empiricist conception of the real the new antagonistic discourse affirms at every point that the real is a construct and aims to demonstrate the varying terms of that construction. Undeniably, as in the case of Hindess and Hirst, the empiricist real is deconstructed via procedures and discursive traditions imported from French rationalism, for example in the way they deny 'facts' in the name of 'concepts'. Such rationalist arguments are inevitably attended by risks (idealism is the name of one) but against this has to be considered the radical effectivity of rationalist arguments when inserted into a tradition so depressingly assured that the real is self-evident.

That shock can be measured, for example, in the way art historians reviewed Norman Bryson's *Vision and painting*. While acknowledging as they surely must that painting constructs its visual effects, they felt sufficiently threatened by Bryson's argument to have to insist on the reality of the extra-discursive. Rudolf Arnheim in the *Times Literary Supplement* (7 October 1983) linked knowledge of the real with the essential human subject, hoping to refute the book with the rhetorical question, "what then is the objective base to which we owe our cherished universal vision?" Michael Podro went out of his way to affirm that "culture is constrained by something outside its own proposing and assuming — what we may term reality" (1984, p. 245) and Peter

Fuller in *New Society* (30 June 1983) cried out against Bryson "despite his idealist assertions to the contrary, there *is* a knowable external reality" (italics original). Quite simply, the existence of an extra-discursive reality is *never doubted* in *Vision and painting*; I take each of these responses to the book as symptoms of the English obsession with the real which is valuably challenged by a post-structuralist argument departing from the view that, since all experience of the real is constructed, art history cannot understand its particular object by assuming it is an Essential Copy.

Critical engagement engages as well as criticises, *must* engage *to* criticise. British post-structuralism necessarily entered the terrain of the national culture in an attempt to transform it. Symptomatic of this are the defensive gestures by which Hindess and Hirst feel impelled to make clear that their position on epistemology does not "cause us intellectual discomfort when we refrain from walking out of the top windows of high buildings" (1977, p. 8) or the collective writers of *Changing the subject* that "we have not thrown out the real" (Henriques *et al.* 1984, p.100). Symptomatic also is the very fact, noted appropriately along the way, that writers have found it important to argue about the possibility of knowledge of reality (in specific forms). That argument itself partakes of the cultural heritage almost unthinkingly, is to this extent an appropriation by it, though for this the trade-off is an effective critical discourse, one strengthened because it can claim to have an account of referentiality and which has certainly escaped the facile alternatives elsewhere on offer (either absolute knowledge outside discourse or no knowledge at all, etc.)

Since the question of the real will not be returned to, it may be best to leave it with a quotation from Derrida:

> what happens to science when the metaphysical value of truth has been put into question, etc? how are the effects of science and of truth to be reinscribed? [Derrida refers to Nietzsche]...it goes without saying that in no case is it a question of a *discourse against truth* or against science. (This is impossible and absurd, as is every heated accusation on this subject.) And when one analyses systematically the value of truth as *homoiosis* or *adequatio*, as the certitude of the *cogito* (Descartes, Husserl), or as a certitude opposed to truth in the horizon of absolute knowledge *(Phenomenology of the Mind),* or finally as *aletheia*, unveiling or presence (the

Heideggerean repetition), it is not in order to return naively to
a relativist or sceptical empiricism...*we must have truth*...we
must recognise in truth 'the normal prototype of the fetish'.
How can we do without it? (1981a, p. 105)

Over the subject a similar argument must be entered as over the
real. On the one hand British post-structuralism — unlike
comparable versions in America — founded itself and defined itself
(as it has been defined in this present work) as a critique of the
subject. And this measures the radicalism of the discourse when
inserted into the context of the national culture with its moralising
assumption of the co-substantiality of a transcendent subject and a
transcendent real. At the same time there is a respect in which this
deconstruction of the subject reproduces the mode of the discursive
formation it appears within. That sustained engagement with the
subject — in *Screen*'s project of following through Althusser's
essay on ideology, in Hirst's attack on Thompson, in *Changing the
subject* — had as its condition of existence the notion of the
sovereignty of the subject as the heart of the real. If analysis of
national cultures shows it was inevitable that American
post-structuralism would concern itself with irony and
undecidability, it was equally inevitable that British
post-structuralism should talk about the self.

Thirdly, against the prevailing conception of discourse as
essentially transparent, British developments affirmed the
materiality of discourse and discursive forms, specifically and in
detail, both through analysis of the discourses of knowledge in
psychology and through analyses of specific signifying practices —
of film, television, the history of painting, of music, novels, plays,
poetry. This is at the level of content. But also at the level of
discursive form itself post-structuralism in Britain intervened in a
potentially radical way through its own stylistic. This was noted in
the case of the *New Left Review* versus Raymond Williams, as well
as Hirst versus Thompson. The radical edge of its discourse (not in
any case homogeneous) can be measured in its willingness to
pursue the logic of an argument beyond the bounds of common
sense, at the risk of condemnation as "jargon" or "silly".

This brings the attempted assessment to a most interesting issue.
It is one which has not surfaced often but when it has, for example
in the Southampton debate when the American was told he was not
serious, a definite aspect becomes apparent in which the new
discourse has merely reproduced and not challenged the inherited

culture. The opposition serious/silly has been perpetuated; British post-structuralism remains overwhelmingly serious. This ensues from its relation to the parent discourse of Marxism, to a commitment to political purposes and, in the end, to changing not just the subject but the world. But the degree to which it repeats traditional British moral seriousness must count as a certain limitation on the project.

The post-structuralist intervention, 1968–1988

English national culture, it was argued, operates through a strategy of containing and negotiating conflict wherever the opposing position could be so contained: 'include if we can, exclude if we must'. Marxism is a limit case for that strategy. Post-structuralism, taken up within Marxism (as has been documented), comes to occupy a similar discursive space to Marxism as a radically oppositional discourse. How effective that opposition has been may be reviewed if we revisit Anderson's 1968 admittedly academicist account of the national culture (see above, pp. 10–12).

Anthropology has not been part of the present discussion. Philosophy remains the discipline least affected by post-structuralism as represented by Derrida. History writing has felt the impact of work by Hirst, though as was suggested in Chapter 6, the national culture weighs particularly heavily in that realm. Compared to the situation Anderson viewed in 1968, gains certainly have to be recorded in both social sciences and psychology — in the latter Anderson can foresee the introduction of an argument showing the constitution of the subject as determined by social and economic forces but not its constitution within discourse — which is the point of the leverage exerted by *Changing the subject*, a text which (to refer to another of Anderson's disciplines) has the consequence of eroding the existing apartheid between psychology and psychoanalysis. What he does not foresee is the range and force of work in the area of what he lumps together as "Aesthetics", film, art history, music, literature, nor the important innovation of cultural studies, an area that works between social studies and theories of signifying practices.

Though Anderson's account is limited in its assumption that different interventions in different subject areas need to be assessed in terms of their totalising capacity his essay did correctly anticipate that the work of Leavis was potentially the most radical opening. For Leavis directly provoked the counter-intervention of Raymond Williams, and the work of Williams on cultural studies opens the space which comes to be occupied in the early 1970s by *Screen* and its work on cinema. This led to two things. *Screen*, by importing into England the writing of Althusser, Lacan, Barthes and others, and especially by working its conceptualisations through in detailed application to a specific area, becomes the precedent whose influence — as has been one of the main themes here — subsequently carries through into many other areas. And *Screen*, by moving between literature and film, not only affected cultural studies but helped to make possible the analysis of a whole range of discourses, visual, written, even musical, as forms of signifying practice.

Meanwhile, since Anderson wrote, the political conjuncture at which post-structuralism in Britain took off around 1974 (and which has not been mentioned since Chapter 2) has been transformed, and this with effects that must now be considered.

The changed conjuncture of the 1980s

A linear order of exposition is always unsatisfactory, manifestly so at this point in the present exposition. For during the decade from 1977 to 1987 when most of the work discussed in the preceding chapters was produced, the very frame in which developments took place in Britain changed. With the election of the first Thatcher government in 1979 there was a radical shift in political direction away from social democracy and back towards the entrepreneurial capitalism of the pre-war period. The chronic economic crisis worsened but was now presented through the revival of an older mode. A cut in the 'social wage' (benefits in housing, health and education provided by the 'welfare state') together with a cut in wages for the newly unemployed (3.5 million more of them since 1979) was managed (with the help of the oil bubble) by mobilising 'people' and 'nation' against the previous social democratic ideas of 'class' and 'state', mobilising, that is, a sufficient minority to secure re-election in 1983 and 1987. From this newly established vantage-point the two decades from 1950 to 1970 appear a golden interregnum within 'business as usual'.

For post-stucturalism in Britain the new conjuncture was marked by at least three consequences. As the 1970s gave way to the '80s there was both, in the title of Ellen Meiksins Wood's book, "The retreat from class" (1986) and class politics, and an advance into gender politics. To the extent that this move (evidenced for example in the feminist commitment of *Changing the subject* and of *Screen* after 1980) confronted new issues it was an advance, to the extent that gender politics *replaced* class politics it was an effect of defeatism (there is *much* more to be written on this but it may well be too early to assess satisfactorily).

Secondly, in the 1980s the moment of theory came to an end. A decade earlier every month brought news of a new name from Paris — Althusser, Barthes, Derrida, Foucault — while the next promised to fill the gaps in the alphabet. Now Barthes, Lacan and Foucault are dead, Althusser has finally succumbed to the insanity he fought against all his life, Kristeva turned from literature and politics to the practice of psychoanalysis. Derrida survives, Lyotard is perhaps magnified by the space he was expected to fill (and Baudrillard certainly is). By 1980 the theoretical re-thinking had been done, as Perry Anderson noted:

> Much of the work of *New Left Review* in this period was devoted to a conscious attempt to start, in some sense, to remedy this native deficiency — by publishing and discussing, often for the first time in Britain, the work of the most salient theorists from Germany, France and Italy. This programme, pursued methodically, was reaching its end by the early '70s. (1980, p. viii)

Both the intellectual excitement of the previous decade and its associated theoreticism came to an end as attention, concentrated in part by the ascendence of the right, turned to working through theory in application.

Thirdly, the new political situation was accompanied by a theoretical crisis for the left, one which has already been referred to at the end of Chapter 3 and elsewhere.

Erosion of the base/superstructure model

In the mid-1960s the New Left had derived confidence both from the promise of the conjuncture but also the conviction that Althusser's account of relative autonomy (an issue which remained insoluble to the Williams of *Culture and society* in 1958) had solved the difficulty and could be drawn on without hesitation as a means to analyse the social formation, including ideological practice. This faith was gradually eroded, as several writers have testified.

Colin MacCabe in 1985 writes retrospectively of the confidence given to the work of *Screen* in undertaking analysis of a specific cultural form by the work of Althusser, especially as this led to the conviction that the specificity of cinema could be related to the fundamental divisions of capital and labour which, according to the conditions of relative autonomy, were produced at the level of ideological practice, of which cinema — Nixon–Paramount — was an instance. As MacCabe records, during the late 1970s, belief in Althusser's modified conception of relative autonomy and the base/superstructure model began to fail:

> This tenet of faith became increasingly difficult to uphold as, throughout the '70s, a series of texts were produced by people who had acted as editors of the Althusserian magazine *Theoretical Practice.* Tony Cutler, Barry Hindess, Paul Hirst and Athar Hussain both singly and together produced argument after argument to show the theoretical impasse of Althusser's position. Either the ideological and political are autonomous from the economic and have their own effectivity, in which case any notion of defining the relations of production simply in economic terms becomes ridiculous, or they are not autonomous and then no matter how much 'complexity' is introduced into the analysis, economics will give you the 'real' relations of production and it will simply be a matter of specifying the 'modifications' of those relations introduced by their political or ideological representation, those representations themselves finally being determined in their operation by the 'real' economic relations. (1985, pp. 13–4)

At bottom, the issue is simple: either the superstructure is relative to the economic base or it is autonomous.

The same inexorable logic is spelt out in a recent text by Laclau and Mouffe:

> For, either the structural framework constituted by the basic determinations of society explains not only the limits of autonomy but also the nature of the autonomous entity — in which case that entity is another structural determination of the system and the concept of 'autonomy' is redundant; or else the autonomous entity is not determined by the system, in which case it is necessary to explain where it is constituted. (1985, pp. 139–40)

Eagleton, typically, realising that the paradoxical concept of relative autonomy has comic potential, makes of it a joke which, equally typically, is seriously meant. Conceptions which suppose a base/superstructure model, "essentialist notions of social totality", are "plainly discreditable" while conceptions which treat every aspect of the social formation as autonomous lead only to a "politics of the fragment" and are "ineffective". Eagleton concludes:

> The fact that such matters...are not at the moment susceptible of satisfying theoretical resolution is a sign that they are indeed more than theoretical — that these dilemmas are the mark at the level of theory of certain real deadlocks and difficulties at the level of political history, and in part await for their successful outcome upon developments in that latter realm. (1986a, p. 5)

Thus: the theory that base determines superstructure is said to be discreditable and an explanation for why this is so is then given by drawing on the base/superstructure distinction. The theoretical difficulty said to be insoluble is introduced as already solved to explain why the difficulty hasn't yet been solved. Eagleton's self-referential joke is fully intended.

Meanwhile, there is no evidence at all that the theoretical impasse of classic Marxism has led to an end of political radicalism in Britain in the 1980s (the opposite in fact — the increased polarisations overseen by Thatcherism have greatly extended political will) but there has certainly been a shift in theoretical allegiance from Althusser to Foucault. This will be briefly reviewed. There is a temptation for the approaching closure of a critical text to be accompanied by an apocalyptic tone — this

214

present one will err on the side of caution, accepting that post-structuralism opens many avenues and claiming only that work in England has produced two definite advances in theoretical and applied understanding: a critique of the subject especially relevant to the human sciences; a version of textual analysis in terms of position offered to the reader which has application to all forms of signifying practice.

Between Althusser and Foucault: the critique of the subject

In a paper published in English in 1982 Foucault explained that the concern and object of his continued analysis had been not power but the subject. His opening statement performs a retrospective summary and re-reading of his own work and deserves quotation in full:

> I would like to say, first of all, what has been the goal of my work during the last twenty years. It has not been to analyse the phenomena of power, nor to elaborate the foundations of such an analysis.
>
> My objective, instead, has been to create a history of the different modes by which, in our culture, human beings are made subjects. My work has dealt with three modes of objectification which transform human beings into subjects.
>
> The first is the modes of inquiry which try to give themselves the status of sciences; for example, the objectivising of the speaking subject in *grammaire générale*, philology, and linguistics. Or again, in this mode, the objectivising of the productive subject, the subject who labours, in the analysis of wealth and of economics.
>
> Or, a third example, the objectivising of the sheer fact of being alive in natural history or biology.
>
> In the second part of my work, I have studied the objectivising of the subject in what I shall call 'dividing practices'. The subject is either divided inside himself *[sic]* or divided from others. This process objectivises him. Examples are the mad and the sane, the sick and the healthy, the criminals and the 'good boys'.
>
> Finally, I have sought to study — it is my current work — the way a human being turns him- or herself into a subject. For example, I have chosen the domain of sexuality — how

men have learned to recognise themselves as subjects of 'sexuality'.

Thus it is not power, but the subject, which is the general theme of my research. (1982, pp. 208–9)

That is sufficiently clear statement.

The position Foucault stakes out is defined both by alignment with and distance from that of Althusser. In the first place it goes almost without saying that Foucault begins from concurrence with Althusser's rejection of humanism. The critique covers both the humanism which regards the subject as sovereign and its corresponding formulation in the (Hegelian) attempt to derive the social formation from what Althusser calls an "expressive totality" and which Foucault refers to in this paper when he dismisses the notion "that there is a primary and fundamental principle of power which dominates society down to the smallest detail" (p. 234). Secondly, and consequently, Foucault subscribes to the Althusserian account of the subject as support for a position but only to qualify this view.

For Althusser the subject is defined as such (1) by its submission (2) by its apparent self-presence (Althusser 1977b, p. 169), an analysis Foucault re-writes and underwrites in terms of power: "There are two meanings of the word *subject*: subject to someone else by control and dependence, and tied to its own identity by a conscience or self-knowledge" (p. 212). But Foucault goes on to argue that the subject is always a site for struggle. With Althusser in mind he acknowledges:

I know what objections can be made. We can say that all types of subjection are derived phenomena, that they are merely the consequences of other economic and social processes: forces of production, class struggle, and ideological structures which determine the form of subjectivity.

It is certain that the mechanisms of subject cannot be studied outside their relation to the mechanisms of exploitation and domination. But they do not merely constitute the 'terminal' of more fundamental mechanisms. They entertain complex and circular relations with other forms. (Foucault 1982, p. 213)

The subject is determined, positioned as a support, but cannot be reduced to that positioning because it is active in the reproduction of discursive and social practices.

Power is to be redefined in terms of the subject because that is the only way of taking "the forms of resistance against different forms of power as a starting point" (p. 211). Thus "the term 'power' designates relationships between partners" (p. 217), a relationship which in presuming domination presumes at the same time *someone* to be dominated: "it is nevertheless always a way of acting upon an acting subject or acting subjects by virtue of their acting or being capable of action". In drawing on Hegel's paradigm of the master and slave, Foucault insists on defining power as mastery of a subject, not an object (you cannot exercise power over a tree). Consequently — and against Althusser's functionalism — contestation and resistance is written into the definition: "At every moment the relationship of power may become a confrontation between two adversaries" (p. 226).

British post-structuralism was set in train in the pages of *Screen* by a theoretical commitment to the Althusserian account of the subject as support for a position, constituted to misrecognise itself as constitutive. Underpinned by the concept of relative autonomy, this view was criticised by Paul Q. Hirst for its functionalism, at the same time as the concept of relative autonomy was coming under radical and damaging critique. But the politics of the subject are retained and indeed reinforced by the shift of commitment from Althusser to Foucault. Bracketing the real, the work of Foucault admits causality only in order to treat determination as local and microstructural, exercised across both social and discursive practices. Instead of power originating at a real centre as economic power, Foucault writes that "power is everywhere; not because it embraces everything, but because it comes from everywhere" (1981, p. 93). It is precisely according to the spirit if not the letter of Foucault's work (for *Language and materialism* of 1977 makes no mention of Foucault) that Rosalind Coward signals a crucial re-direction of *Screen*'s project when she writes that emphasis should be placed not on representation as effect of a cause but as cause of an effect, "how systems of representation inscribe (ideological) positions" (1977, p. 95). This is the line subsequently followed by British post-structuralism.

In the main, for three reasons. Only if power is conceived in its articulation in and for the subject can it be theorised outside the Althusserian functionalism which treats the subject as effect but not cause, constituted but disabled from any constitutive resistance: "It is this contradiction in the subject — between the conscious self, which is conscious in so far as it is able to feature in discourse, and the self which is only partially represented there — which constitutes the source of possible change" (Belsey 1980, p. 85). Secondly, so understood, the subject must be seen as a gendered subject, and thus the concept promises to join a politics of gender in with a politics of class. Thirdly, the issue of the subject opens up the question of desire. Even if it is the case (as has been argued) that the order of the unconscious and the order of the social formation cannot be thought together in theoretical coherence, they are nevertheless brought together in any discursive or social practice. Accordingly an analysis can only be reductive if it ignores either.

Against this a more traditional Marxist argument would urge two things. One would be that preoccupation with the subject is a locally Western concern rightly seen as of small importance in the jungles of Nicaragua (epitomised perhaps in the story of the revolutionary about to be shot by a firing squad led by a Paris-educated fascist who tells the prisoner, "Don't take this personally: think of yourself as a support for a position" — though personally if I were in that situation I'd prefer to think of myself as a support who was always already contingent rather than a full subject about to be extinguished once and for all).

To this it can be replied that it is not a wilful and self-regarding first-worldist intelligentsia which has put the subject on the agenda but rather history in the form of the social developments in the advanced capitalist countries in the past two centuries. As Foucault points out in the essay just cited, the growth of modern state power since the time of the French Revolution has been especially a growth in a would-be totalising power over the subject, separating out, disciplining, individualising, internalising, precisely *constituting* the subject. As for contradiction in the subject as site of resistance, this is less a matter of something invented by theory than belated recognition of the movement across the whole range of signifying practices in the West in the opening three decades of this century. Modernism registers a crisis in and of the supposedly autonomous subject, a crisis which post-structuralism has come to analyse at the level of theory decades afterwards, for as usual the owl of Minerva flies only in the twilight.

A second hard-line objection would be that in a classically bourgeois manner prioritising the subject once again substitutes individual consciousness for social being, directing attention away from the objective contradictions in class and social formations towards the personal and subjective. Even though it can be argued that the subject of post-structuralism is a socially constituted subject, this is more difficult to answer.

Although giving priority to the subject and its critique does not necessarily entail an ontological commitment to subjectivity over the objective determinants of the social formation, there is undeniably a risk that, *de facto* if not *de jure*, this will eventuate. There is no conceptualisation or structure of ideas so inherently radical it is immune from recuperation, misrecognition and betrayal. It has in fact been the founding argument of this book that 'ideas' take on meaning only in a specific historical context and tradition, as certain French ideas have done in the context of English political discourse. There can be no guarantees, therefore, that the conception of the subject as defended here, will not be restored to another covert version of liberalism (here American deconstruction offers an instructive warning). But since there can be no such rationalist guarantees — ideas are always taken up in practice — then the social context itself may be the best and only guarantee. As has been amply illustrated, British post-structuralism was sponsored by Marxism and shows no signs of surrendering its engagement with radical politics.

Text and the position of the subject

British post-structuralism has adapted its concern with subjectivity to analysis of signifying practices and the possible effect of texts in positioning their readers. This has been discussed as it has been carried across from *Screen* and film theory to the analysis of literature, of the fine art tradition, of music, and so into the area of cultural studies. But from as early as Paul Willemen's intervention in *Screen* in 1978, the view that a text provides a position for a subject has been challenged by introducing a distinction between implied and actual position, a question taken up in different emphases by other writers.

Regarding the specificity of painting, Norman Bryson shows vividly that any internal features of the text, including those to be analysed in terms of positioning, are realised in interaction with the social formation, as for example codes governing face, body and dress are activated by a Giotto fresco only because they play across the semantic field as a whole. Similarly, Durant's *Conditions of music* only analysed the formal properties of music and the Western tonal system in subordination (perhaps an excessive one) to the practices of musical production and reproduction in which these forms are inserted. And the problem is there also, with different answers prescribed for it, in the post-structuralist literary theories of MacCabe and Belsey, which stress textual effect, and with the alternative emphasis, by the tradition of left deconstruction in Williams, Bennett and Eagleton, which prioritises the institutional practice in which texts are reproduced over any possible textual effect.

The text as structure or the text as act? The reader as textually implied or the reader as actually situated within social and historical practices? We encounter here a dichotomy which is not new. For example, in a paper of 1928 Roman Jacobson and Jurij Tynjanov indicate an end to the trajectory of Russian Formalism when they argue that a structuralist analysis of literature as synchronic system (on the model of Saussure's *langue*) "now proves to be an illusion" (p. 79) since "every system necessarily exists as an evolution, whereas, on the other hand, evolution is inescapably of a systemic nature" (p. 80). They urge therefore a new science which would aim to correlate literature as synchronic system with literature as diachronic effect, analysis of a correlation between what they term "the literary series and other historical series" (p. 81). That new science has not appeared.

I am sorry to disappoint the reader who may have followed the constant deferral of discussion of this issue in the hope that eventually an unprecedented solution would be pulled out of the hat. There is no solution to the non-correspondence between how a text reads its reader and how a reader reads a text. In default of a resolution that recognition itself will have to serve.

It is the theme of William Ray's book on *Literary meaning* (1984), which argues the case with great cogency and is reported here because its argument is surely correct. Ray states that there can be no firm or final dichotomy between literary meaning as objective structure and meaning as subjective act. Rather, there is always a *tension* between

> our two common-sense intuitions of meaning, as both
> historically bound *act*, governed by a particular intention at a
> particular moment, and permanent textual *fact*, embodied in
> a word or series of words whose meaning transcends

particular volition and can be apprehended in its structure by any individual possessed of the language. (p. 2)

This tension manifests itself in such binary oppositions as subject versus object, instance versus system, performance versus competence, event versus structure. Refusing to attribute priority to meaning as either act or text, recognising that they're "reciprocally constitutive notions" (p. 144), *Literary meaning* develops an account of this tension as *dialectical*.

In support of its assertion the text shows that some form of the assumption that meaning is determined by act *and* event runs through much recent theoretical work (to list: the work of Poulet, Sartre, Ingarden, Iser, Norman Holland, David Bleich and E. D. Hirsh). The writers are not refuted but rather their arguments pursued until they undo themselves "according to their own logic" (p. 106). And undo themselves they do, for each offer to define meaning as act is revealed to depend on a notion of intersubjective structure. At this point the book turns back the other way, against structuralism as exemplifed in Culler's 1975 *Structuralist poetics* and Umberto Eco (specifically *A theory of semiotics* and *The role of the reader*). Again their own logic is mobilised against them to show they are driven into an account of meaning as act. *Literary meaning* concludes that we must recognise that "every semiotic fact is an act, every history of events an event in history" (p. 142).

If that is the case, if there is an inescapable dialectic between text as structure and text as act, reader as implied and reader as actual, and there can be no finally satisfactory, theoretically coherent and unified way of discussing both, then the kind of problematic adopted in British post-structuralism is not denied though its limits become clear. To analyse the means by which a text offers a position for the reader confronts textuality while containing an acknowledgement that the reader's position always exceeds any position provided. Two things continue to justify this strategy. One is that the deployment of the Althusserian–Lacanian conception of the subject for textual analysis has evidenced a powerful capacity across a range of different aesthetic discourses to integrate theoretically and make sense of formal properties that otherwise remain unexamined and unexplained. In this the problematic justifies itself by its demonstrable success in analysis at the level of the signifier rather than at that of the signified, not as a hermeneutics but as a poetics of the text. But a poetics, secondly, which in virtue of its fixing on the subject as its concern, as was argued before, cannot easily be divorced from a politics.

One implication needs to be touched on before ending. If it is accepted that post-structuralist writing in England has successfully and effectively intervened in the specific areas of what are conventionally separated off as academically different 'disciplines' each with different 'subjects' while yet maintaining a degree of theoretical coherence and common concern, the political consequences are not merely theoretical but also institutional. Clearly this is the case in carrying through the project of reconstituting 'literary criticism' by opening up analysis across the whole range of signifying practices (film, television, painting, and yes, even those forms traditionally regarded as characterised by literariness). The institutional demarcation between 'Literary Studies' and 'Cultural Studies' is necessarily threatened, as is that larger one between the 'Social Sciences' and 'Humanities', between sociology, historiography, social psychology, and literature, art history, musicology. What has been referred to as the 'problematic' of British post-structuralism calls for institutional transformations within the academy, though it is hard to see this taking place apart from wider institutional change.

APPENDIX I

Textual Practice: One Example

In Britain post-structuralism has not been confined to a merely theoretical intervention; it has also directly influenced forms of textual practice, including the films of Laura Mulvey and Peter Wollen (such as *Penthesilia, Riddles of the Sphinx, Amy*). Because of its importance one novel is singled out here as an example and discussed *hors de concours* in an appendix.

Michael Westlake: *Imaginary women* (1987)

In the film *Alien* (1979), after the ardours of her adventures, the heroine (played by Sigourney Weaver) ends up sleeping in her transparent cocoon accompanied only by her cat. The tasks set to the heroine of *Imaginary women* in finding her identity begin with her alone with her cat — but since she has as yet no name she is referred to in the text as Mac**ash and, to ensure her masculine pet has no more certainty of his identity, he bears indifferently the epic names Adolphus, Amadeus or Augustus.

In the 1970s *Screen* warned against an aesthetics of transgression, which hoped to break entirely with narrative, and urged instead a radical re-working of narrative. It is perhaps most usefully in these terms that we may understand the treatment of narrative in *Imaginary women*. Structured into three "Thirds" each consisting of thirteen short units and so listed at the beginning, the text comprises thirty-nine sections, in triple parallel to each other, repeating, embroidering and modifying themes and figures though not in a mechanical manner — thus number seven in each third is a graph, number two in each extends the cat's tale, the penultimate concerns Gropius, the lover of six women, and so on, though the

223

film sequences of I. 4 (Polanski's *Chinatown*) and II. 4 (Hitchcock's *North by North-West*) find no exact parallel when III. 4 develops the story of Joyce Chan. From these thirty-nine sections, six, the first and last of each third, carry forward the narrative of Mac**ash.

Not only is this narrative already firmly distanced from realism by being woven in with thirty-three units that are not really narrative at all, and not only is it explicitly placed in a parodic frame as the typical plot of a film noir (at least at first — towards the end the genre changes), but it is also a typical, even abstract story, since it enacts very much the construction of identity as understood by psychoanalysis. In his essay of 1931 on female sexuality Freud suggests that on discovering the threat of castration in the site of the mother's body the little girl may: (1) give up sexuality altogether; (2) refuse to believe she has not got the phallus; (3) seek to re-find the phallus in the father and so, indirectly, in another man (the bridegroom). One way to epitomise Mac**ash's attempt to trace a figure (her own identity) would be to say that of these three trajectories she pursues neither the first nor the third, and ends up neither dead nor married. What she does do — what happens to her — is rather more complexly suggestive.

She does begin by losing the phallus (it is eaten by Adolphus, in fact). At the end of the first third she is asked by a pretty masculine mother-figure (Sophie, alias The General) if she will "accept any gift you are offered" (p. 58), the gift turning out to be a microfilm blueprint (retrieved from Adolphus in II. 1. in the least distasteful manner possible), a blueprint of the missile bunker under the hills "to the east of our city", concealing the world's central warfighting computer (its software has been implanted with a self-replicating feminist programme called Absolution Nihilating Nuclear Armageddon or "ANNA" whose function is to render all binary military orders undecidable). But the gift also turns out, in II. 13, to be a black bird like that in *The Maltese falcon*. This is lost in its turn when Mac**ash parachutes into the hills, is captured and tortured by the General until her head is cut off with an axe by her own simulacrum — at which point she becomes a copy of herself and, in III. 13, is introduced into identity and the family by finding a name as Anna Mac Xi-ash (her grandmother is discovered to have been Chinese).

Some elucidating comments can be offered. Via the blueprint and her name Anna, this quest for personal identity is linked to the epic, indeed global narrative of our times, as it is in Pound's

Cantos, and, more cogently, in Thomas Pynchon's *Gravity's rainbow*, when Tyrone Slothrop's sexual career becomes intimately linked with the age of the nuclear missile. As speculated by Freud in a famous paper ("On transformations of instinct"), the phallus easily appears equated in a symbolic series with faeces (money, gift) and baby (here indiscriminately Adolphus, the blueprint he excretes, the black bird).

"Thus the symbol manifests itself first of all as the murder of the thing, and this death constitutes in the subject the eternalization of desire" (Lacan 1977a, p. 104): if read in relation to the psychoanalytic account of the construction of identity it is not at all surprising that Mac**ash should become herself as a copy of herself, "a perfect simulacrum" (p. 132) — if identity is situated in a fictional direction, then self-identification is a simultaneous entry into language and death. What is surprising is that she acquires adult heterosexual desire (specifically, at the end, for the towering figure of Carrefour) through the intervention of the General and eleven other imaginary women, among whom as Anna/Ariadne she takes the place of the thirteenth. If identity and sexual difference are defined with reference to the phallus and if the phallus is a symbol, a signifier (*the* signifier), then it (and identity) may be granted in the name of the mother (as it is to Lily Briscoe in Virginia Woolf's *To the lighthouse*) but only perhaps on condition that a matriarchal grouping now has a power comparable (though different) to that of patriarchy. And this may be the necessity, both structural and thematic, which binds together the other thirty-three sections in creating imaginary women epitomised at the end in the uncovering for the first time of the so-far repressed thirteenth sign of the Zodiac, Arachne the spider. (Of course. How have we managed without her so far?)

The text refers in III. 5. to "narrative, with its plot-obsessed paranoia", and up to now this present account has pursued the same old obsession. Nevertheless some account first has to be given of the narrative because to give a summary of the rest of *Imaginary women* requires an act of prioritising the text resists — all the other sections are equal in importance (but importance to what? to making possible Mac**ash's narrative). From the other thirty-three sections I shall select three motifs or themes or figures or modes of discourse to represent the rest.

One is mathematics. It is asserted that "mathematics fundamentally figures female absence" (p. 34), a view expanded in the paragraph detailing ways in which 12 is "the patriarchal number" (p. 190). The discourse of mathematics therefore constantly recurs across the text in a double significance — as a way in which the masculine imagination seeks to fix the feminine in place, as the possibility a non-Europocentric logic of order (for this Chinese culture is explored) may postulate an order for this other. Hence the centre of each third (ie. I. 7, II. 7, III. 7) plots points on an *x*/*y* axis (sex/die?) culminating in a graph named as "woman <> mathematics" (<> being the symbol for 'greater or less than' but also the diamond in cards and the 'punch' symbol used by silversmiths for authenticity and by Lacan, see 1977a, p. 315). Hence also a text consisting of thirty-nine sections whose internal resonances work to subvert its programmatic ordering (the formula *delta t* as a structuring paradigm in *Gravity's rainbow* is well discussed by Joseph Slade, 1974, pp. 217–20).

A second figure which can be traced — by a reader — in the weaving together of the text is that presented in the narrative when Mac**ash is apparently decapitated by herself. This surfaces constantly elsewhere as the woman sawn in half by the magician and seemingly rejoined at the waist by a tattooed belt of film sprocket holes (35mm) (II. 8 and again III. 11) (this leading into the woman covered in tattoos of tropical fish in I. 3), as the double fate of the Whole Hog who in II. 6 is both killed by Sara Bella's sword *and* in another continuum transformed by the same stroke from a werehog back into a handsome prince, as the doubling of Sara's friends, Groundrat and Foundflat, in I. 10, together with the doubling of Mac**ash's enemies, later intimate friends, Mex and Booris (II. 1).

A third, minor trope is made up by a stuttered initial letter "f". Introduced on the second page ("Our f-f-f", p. 4), the motif belongs to Evelyn Mulwray (Faye Dunaway) in *Chinatown* who refers to her incestuous object of desire as "my f-f-father" (p. 21), becomes the copy of the Falcon given to Mac**ash ("a f-f-fake", p. 123), is expanded in III. 8 with its account of the exhibition of Matisse paintings (all of imaginary women) which may be artistic "f-f-forgeries" and "f-f-fabrications" (p. 159) and concludes, more or less, in the (non-fictional) name of the sculptress Niki de Saint Phalle ("F for Faker or Saint Ph-Ph-Phalle", p. 173) who paints death as a microcephalous woman in a red swimsuit riding a horse. Sexuality, incest, death, fictionality, art: from this imitated slip associated meanings reach out to intersect with the tropical fish tattooed on Molly, fish eaten by John Huston and Jack Nicholson in the Albacore Club in *Chinatown* as well as the "flawed fish" eaten by Cary Grant and Eva Marie Saint in *North by North-West*, the "f" inserted by J. J. Case (by mistake?) into "MacFlash" (p. 54), La Jefe's international state combine "FF&F (Fish, Forestry and Finance)" (p. 154), intersecting indeed with almost every occurrence of the phoneme /f/ in the text making it liable to resonate in sympathy with those occurrences which are manifestly instances of meaning.

> But one has only to listen to poetry, which Saussure was no doubt in the habit of doing, for a polyphony to be heard, for it to become clear that all discourse is aligned along the several staves of a score. There is in effect no signifying chain that does not have, as if attached to the punctuation of each of its units, a whole articulation of relevant contexts suspended 'vertically', as it were from that point. (Lacan 1977a, p. 154)

Imaginary women is a text which secures for the reader no centre or anchoring-point round which it is structured and he or she will be positioned. In the main, two modes of discourse are played off against each other, the six narrative sections, the thirty-three others. They constitute the two axes of the text, the syntagmatic axis developing as it were horizontally and the paradigmatic developed vertically from points in the narrative. Or better, in Lacan's example, like polyphonic music in which a theme is harmonised, varied, repeated in other modes above and below the single line. As this analysis has sought to suggest, in this text each term (trope, figure, narrative event) is connected synaptically in many-tracked association with (ultimately) every other.

Linearity in the syntagmatic chain, as Lacan writes in the same passage, "is necessary" as the place for identity, "a single voice", and for the reader of *Imaginary women* that position is afforded by the consecutive and coherent narrative in which Mac**ash finds herself. But if the text provides this as the point of necessary stability for the conscious ego, it does so only by revealing the constructed dependencies of which this temporary fixity is an effect. A short way to suggest this is by pointing to this as a comic text, a sustained instance of the joke which is the consequence, Freud argues, when, *"a preconscious thought is given over for a moment to unconscious revision and the outcome of this is at once grasped by conscious perception"* (1976, p. 223). Many of the jokes and examples of verbal play in *Imaginary women* work by opening the signifier to unconscious meaning which exceeds retrieval in any subsequent conscious perception (in this respect "f-f-f" is no joke).

Dependency within the subject of ego on id, dependency of signified on signifier: it hardly needs to be insisted that *Imaginary women* is artificial, constantly posing its reader in a position of self-reflection, drawing attention to the operation of the signifier (both verbal and written, mathematical and graphic) through which its signified meanings are brought about. Inscribed throughout is the effect of its own assertion that the text is a fabrication, "of which the common root of the words 'text' and 'textile' is the clue" (p. 147). A third dependency is harder to speak of, for the claim that this text articulates itself in relation to a social other can only be validated over time. Sufficient perhaps to suggest that the re-working of feminine identity, of the relations between patriarchy and (possible) matriarchal power, of the transformation of world order envisaged in the manifestoes of Anna 1 and Anna 2 in III. 6 catch up some of the deepest concerns of our time and point forward to a time when they achieve more satisfactory resolution.

Imaginary women is a novel which would not have been possible without the modernism of Joyce and the post-modernism of Nabokov, Vonnegut and Pynchon, but it also achieves its place in the context of British post-structuralism. It is the most significant addition to the English novel since the publication here of Beckett's *Murphy* in 1938.

APPENDIX II

A Note on Institutions

British post-structuralism was developed especially in the years following the conjuncture of 1974. It was brought about in a process of working through which was at best genuinely collective and which depended upon a material basis in a number of institutions. These consisted partly of conferences, partly journal publications.

Conferences

On 29–31 March 1974 the Department of English and History at Manchester Polytechnic sponsored a conference on "English Studies — the Socio-historical and Literary-critical Approaches", essentially Marxist approaches (speakers were Terry Eagleton and David Craig) versus authorial approaches. This initiative had two definite consequences. One was that Peter Widdowson and others decided to start the journal *Literature and History*, the other was the running of a second conference in 1975 by Thames Polytechnic which led on to the inauguration of the Essex conferences from 1976.

Through the extraordinary efforts of David Musselwhite, Francis Barker, Peter Hulme and other members of the School of Literature at the University of Essex, a series of conferences was organised under the title "The Sociology of Literature". This in fact became the main Marxist literature conference and continued to run from 1977 to 1984 (with a lacuna in 1979) and attracted participants from languages and various social science departments as well as from English. After 1976 the conference set out to examine texts, aesthetic and theoretical, around a number of conjunctures: 1848 in

1977; 1936 in 1978; 1642 in 1980; 1789 in 1981. At the same time, from 1979 onwards the papers of the previous year were published by the University of Essex.

In the first years, led by Stuart Hall, Raymond Williams and Terry Eagleton, the conference was exciting and took itself very seriously as the moment of British Marxism from 1974 worked its way through in a confrontation at the level of theory with the range of recent Marxist work: from the Frankfurt school through to Goldmann, to Althusser and Macherey (Macherey himself was a visiting speaker in 1976 and Renée Balibar in 1977 — in 1978 Julia Kristeva failed to arrive). But by the early 1980s the Essex conference, in common with other projects launched around 1974, was beginning to find that its trajectory seemed to be completed. In 1982 the troops were assembled once more, not for a conjuncture, but a grand retrospective on "The Politics of Theory", though the aim of demonstrating advance showed as many cracks as it did evidence of achievement. In 1983 the conjuncture was 1983 ("Confronting the Crisis"), in 1984 the topic was colonial discourse and in 1985 the conference was replaced by another on cultural production. It was at Essex in 1976 that a theorist, having illustrated theory from analysis of a text and being told unequivocally that his reading of the text was factually incorrect, extemporised the unanswerable reply, "According to the inexorable logic of my theory that fact is impossible" (for a fuller history of Essex, see Barker *et al.*, 1986).

The degree to which Essex represented novelty, theoretical seriousness and political radicalism can be measured by contrasting it with the traditional conference for university teachers of English, the UTE conference. By 1979 when it was held at Edinburgh on 28–31 March UTE had reached such a state of desiccation that someone could lecture serenely about "the future of Coleridge research over the next fifty years" secure in the certainty that this would continue exactly as it had done in the previous half-century. In fact the only disturbance was not so much actual as symptomatic. A specially invited speaker denounced semiology, sociology, semiotics, Marxism and Macherey (pronounced "Mackeray") to an audience almost all of whom were hearing the forbidden names for the first time.

Quite soon even UTE changed. In 1982 it began to address the issue of theory, including Marxism and post-structuralism (Peter Widdowson was the first person from a polytechnic ever asked to speak at this conference in that year) and thereafter the conference renamed itself the Higher Education Teachers of English conference (HETE). At Newcastle in 1983, Reading in 1984, Liverpool in 1985, Brighton in 1986 and Canterbury in 1987 HETE has become a genuine forum for debate in literary studies, though at the price of losing its general constituency among English lecturers and becoming ever more a self-selecting group interested in 'the new criticism'.

The Literature/Teaching/Politics group (LTP) originated as a meeting at Thames Polytechnic in 1979 and held its first conference at Cardiff in 1980. It is a decentred structure of loosely affiliated groups concerned with socialist/feminist strategies as much in the pedagogy of English teaching as in its syllabus design, and though it does have an annual conference (at Cambridge in 1981, Birmingham 1982, Sunderland 1983, Ilkley 1984, Bristol 1985, and Glasgow 1986), the meeting aims to avoid formal papers and the disciplined examination of a topic. Post-structuralism has figured along the way in conjunction with an overriding Marxism. The group also publishes the LTP journal, this providing papers from the regional group who have organised the conference, or, in a more traditional way, collecting papers given at the conference (for, *de facto*, papers are given). For a fuller account, see Taylor 1987 (Helen Taylor at Bristol Polytechnic is the nearest LTP has got to a 'contact name').

On 10–11 July 1981 a conference sponsored by the people working in and around the *Oxford Literary Review* took place at the University of Southampton, "Theory and Text: New Developments in the Study of Literary Language". Although some of the speakers usual at Essex were invited (Colin MacCabe, Catherine Belsey), the conference, concerned with literature rather than politics, was in fact the first public declaration and celebration of American deconstruction in Britain. Two years later a second Theory and Text conference ("Post-structuralism and the Question of History", 8–9 July 1983) imported Barbara Johnson, Richard Rand and Rodolphe Gasché. Its opening session included an attack on Marxism which showed how the discourse of historical materialism drew on certain metaphors, though the conference was closed with a paper from Tony Bennett (papers published in Attridge *et al.*, 1987). Again a questioner — another questioner — asked Richard Rand if he was serious, prompting the observation that people who ask Richard Rand if he is serious are getting younger every year. By 1983 Theory and Text seemed clearly to have taken over the initiative once held by Essex and to attract the interest if not commitment that

that once did. An intended conference in 1985 on the language of poetry was replaced by one on sexual difference (papers published in *OLR* for 1986). This was one of the largest and best-attended of its kind. There was no Theory and Text conference in 1987.

Journals

Because university prestige is not strongly tied to journal publication and because the whole enterprise tends against the political mainstream, British post-structuralism has survived effectively without a journal at its centre. This has been compensated for by its dispersal across different disciplinary areas.

All the more remarkable therefore that *New Left Review* has continued to publish vigorously, attaining no.163 in May in 1987. It also continues to find a space for material in aesthetics, notably essays by Terry Eagleton. *Radical Philosophy* was started in 1972 and has continued to flourish with little visible means of support. It has consistently published work in the area of post-structuralism in an open-handed and critical manner, matching David Wood's "Introduction to Derrida" in the issue of Spring 1979 with a heavy-handed attack on Lacan in that of Winter 1979.

Between 1971 and 1973 a remarkable political journal was published, *Theoretical Practice* (the editorial group included Tony Cutler, Barry Hindess, Paul Hirst and Athar Hussain). It would not be unfair to characterise the strategy of this intervention as one of total theoreticism: that is, to analyse out the necessarily correct theoretical account of the conjuncture at which point revolution became inevitable. On the one hand *TP* aimed to re-build the study groups, conferences and active support *NLR* abandoned (stories still circulate of the fearsomely demanding reading lists whose completion led to initiation into such groups); on the other, as Hirst admits, *TP* exhausted itself in an intense struggles "about the correct line of theoretico-political work" (Hirst 1986, p. 5). Some of the energies that went into *TP* were subsequently diverted into *Economy and Society*, a journal published by Routledge & Kegan Paul since 1972 and in which Hirst's review of Thompson first appeared in 1979, as well as, for example, Eagleton's 1984 defence of post-structuralism in reply to Perry Anderson, "Marxism, structuralism and post-structuralism" (reprinted Eagleton 1986a).

It is said that a conscious decision was made around 1970 by those active around *New Left Review* that theoretical struggle in the domain of aesthetic practice would be better carried out elsewhere and that this was the initiative for co-opting *Screen*. Before 1971 it was a moderately dull film journal published in conjunction with *Screen Education* by the Society for Education in Film and Television, an independent body with a grant-in-aid from the British Film Institute. Sam Rohdie became editor of *Screen* in 1971, followed by Ben Brewster (1974–6) and Geoffrey Nowell-Smith (1977–8). During its heroic period (say, 1973–7) *Screen* successfully permeated British intellectual life in a series of practical forms: regional groups, reading groups (such as that in Manchester to which *Film theory: an introduction* (1988) by Rob Lapsley and Michael Westlake is dedicated), the BFI summer school, *Screen* readers' meetings in London, weekend schools both in London and the provinces, the film 'event' at the Edinburgh Film Festival. The generalisation may be hazarded that the theoretical effectivity of journals, at least would-be radical journals, rests on their willingness to encourage such practical participation (supporting evidence here being the old Left Books and Left Book clubs of the 1930s). Certainly, a change in *Screen* coincided with a decline of this participation, and though the journal continues to make an important contribution, drawing on past work, it is now much more narrowly concerned with cinema and its politics stresses feminism more than socialism.

In the mid-1970s *Screen* was boosted to its apogee by the seemingly endless stream of new names arriving across the Channel each quarter. Moving out from a basis in Russian Formalism, Brecht and Althusser, *Screen* was able to introduce Metz, Bellour, Lacan, Kristeva and Foucault, hot from the bookshops of the Left Bank. Thus, "The imaginary signifier" by Metz appeared in *Communications* no. 23 in May 1975 and was translated for *Screen* in its issue of Summer 1975. As earlier pages here have testified, the magazine with the greatest effect in disseminating post-structuralism in Britain was *Screen*.

In March 1975 a group based at Thames Polytechnic founded *Literature and History*, a journal taking the relations between literary study and historical study as its structuring problematic and publishing essays deriving from each side but aiming, as the Editorial Preface said in the first issue, "to indicate kinds of possible exchange and interrelationship" (in practice, a majority of the articles have been literature-based). In 1976 came the first issue of *Red Letters*, the Communist Party literature journal which has continued to be produced somewhat sporadically since then, reaching its tenth anniversary issue, *RL* no. 20, in December 1986, and having become transformed in the meantime from being a literature journal into "a journal of cultural politics" (there was for a short period in 1978 a rival Trotskyist literature magazine called *Wedge*, though it came and went very quickly).

With its immaculately respectable title, the *Oxford Literary Review* was started in Oxford by Robert Young, Ian McLeod and Ann Wordsworth, among others. At first it was a left-leaning post-structuralist journal (publishing Macherey, for example), but after a refashioning in 1978 in a new format and with an Honorary Presidential Committee including Harold Bloom, Geoffrey Hartman and J. Hillis Miller it directed itself more obviously at an American readership and was dedicated in the main to work in the line of Derrida as he is read by his American interpreters. *OLR* has printed for the first time in England a number of important texts by Derrida, Foucault, Lyotard and others. Except where it has reprinted papers from the Southampton conference it has also increasingly moved away from specifically literary analysis towards more general issues in and around deconstruction. *OLR* is the only journal in Britain that can genuinely claim after its own fashion to be post-structuralist and only post-structuralist.

Ideology and Consciousness (the title itself making an interesting distinction) appeared only between May 1977 and Autumn 1979. Its importance is indicated by its editorial collective, which included Julian Henriques, Couze Venn and Valerie Walkerdine, who went on with others to edit *Changing the subject*. *Ideology and Consciousness* introduced critical writing and a concern in English with the work of Foucault that led on to this major critique of social psychology. The engagement and relative disengagement of the journal from the problematic of Althusserian Marxism can be plotted through a series of articles, including Stuart Hall's "Debate" with the editorial collective in *IC* no. 3 (Spring 1978).

Two feminist journals founded in the late 1970s, *m/f* (from 1976) and *Feminist Review* (from 1979), have carried significant post-structuralist writing. *Feminist Review*, as part of its wider concern with the political struggles of women, has printed a number of articles, particularly those drawing on psychoanalysis, to which the general term applies. The journal *m/f*, now regrettably discontinued, was even more explicitly committed to a post-structuralist perspective.

A new orthodoxy?

Within the minor relative autonomy of journal production it looks as though a conjuncture was negotiated in 1985. Perhaps the demise of social democracy in Britain became urgently apparent in this summer after the end of the coal dispute of 1984–5 or perhaps the 'new criticism' had genuinely achieved an advance of its own against the prevailing dominance. Nevertheless, two journal issues were conspicuously significant, not least because of their independence from each other. *PN Review*, a curiously English poetry magazine devoted both to finding a social mission for poetry and with it a vaguely conservative politics, published an issue, no. 48 (1985), consisting entirely of brief responses to what it termed "A New Orthodoxy". Thus the new orthodoxy "ignores the case for literature as a distinctive area of imaginative experience" and "sanctions, by its unjustified insistence that language constructs reality and the individual subject, the contemptuous dismissal of versions of reality — and individual subjects — that challenge its hegemony" (p. 1). In response, urge the editors, Nicolas Tredell and Michael Schmidt, "this orthodoxy must be challenged". Though post-structuralism is nowhere near an orthodoxy, still less a hegemony in English intellectual life, the very fact of this attack shows the inroads it has made.

Critical Quarterly was founded in 1959 by C. B. Cox and A. E. Dyson with, as its Foreword said, "no new critical manifesto" (p. 3) but a vaguely Leavisite interest in twentieth-century literature, it has trundled along in the literary critical mainstream ever since. Suddenly, in the Spring and Summer issues of 1986, in volume 28, nos 1 and 2, all was changed utterly: Colin MacCabe was invited to take over as guest editor as the journal was surrendered to twelve essays in the new criticism (to be republished as *Futures for English* by Manchester University Press). If these two issues are read together it looks as though something has changed at a deeper level. This is confirmed by the willingness of Methuen, spurred on by the success of their 'New Accents' and University Paperback publications, to underwrite not one but three new journals in 1987: *Textual Practice, New Formations, Cultural Studies.*

Appendix III

An Interview with Jacques Derrida

In 1980 when Derrida visited Edinburgh he was interviewed in English by James Kearns and Ken Newton, lecturers in French and English respectively at Dundee University. The interview was published in the *Literary Review*, no. 14 (April/May 1980), pp. 21-2, and is reproduced below.

JK. May we begin by asking you to outline the present state of your research, particularly as it relates to your theory of 'différance'?

JD. In March, I shall publish a book entitled: *The Postcard from Socrates to Freud and Beyond* which will deal with this theme of 'différance' in a field situated between psychoanalysis and telecommunications. It is a close reading of Freud's *Beyond the Pleasure Principle* in which I discuss a set of problems on the nature of telecommunications, problems concerning not only the technology of telecommunications in relation to the development of psychoanalysis but also epistolary literature: what is a destination? an addressee? what is it to send a message? to receive a message? what is the identity of the sender? of the receiver? what is correspondence? what remains, what is destroyed in correspondence? The book begins with a fictional correspondence of which a description of a picture-postcard forms the thread. I discovered the postcard in Oxford three years ago and was fascinated by it. It is a reproduction of an illustration in a thirteenth-century book on fortune-telling and shows Socrates writing and Plato standing behind him, pointing. The fictional correspondence is entitled 'envoi', a play on words between the literary envoy and act of sending, and discusses the Heideggerian interpretation of history as 'Geschick', sending. It formulates the problem of the relationship between

236

telecommunications and serves as a preface to an analysis of the 'Fort-Da' in *Beyond the Pleasure Principle*. I try to show the ways in which psychoanalysis is conditioned by a given situation in the technology of telecommunications and since you raise the question of 'différance' with an 'a', 'différance' is here postal relay of delay ('relais ou délai postal'), relay station or waiting period.

JK. May we turn to the implications for literary analysis of your theory of deconstruction. You have defined deconstruction as a two-fold strategy of overthrow and displacement. In order to deconstruct the literary text, one must locate the verbal and semantic elements which resist, disorganise the classical philosophical oppositions but without being drawn into a hegelian-type dialectic in which these oppositions are sublimated in a third term. You call these elements the 'undecidables'. Verbal signifiers are opened up for our active interpretation. The absence of a transcendent signifier results in the play of signification stretching infinitely. First of all, would you accept this account of your theory of deconstruction?

JD. Yes, certainly.

JK. The question then is: how does one decide which of the infinite number of possible plays of signification to retain? How does one decide that certain terms are 'undecidable?'

JD. It is not a matter of decision. In certain historical and theoretical situations, some terms can appear to have this indeterminacy. In order to discover and exploit their indecidability, however, you must yourself be inscribed in a certain situation. It was not possible, for example, to propose my analysis of terms such as 'supplement', 'hymen', 'pharmakon' in another situation from that in which I attempted to analyse them. There are many different kinds of conditions which determine this (the stage of research, the historical and theoretical situation in a given field for instance), which permit you to discover and exploit this indecidability. For myself, I could not have formulated the problem in this way had I not been prepared by, for example, the Husserlian reflection on 'écriture' and on ideal objectivity and by the modern mathematical model of the undecidable. So it is not a matter of decision. It is not a matter of method. There is no rule for this if by rule you mean a set of formal devices.

KN. It might be argued that deconstruction inevitably leads to pluralist interpretation and ultimately to the view that any interpretation is as good as any other. Do you believe this and how do you select some interpretations as being better than others?

JD. I am not a pluralist and I would never say that every interpretation is equal but *I* do not select. The interpretations select themselves. I am a Nietzchean in that sense. You know that Nietzsche insisted on the fact that the principle of differentiation was in itself selective. The eternal return of the same was not repetition, it was a selection of the more powerful forces. So I would not say that some interpretations are truer than others. I would say that some are more powerful than others. The hierarchy is between forces and not between true and false. There are interpretations which account for more meaning and this is the criterion.

KN. You would reject then the view that meaning is any response whatever to a sign? that meaning is determined by the person who reads the sign?

JD. Yes, of course. Meaning is determined by a system of forces which is not personal. It does not depend on the subjective identity but on the field of different forces, the conflict of forces, which produce interpretations.

KN. You would, therefore, reject the theory of authorial intention as determinate of meaning?

JD. Yes. I would not say that there is no interest in referring to the intentional purpose. There are authors, there are intentionalities, there are conscious purposes. We must analyse them, take them seriously. But the effects of what we call author's intentions are dependent on something which is not the individual intention, which is not intentional.

JK. There is a pragmatic aspect to this question of intentionality. It has been suggested that it is only in the field of literary theory that reader-based theories of interpretation are taken seriously, that all other fields of discourse accept author-based meaning intention. Reader-based theories of interpretation tend, therefore, according to this view, to partition off literary speculation from the rest of experience and thus to trivialise literary speculation. What are you views on this?

JD. I do not accept this opposition between reader-based and author-based meaning. It comes from a misunderstanding of deconstruction, one which sees deconstruction as free interpretation based only on the fantasies of the reader. No one is free to read as he or she wants. The reader does not interpret freely, taking into account only his own reading, excluding the author, the historical period in which the text appeared and so on.

KN. So you would not consider yourself an anti-historicist?

JD. Not at all. I think that one cannot read without trying to reconstruct the historical context but history is not the last word, the final key, of reading. Without being anti-historicist, I am suspicious of the traditional concepts of history, the hegelian and the marxist concepts.

JK. In *Positions,* published in 1972, you expressed the view that a meeting ("rencontre") between your critique of Western metaphysics and the texts of Marxism was necessary and that your own reflection on this problem was still to come. Since *Positions* has the meeting come closer in your view?

JD. I have not written anything on this subject. Marxism, of course, is not an entity. There is not one marxism, there is not one marxist practice, so to answer your question I should first have to differentiate many sorts of marxist theory and practice and that would be a very long process. But I would reaffirm that there is some possible articulation between an open marxism and what I am interested in. I insist upon the *open* marxism. As you probably know, the situation has changed completely in France since *Positions.* At that time, as marxism was the dominant ideology among French intellectuals I was anxious to mark the distance between marxism and what I was interested in so as to maintain the specificity of may own work. In the space of four or five years, however, marxism has ceased to be the dominant ideology. I don't want to exaggerate but I would say that marxists are now almost ashamed to call themselves marxists. Though I am not and have never been an orthodox marxist, I am very disturbed by the antimarxism dominant now in France so that, as a reaction, through political reflection and personal preference, I am inclined to consider myself more marxist than I would have done at a time when Marxism was a sort of fortress.

JK. Could you define the term "open Marxism"?

JD. It is a tautology. Marxism presents itself, has presented itself from the beginning with Marx, as an open theory which was continually to transform itself and not become fixed in dogma, in stereotypes. It is also true that it is a theory which, for political reasons which require to be analysed, has had a greater tendency than other theories to scholasticism, to refuse transformations which were taking place in the sciences, in pyschoanalysis at a particular period, in a certain type of linguistics. This seemed to

239

me an anti-marxist gesture on the part of those who called themselves marxists. Opening up has been a very slow, uneven, irregular process and this seemed to me unfaithful to the premisses of marxism. So an open marxism is one which, without giving way, obviously, to empiricism, pragmatism, relativism, nevertherless does not allow theoretical restrictions to be imposed upon it by a particular political situation, by a particular political power, as has sometimes been the case in the Soviet Union, and in France too. It is one which does not refuse *a priori* developments of problematics which it does not believe to have itself engendered, which appear to have come from outside. I believe that it is possible, on account of laws which marxism itself should be able to analyse, for problematics to develop outside marxist theory, outside societies dominated by this theory.

JK. This evening, you have given a talk entitled: "Should philosophy be taught in schools?" Would you like to summarise the main points for the readers of *The Literary Review*?

JD. I began by describing the situation in France to see if analogies could be made between the French situation and that of other Western, industrial societies. At the moment, they all have in common the desire to reduce their teaching of philosophy for reasons which, as I tried to explain, are both techno-economic, the profitability argument, and political, since philosophy is often thought, rightly or wrongly, to be politically dangerous. In order to resist in practical and theroretical terms this regression in philosophy teaching, we formed in France the G.R.E.P.H. *(Group de Recherche sur L'Enseignement Philosophique)* and I explained at some length our analyses of the French situation. To us it seemed that the principal means of transforming this situation was to extend philosophy teaching in schools throughout the curriculum, that the prejudice according to which philosophy should be reserved for sixth-form pupils and university students in fact supported powerful interests which we are attempting to analyse. I tried to show that this question of the age at which philosophy could be taught is not an isolated question, is not simply one question among others, but that it is related to the educational system in its totality so that to question the age at which philosophy could be taught was to question the whole organisation of teaching, in philosophy and elsewhere.

Bibliography

Althusser, Louis (1972) *Politics and history* (London: New Left Books)
—— (1976) *Essays in self-criticism* (London: New Left Books)
—— (1977a) *For Marx* (London: New Left Books)
—— (1977b) *Lenin and philosophy and other essays*, 2nd edn. (London: New Left Books)
—— and Balibar, Etienne (1975) *Reading Capital* (London: New Left Books)
Anderson, Perry (1964) "Origins of the present crisis", *New Left Review*, no. 23 (January/February), pp. 26–53
—— (1968) "Components of the national culture" *New Left Review*, no. 50 (July/August 1968), pp. 3–58
—— (1976) *Considerations on western Marxism* (London: New Left Books)
—— (1980) *Arguments within English Marxism* (London: NLB and Verso)
Arnold, Matthew (1960) *Culture and anarchy*, ed. J. Dover Wilson (Cambridge: Cambridge University Press)
Attridge, Derek, Bennington, Geoff and Young, Robert (eds) (1987) *Post-structuralism and the question of history* (Cambridge: Cambridge University Press)
Baldick, Chris (1983) *The social mission of English criticism, 1848–1932* (London: Oxford University Press)
Barker, Francis (1984) *This tremulous private body* (London: Methuen)
—— Hulme, Peter, Iversen, Margaret, and Loxley, Diana (eds) (1986) *Literature, politics and theory, Papers from the Essex Conference, 1976–1984* (London: Methuen)
Barry, Peter (1981) "Is there life after structuralism?", *Critical Quarterly* 23, no. 3 (Autumn), pp. 72–7
Barthes, Roland (1967) *Elements of semiology* (London: Cape)
—— (1972) *Critical essays* (Evanston: Northwestern University Press)
—— (1973) *Mythologies* (London: Paladin)
—— (1975) *S/Z* (London: Cape)
—— (1976) *The pleasure of the text* (London: Cape)
—— (1977) *Image–music–text* (London: Fontana/Collins)
Bellour, Raymond (1975) "The unattainable text", *Screen, 16*, no. 3 (Autumn), pp. 19–27
Belsey, Catherine (1980) *Critical practice* (London: Methuen)
—— (1985) *The subject of tragedy: identity and difference in Renaissance drama* (London: Methuen)
Bennett, Tony (1979) *Formalism and Marxism* (London: Methuen)
—— (1981a) "Popular culture: defining our terms", Units 1/2, Course U203 (Milton Keynes: Open University Press)
—— Boyd-Bowman, Susan, Mercer, Colin and Woollacott, Janet (eds) (1981b) *Popular film and television* (London: BFI/Open University Press)

—— Martin, Graham, Mercer, Colin and Woollacott, Janet (eds) (1981c) *Culture, ideology and social process* (London: Batsford)

—— Mercer, Colin, and Woollacott, Janet (eds) (1986) *Popular culture and social relations* (Milton Keynes: Open University Press)

—— and Woollacott, Janet (1987) *Bond and beyond* (London: Macmillan)

Benton, Ted (1984) *The rise and fall of structuralist Marxism* (London: Macmillan)

Bloom, Harold, 1979. "The breaking of form", in H. Bloom, P. de Man, J. Derrida, G. Hartman and J. Hillis Miller (eds), *Deconstruction and criticism* (London: Routledge & Kegan Paul)

Boswell, James (1945) *Life of Dr Johnson* (New York: Scribners)

Bourne, Geoffrey (1981) "Meaning, image and ideology", Unit 14, Course U203 (Milton Keynes: Open University Press)

Brecht, Bertolt (1964) *Brecht on theatre*, ed. J. Willett (London: Methuen)

—— (1965) *The Messingkauf dialogues*, tr. J. Willett (London: Methuen)

Brewster, Ben (1977) "Notes on the text of John Ford's 'Young Mr. Lincoln' by the Editors of Cahiers du Cinéma", in John Ellis (ed.) *Screen Reader 1,* (London: Society for Education in Film and Television)

Bryson, Norman (1983) *Vision and painting: the logic of the gaze* (London: Macmillan)

Carroll, Noel (1982) "Address to the heathen", *October, 23* (Winter), pp. 89–163

Chanan, Michael (1981) "The trajectory of western music", *Media, Culture and Society, 3*, no. 3 (July), pp. 219–42

Clark, Timothy J. (1980) "Preliminaries to a possible treatment of 'Olympia'", *Screen, 21*, no. 1 (Spring), pp. 18–41

Colls, Robert, and Dodd, Philip, (eds) (1986) *The ideology of Englishness: national identity in the arts, politics and society, 1880–1920* (London: Croom Helm)

—— (forthcoming) *English identities, 1789–1989* (Oxford: Blackwell)

Coward, Rosalind (1977) "Class, 'culture' and the social formation", *Screen, 18*, no. 1 (Spring), pp. 75–105

—— (1977/8) "Response", *Screen, 18*, no. 4 (Winter), pp. 120–2

—— (1984) *Female desire* (London: Paladin)

—— and Ellis, John (1977) *Language and materialism: developments in semiology and the theory of the subject* (London: Routledge & Kegan Paul)

Cubitt, Sean (1986) "Cancelling popular culture", *Screen, 27*, no. 6 (November/December), pp. 90–3

Culler, Jonathan (1983) *On deconstruction: theory and criticism after structuralism* (London: Routledge & Kegan Paul)

Cusin, Michel (1985) "'Poetry as discourse'", *Etudes Anglaises, 18*, no. 2 (April/June), pp. 230–1

Davies, Tony (1987) "Damning the tides: the new English and the reviewers", in M. Green (ed.), *Broadening the context* (London: Murray)

de Man, Paul (1979) *Allegories of reading* (New Haven: Yale University Press)

—— (1983) *Blindness and insight*, 2nd rev. edn (London: Methuen)

—— (1986) *The resistance to theory* (Manchester: Manchester University Press)

Derrida, Jacques (1973) "Avoir l'oreille de la philosophie" in L. Finas, S. Kofman, R. Laporte and J.M. Rey (eds), *Ecarts: Quatre essais à propos de Jacques Derrida* (Paris: Fayard)

—— (1976) *Of grammatology*, tr. G. Spivack (Baltimore: Johns Hopkins University Press)

—— (1978) *Writing and Difference*, tr. A. Bass (London: Routledge & Kegan Paul)

—— (1980) "An interview with Jacques Derrida", *Literary Review*, no. 14, pp. 21–2 (reprinted here in Appendix III)

—— (1981a) *Positions*, tr. A. Bass (London: Athlone Press)

—— (1981b) *Dissemination*, tr. B. Johnson (London: Athlone Press)

—— (1982) *Margins of philosophy*, tr. A. Bass (Brighton: Harvester)

Dollimore, Jonathan (1984) *Radical tragedy* (Brighton: Harvester)

—— and Sinfield, Alan (eds) (1985) *Political Shakespeare, new essays in cultural materialism* (Manchester: Manchester University Press)

Donald, James, and Mercer, Colin (1981) "Reading and realism", Unit 15, Course U203 (Milton Keynes: Open University Press)

Doyle, Brian (1982) "The hidden history of English studies", in P. Widdowson (ed.), *Re-reading English* (London: Methuen)

Drakakis, John (ed.) (1985) *Alternative Shakespeares* (London: Methuen)

Durant, Alan (1984) *The conditions of music* (London: Macmillan)

Eagleton, Terry (1975) *Myths of power, a Marxist study of the Brontës* (London: Macmillan)

—— (1976) *Criticism and ideology* (London: New Left Books)

—— (1978) "Aesthetics and politics", *New Left Review*, no. 107 (January/February), pp. 21–34

—— (1979) "What is literature?", *New Statesman*, 6 July

—— (1981) *Walter Benjamin: towards a revolutionary criticism* (London: Verso/NLB)

—— (1983) *Literary theory: an introduction* (Oxford: Blackwell)

—— (1984a) *The function of criticism* (London: Verso)

—— (1984b) "The *Oxford Literary Review* (double issue, volume 5,nos 1 and 2)", *Literature and History, 10*, no. 1 (Spring), pp. 134–6

—— (1986a) *Against the grain: essays 1975–1985 (London: Verso)*

—— (1986b) *William Shakespeare* (Oxford: Blackwell)

Easthope, Antony (1979) "Liberal and theoretical discourse: an opposition assessed", *Social Praxis, 6,* nos 3/4, pp. 217–35

—— (1983a) *Poetry as discourse* (London: Methuen)

—— (1983b) "The trajectory of *Screen*, 1971–1979", in Francis Barker, Peter Hulme, Margaret Iversen and Diana Loxley (eds), *The politics of theory* (Colchester: University of Essex)

—— (1986) *The masculine myth in popular culture* (London: Paladin)

—— (forthcoming) "The subject of literature, the subject of cultural studies", in D. Morton and M. Zavarzadeh (eds), *Theory/pedagogy/politics*

Eco, Umberto (1977) *A theory of semiotics* (London: Macmillan)

—— (1982) "The narrative structure in Fleming", in B. Waites, T. Bennett and G. Martin (eds), *Popular culture: past and present* (London: Croom Helm)

Eliot, T.S. (1962) *Notes towards the definition of culture* (London: Faber)

Elliott, Gregory (1986) "The Odyssey of Paul Hirst", *New Left Review*, no. 159 (September/October), pp. 81–103

Ellman, Maud (1987) *The poetics of impersonality: the question of the subject in T. S. Eliot and Ezra Pound* (Brighton: Harvester, 1987)

Emerson, R. W. (1950) *The complete essays* (New York: Random House)

Fish, Stanley E. (1974) *Self-consuming artifacts: the experience of seventeenth century literature* (Berkeley: University of California Press)

Flinn, Carol (1986) "The 'problem' of femininity in theories of film music" *Screen*, 27, no. 6 (November/December), pp. 56–72

Foucault, Michel (1977a) "What is an author?", *Screen*, 20, no. 1 (Spring 1979), pp. 13–33

—— (1977b) *Language, counter-memory, practice*, tr. D. F. Bouchard and S. Simon (Ithaca: Cornell University Press)

—— (1979) "My body, this paper, this fire", *Oxford Literary Review*, 4, no. 1 (Autumn), pp. 9–28

—— (1981) *The history of sexuality*, vol. 1., "An introduction" (Harmondsworth: Penguin)

—— (1982) "Afterword: the subject and power" in H. L. Dreyfus and P. Rabinow (eds), *Michel Foucault: beyond structuralism and hermenutics* (Brighton: Harvester)

Formations (1984) "Formations of nation and people" (London: Routledge & Kegan Paul)

Freud, Sigmund (1975) *New introductory lectures* (Harmondsworth: Penguin) (PFL vol.2)

—— (1976) *Jokes and their relation to the unconscious* (Harmondsworth: Penguin) (PFL vol. 6)

Gardner, Helen (1982) *In defence of the imagination* (London: Oxford University Press)

Gombrich, Ernst (1960) *Art and illusion: a study in the psychology of pictorial representation* (Oxford: Phaidon)

Goulden, Holly, and Hartley, John (1982) "'Nor should such Topics as homosexuality, masturbation, frigidity, premature ejaculation or the menopause be regarded as unmentionable'", *Literature/Teaching/Politics*, no. 1 (1982), pp. 4–20

Hall, Stuart (1980) "Recent developments in theories of language and ideology: a critical note", in S. Hall, D. Hobson, A. Lowe and P. Willis (eds), *Culture, media, language* (London: Hutchinson)

—— Chambers, Iain, Clarke, John, Connell, Ian, Curti, Lidia, and Jefferson, Tony (1977) "Marxism and culture", *Screen*, 18, no. 4 (Winter), pp. 109–19

Hammett, Dashiell (1964) *The Maltese falcon* (New York: Vintage)

Hartz, Louis (1955) *The liberal tradition in America*, (New York: Harcourt Brace & World)

Heath, Stephen (1974) "Lessons from Brecht", *Screen*, 15, no. 2 (Summer), pp. 103–28

—— (1975) "Film and system: terms of analysis", Part 1, *Screen, 16*, no. 1 (Spring), pp. 7–77; Part 2, *16*, no. 2 (Summer), pp. 91–113

—— (1976) "Anata mo", *Screen, 17*, no. 4 (Winter), pp.49–66

—— (1977) "Notes on suture", *Screen, 18*, no. 4 (Winter), pp. 48–76

—— (1978) "Difference", *Screen, 19*, no. 3 (Autumn), pp. 51–112

—— (1981) *Questions of cinema* (London: Macmillan)

Henriques, Julian, Hollway, Wendy, Urwin, Cathy, Venn, Couze, and Walkerdine, Valerie (1984) *Changing the subject: psychology, social regulation and subjectivity* (London: Methuen)

Hindess, Barry, and Hirst, Paul Q. (1975) *Pre-capitalist modes of production* (London: Routledge & Kegan Paul)

—— (1977) *Mode of production and social formation* (London: Macmillan)

Hirst, Paul Q. (1979) *Law and ideology* (London: Macmillan)

—— (1986) *Marxism and historical writing* (London: Routledge & Kegan Paul)

—— and Woolley, Penny (1982) *Social relations and human attributes* (London: Tavistock)

Hodgson, Geoff (1981) *Labour at the crossroads* (Oxford: Martin Robertson)

—— (1984) *The democratic economy* (Harmondsworth: Penguin)

Hume, David (1911) *A treatise of human nature*, 2 vols (London: Dent)

Jakobson, Roman (1971) "Shifters, verbal categories, and the Russian verb", in *Word and language* (The Hague and Paris: Mouton)

—— and Tynjanov, Jurij (1971) "Problems in the study of literature and language" (1928), in L. Matejka and K. Pomorska (eds), *Readings in Russian poetics* (Cambridge, Mass.: MIT Press)

James, Allison (1982) "Confections, concoctions and conceptions", in B. Waites, T. Bennett and G. Martin (eds), *Popular culture: past and present* (London: Croom Helm)

James, Susan (1987) "Althusserian materialism in England", in C. Crossley and I. Small (eds), *Studies in Anglo-French relations* (London: Macmillan)

Jameson, Fredric (1983) *The political unconscious* (London: Methuen)

Jardine, Lisa (1986) "'Girl talk' (for boys on the Left), or marginalising feminist critical practice", in 'Sexual difference', *Oxford Literary Review, 8*, nos 1–2, pp. 208–17

Johnson, Richard, McLennan, George, Schwarz, Bill, and Sutton, David (eds) (1982) *Making histories: studies in history writing and politics* (London: Hutchinson)

Karolyi, Otto (1965) *Introducing music* (Harmondsworth: Penguin)

Kearney, Richard (1984) *Dialogues with contemporary continental thinkers* (Manchester: Manchester University Press)

Kristeva, Julia (1976) "Signifying practice and mode of production", *Edinburgh Magazine, 76*, pp. 60–76

—— (1984) *Revolution in poetic language*, tr. Margaret Woller (New York: Columbia University Press)

Lacan, Jacques (1966) *Ecrits* (Paris: Editions du Seuil)

—— (1977a) *Ecrits: a selection* (London: Tavistock)

—— (1977b) *The four fundamental concepts of psycho-analysis* (London: Hogarth Press)

Laclau, Ernesto, and Mouffe, Chantal (1985) *Hegemony and socialist strategy: towards a radical democratic politics* (London: Verso)

Lapsley, Rob, and Westlake, Michael (1988) *Film theory: an introduction* (Manchester: Manchester University Press)

Leitch, Vincent B. (1983) *Deconstructive criticism, an advanced introduction* (New York: Columbia University Press)

Lentricchia, Frank (1980) *After the new criticism* (London: Athlone)

Llewelyn, John (1986) *Derrida on the threshold of sense* (London: Macmillan)

Locke, John (1947) *An essay concerning human understanding* (London: Dent)

Lodge, David (1981) "*Middlemarch* and the idea of the classic realist text", in A. Kettle (ed.), *The nineteenth century novel, critical essays and documents* (rev. edn.) (London: Heinemann)

Lyotard, Jean-François (1983) *The postmodern condition* (Manchester: Manchester University Press)

MacCabe, Colin (1975) "The politics of separation", *Screen, 16*, no. 4 (Winter), pp. 46–61

—— (1976) "Principles of realism and pleasure", *Screen, 17*, no. 3 (Autumn), pp. 7–27 (reprinted 1985, pp. 58–81)

—— (1978) *James Joyce and the revolution of the word* (London: Macmillan)

—— (1985) *Theoretical essays* (Manchester: Manchester University Press)

McDonnell, Kevin, and Robins, Kevin (1980) "Marxist cultural theory: the Althusserian smokescreen", in S. Clarke, T. Lovell, K. McDonnell, K. Robins and V.J. Seidler (eds), *One-dimensional Marxism, Althusser and the politics of culture* (London: Allison & Busby)

Macherey, Pierre (1978) *A theory of literary production* (London: Routledge & Kegan Paul)

Macksey, R. and Donato, E. (eds) (1970) *The structuralist controversy* (Baltimore: Johns Hopkins University Press)

McLennan, Gregor (1984) "History and theory: contemporary debates and directions," *Literature and History, 10*, no. 2 (Autumn), pp. 139–64

Martin, Graham (1981) "Readers, viewers and texts", Unit 13, Course U203 (Milton Keynes: Open University Press)

Marx, Karl (1971) *Introduction to A Critique of Political Economy*, ed. Maurice Dobb (London: Lawrence & Wishart)

—— (1973) *Grundrisse* (Harmondsworth: Penguin)

—— (1974) *Capital*, vol. 1 (London: Lawrence & Wishart)

—— and Engels, Friedrich (1947) *Marx and Engels on literature and art* (Calcutta: no publisher given)

—— and Engels, Friedrich (1950) *Selected works*, 2 vols (London: Lawrence & Wishart)

—— and Engels, Friedrich (1970) *The German ideology*, tr. C. J. Arthur (London: Lawrence & Wishart)

Mauss, Marcel (1970) "A category of the human mind: the nature of person, the nature of 'self'", in *Sociology and psychology*, tr. B. Brewster (London: Routledge & Kegan Paul)

Mercer, Colin (1981) "Pleasure", Unit 17, Course U203 (Milton Keynes: Open University Press)

Metz, Christian (1975) "The imaginary signifier", *Screen, 16,* no. 2 (Summer), pp. 14–76

Mill, John Stuart (1965) *Mill's essays on literature and society*, ed. J. B. Schneewind (New York: Macmillan)

Miller, J. Hillis (1977) "The critic as host", *Critical Inquiry, 3,* no. 3 (Spring), pp. 439–47

Mitchell, Juliet (1975) *Psychoanalysis and feminism* (Harmondsworth: Penguin)

Moi, Toril (1985) *Sexual/textual politics* (London: Methuen)

Montefiore, Alan (ed.) (1983) *Philosophy in France today* (Cambridge: Cambridge University Press)

Mulvey, Laura (1981a) "Visual pleasure and narrative cinema", in T. Bennett, S. Boyd-Bowman, C. Mercer and J. Woolacott (eds), *Popular television and film* (London: BFI/Open University Press). (Selections; full version in *Screen, 16,* no. 3 (Autumn 1975), pp. 6–18)

—— (1981b) "Afterthoughts on 'Visual pleasure and narrative cinema' inspired by *Duel in the sun* (King Vidor, 1946)", *Framework,* nos 15, 16 and 17, pp. 12–15

Nairn, Tom (1964) "The English working class", *New Left Review,* no. 24 (March/April), pp. 43–57

—— (1977) *The break-up of Britain: crisis and neo-nationalism* (London: New Left Books)

Neale, Stephen (1980) *Genre* (London: British Film Institute)

Norris, Christopher (1982) *Deconstruction: theory and practice* (London: Methuen)

—— (1983) *The deconstructive turn: essays in the rhetoric of philosophy* (London: Methuen)

—— (1985) *The contest of faculties* (London: Methuen)

Parker, Rozsika, and Pollock, Griselda (1981) *Old mistresses* (London: Routledge & Kegan Paul)

Parrinder, Patrick (1987) *The failure of theory* (Brighton: Harvester)

Podro, Michael (1984) "Misconceived alternatives", *Art History, 7,* no. 2 (June), pp. 243–7.

Rajchman, John, and West, Cornel (eds) (1985) *Post-analytic philosophy* (New York: Columbia University Press)

Rand, Richard (1982) "o'er-brimmed" *(sic), Oxford Literary Review, 5,* nos. 1/2, pp. 37–58

Ray, William (1984) *Literary meaning* (Oxford: Blackwell)

Rosen, Charles (1976) *Schoenberg* (London: Fontana/Collins)

Samuel, Raphael (ed) (1981) *People's history and socialist theory* (London: Routledge & Kegan Paul)

Sartre, Jean-Paul (1963) *The psychology of the imagination*, tr. Bernard Frechtman (New York: Citadel Press)

Saussure, Ferdinand de (1959) *Course in general linguistics*, tr. Wade Baskin (New York: Philosophical Library)

247

Schwarz, Bill (1977) "On ideology", *Working Papers in Cultural Studies,* no. 10 (Birmingham: Centre for Contemporary Cultural Studies)

Shepherd, John (1977) "The musical coding of ideologies", in J. Shepherd, P. Virden, G. Vuillamy and T. Wishart (eds), *Whose music? A sociology of musical languages* (London: Latimer)

Skinner, Quentin (ed.) (1985) *The return of grand theory in the human sciences* (Cambridge: Cambridge University Press)

Slade, Joseph W. (1974) *Thomas Pynchon* (New York: Warner Books)

Stallybrass, Peter, and White, Allon (1986) *The politics and poetics of transgression* (London: Methuen)

Tarski, Alfred (1949) "The semantic conception of truth", in H. Feigl and W. Sellar (eds), *Readings in philosophical analysis* (New York: Appleton–Century–Crofts)

Taylor, Helen (1987) "'Are we talking about literature?': A history of LTP", *Literature/Teaching/Politics* (Changing the subject), no. 6, pp. 7–11

Thompson, Edward (1978) *The poverty of theory and other essays* (London: Merlin)

Thompson, John O. (1982) "Popular culture: the pleasure and the pain", *Screen Education, 41* (Winter/Spring), pp. 43–52

Waites, Bernard, Bennett, Tony, and Martin, Graham (eds) (1982) *Popular culture: past and present* (London: Croom Helm)

Weber, Samuel (1983) "Capitalising history: notes on *The Political Unconscious"*, in F. Barker, P. Hulme, M. Iversen and D. Loxley (eds), *The politics of theory* (Colchester: University of Essex), pp. 248–64

Weedon, Chris (1987) *Feminist practice and poststructuralist theory* (Oxford: Blackwell)

Westlake, Michael (1987) *Imaginary women* (Manchester: Carcanet)

Widdowson, Peter (ed.) (1982) *Re-reading English* (London: Methuen)

Willemen, Paul (1978) "Notes on subjectivity", *Screen, 19,* no. 1 (Spring), pp. 41–69

—— (1983) "Remarks on *Screen,* introductory notes for a history of contexts", *Southern Review* (Adelaide), *16,* no. 2 (July), pp. 292–311

Willey, Basil (1962) *The eighteenth-century background: studies on the idea of nature in the thought of the period* (Harmondsworth: Penguin)

Williams, Raymond (1965) *The long revolution* (Harmondsworth: Penguin)

—— (1963) *Culture and society, 1780–1950* (Harmondsworth: Penguin)

—— (1977) *Marxism and literature* (London: Oxford University Press)

—— (1980) *Problems in materialism and culture* (London: Verso)

Williamson, Judith (1978) *Decoding advertisements* (London: Marion Boyars)

Wittgenstein, Ludwig (1958) *The blue and brown books* (Oxford: Blackwell)

Wollen, Peter (1976) "'Ontology' and 'materialism' in film", *Screen, 17,* no. 1 (Spring), pp. 7–23

Wood, David (1979) "An introduction to Derrida", *Radical Philosophy,* no. 21 (Spring), pp. 18–28

—— (ed.) (1985) *Derrida and Différance* (Warwick: Parousia)

Wood, Ellen Meiksins (1986) *The retreat from class: a new 'true' socialism* (London: Verso)

Woolf, Virginia (1979) *Women and writing* (London: Women's Press)

Wordsworth, Ann (1982) "Household words: alterity, the unconscious and the text", *Oxford Literary Review, 5,* nos 1/2, pp. 80–95

Young, Robert (ed.) (1981) *Untying the text: a post-structuralist reader* (London: Routledge & Kegan Paul)

—— (1982) "Post-structuralism: the end of theory", *Oxford Literary Review, 5,* nos 1/2, pp. 3–20

—— (forthcoming) *The politics of theory* (London: Routledge)

Index

Index